Liberal Education in a
Knowledge Society

Liberal Education in a Knowledge Society

EDITED BY

BARRY SMITH

Julian Park Professor of Philosophy and
Member of the Center for Cognitive Science
at the University at Buffalo

OPEN COURT
Chicago and La Salle, Illinois

To order books from Open Court, call toll free 1-800-815-2280.

Open Court Publishing Company is a division of Carus Publishing Company.

Copyright © 2002 by Carus Publishing Company

First printing 2002

Printed and bound in the United States of America

Library of Congress Cataloging-in-Publication Data

Liberal education in a knowledge society / edited by Barry Smith.
    p. cm.
   An essay by Carl Bereiter, followed by comments on his work by other writers and Bereiter's response to these writers.
   Includes bilbliographical references and index.
   ISBN 0-8126-9508-9 (alk. paper)—ISBN 0-8126-9509-7 (pbk. alk. paper)
   1. Education, Humanistic. 2. Education—Aims and objectives. 3. Education—Philosophy. 4. Culture—Study and teaching. I. Smith, Barry. Ph.D. II. Bereiter, Carl .

LC1011 .L46 2002
370.11'2—dc21

2002070416

For Blouke Carus

Es wäre nicht der Mühe wert siebzig Jahr alt zu werden,
wenn alle Weisheit der Welt Torheit wäre vor Gott.

Contents

Liberal Education in a
Knowledge Society

1
Introduction:
A New Definition of
Liberal Education

Harold Henderson and Barry Smith

From Plato versus Isocrates to Snow's 'Two Cultures' to our present 'culture wars', the problem of general or 'liberal' education has been one of the central controversies in educational thought. The debate has pertained mainly to elite education, since until the past century only members of an elite were thought to be worth educating beyond the basics. In the new millennium, the old problem has acquired a desperate urgency, partly because it has come to seem insoluble.

Four trends have changed the problem of liberal education beyond recognition in recent decades: 1. knowledge is growing so rapidly and uncontrollably that the very idea of an 'all-round' (or 'general') education is coming to seem unfeasible; 2. nonetheless, it seems increasingly obvious that knowledge skills of some kind are essential in a society where 'knowledge work' has become the most productive and highly remunerated kind of work; 3. moreover, it seems clear that these knowledge skills, whatever they are, can't be confined to an elite, but must be imparted to everyone; 4. in a pluralistic society, the old classical model of learning knowledge skills (illustrated for example by European elite education) is challenged by some groups in society who reject the culture in which such education has been embedded.

Liberal Education in a Knowledge Society contains papers presented at a conference constructed around a new approach to these dilemmas, an approach put forward by Carl Bereiter in the title paper of the conference (and of this volume).[1] Bereiter's position does not fit neatly into any of the familiar schools of thought about liberal education, though it makes contact with several. It is based on a new theory of mind, replacing the once-dominant folk theory in which the mind is regarded as a container with knowledge forming part of its content. In the new theory Bereiter employs—a theory inspired by connectionist models—the emphasis shifts from knowledge regarded as mental content to more informal kinds of knowledgeability. Among the things which people can become knowledgeable about, however, are the items traditionally regarded as mental content: abstract objects like ideas, theories, historical narratives—the sorts of entities that the philosopher Karl Popper, following Gottlob Frege, called 'World 3', to distinguish it from 'World 1' (of physical things and events) and 'World 2' (of subjective mental states).

While rejecting or leaving aside Popper's philosophical ideas, especially his realism, Bereiter uses 'World 3' as a term of convenience by which to name the object of liberal education; we should regard liberal education, he argues, as an "enculturation into World 3." By 'enculturation' he means not the possession of literal, formal knowledge of ideas in World 3, but the acquisition of a more informal knowledgeability, learning to find one's way around the world of ideas, getting to be on intimate terms with some of what is there, and, more generally, learning how to function effectively in creating, interpreting, and improving World 3 objects. Though it does not specify what particular content such 'enculturation' is to be exercised upon, such a conception is entirely consistent with traditional views about liberal education as the transmission of cultural knowledge, characteristic of European high culture. On the other hand, Bereiter's conception also has obvious resonance with much

---

1. The approach has been previously described, for other purposes, in Bereiter and Scardamalia 1996, in Bereiter 1997, and is also the subject of a book-length treatment in Bereiter 2002.

of what is being said today about the so-called 'knowledge economy' and the 'information age'.

The responses in this volume to Bereiter's proposal vary widely. They come from a number of different subject areas, from education to economics to philosophy. And they run the gamut from rejection of Bereiter's ideas to partial endorsement. In Bereiter's own field of education, two contributions come from Bereiter's own Toronto colleagues. Marlene Scardamalia, Bereiter's long-time collaborator in the development of classroom technology designed to implement the ideas Bereiter proposes, describes their joint project, *Knowledge Forum*, a computer-supported classroom environment for knowledge building, and gives evidence of its effectiveness in deepening students' engagement with intellectual content. Gordon Wells criticizes Bereiter's instrumental view of knowledge, urging a stronger focus on the community of knowledge-seekers itself, especially in educational settings, in place of Bereiter's stress on knowledge as an artifact or commodity. Shifting the focus to higher education, James Miller recounts his own experiences in attempting to implement something like liberal education in a hostile setting, and shares Wells's suspicions of Bereiter's apparent complacency toward the instrumentalization of knowledge which is implicit in much currently modish business literature.

Jeremy Edwards and Sheilagh Ogilvie, economists at the University of Cambridge, argue that the whole idea of a 'knowledge economy' or 'information society' is greatly exaggerated. The value of a general education, they suggest, is to be sought not in its *productive* value, as an investment in human capital, but rather in its role as an investment in more efficient *consumption*. This idea is explored further by A.W. Carus, who proposes that we view such investment in better consumption as an *expertise* like that studied by cognitive scientists, and discussed by Bereiter and Scardamalia in their book about this research, *Surpassing Ourselves: An Inquiry into the Nature and Consequences of Expertise*. This view of 'moral expertise' has many echoes in traditional views of liberal education, but though he endorses Bereiter's and Scardamalia's practical program, Carus argues that there is no existing social practice into which any traditional form of liberal education could represent an enculturation.

Erich Reck, a philosopher at the University of California at Riverside, argues finally that Bereiter cannot have Popper's terminology of three 'worlds' without the philosophical baggage. In particular, he argues that a 'World 3' consisting of as heterogeneous a collection of abstract objects as Popper proposes would be self-contradictory and thus not of much practical use, even for Bereiter's limited purposes.

Bereiter forcefully rejects this and the other criticisms in his replies, in which he restates his position and reminds his critics of the practical orientation of his proposal and its location in current debates about education, particularly about educational technology. Nonetheless, he attempts to build bridges between his viewpoint and those of his critics.

For completeness this volume also contains a paper on related themes by Bereiter and Scardamalia, 'Schooling and the Growth of Intentional Cognition: Helping Children Take Charge of Their Own Minds'. This paper was first published in 1983, but only in Hebrew;[2] the original typescript circulated widely and was the object of much discussion, not least within the school division of Open Court Publishing Company, whose Education Director Bereiter was at the time and for many years thereafter. There was often talk of publishing it, perhaps as a separate pamphlet to help deepen the understanding of editors and other employees about Open Court's educational goals, but nothing ever came of these plans. It has aged surprisingly little, and is referred to by one of the contributors (Carus) in relation to Bereiter's target paper in this volume. Since it gives additional depth and background to that paper, and has not been published elsewhere, it is included here, its first publication in its original language.

*   *   *   *   *

Bereiter's and Scardamalia's classroom software and associated ideas arise from many decades of thoughtful involvement in elementary education. In much of this activity, they have worked together with Blouke Carus, who has devoted his life to the idea of

---

2 Bereiter and Scardamalia 1983.

liberal education—in textbook publishing and in his work on behalf of the International Baccalaureate, youth apprenticeship, and state-level accountability. As Blouke has often argued, we are jeopardizing the future of our civilization if we do not invest the time and resources needed to overhaul our educational institutions so that they can provide the basis for serious general education for *all* students.

This book and the conference from which it arose are dedicated to Blouke Carus and what he has stood for in his tireless efforts to change educational institutions. The seminar was held in the Carus-Hegeler Mansion in La Salle, Illinois, and the book is published by Open Court Publishing Company, which has been owned by the Carus family since it was started in 1887. Both mansion and publisher date from the late nineteenth century, so it may be worth adding a few words here about the history of the Carus family, and the roots of Blouke's work in the family's cultural mission.

Blouke Carus's work continues a thread in the cultural tapestry of America which began with the arrival of the young Edward Hegeler from Germany in 1856. When he settled in La Salle, Illinois, and started a zinc factory there, it was by no means obvious that this thread would ever become intertwined with the history of American education. There are three major strands, though, that hold this thread together and connect Hegeler's work with Blouke's program of reform a century later: an engineering mindset, a pragmatic approach, and a peculiar combination of internationalism and rootedness.

The engineering mindset. Edward Hegeler made his name and his fortune by re-engineering the manufacture of zinc. From there, he moved on to something he had no special training in, but knew to be of vital importance: the reconciliation of religion and science. A century later, Blouke made his name and his business by re-engineering the manufacture of potassium permanganate. From there he moved on to something he had no special training in, but knew to be of vital importance: the re-engineering of education.

Both men broke with the orthodox beliefs of their day just as they had broken with engineering orthodoxies, but neither broke with the idea of orthodoxy itself. Paul Carus, Hegeler's son-in-law and ideological right hand (and Blouke's grandfather) wrote disparagingly of liberals who "attempt to reject the errors of the past, but in the vain hope of attaining infallibility themselves. . . . reject also the aspiration of having definite opinions." Both men brought to their endeavors beyond engineering the same energy and attitude they had displayed within it. It was taken for granted that if your mousetrap works better, if your Religion of Science works better, if your reading program works better, then sooner or later the world will beat a path to your door. This doesn't mean you should do nothing to promote it; on the contrary. But your main selling point, as an engineer, is not surface glitz or clever positioning but product integrity. People in marketing departments everywhere, now and a century ago, stand ready to explain just how naive this attitude is. But then these same people would have told Edward Hegeler and Blouke Carus to stick to their chemicals.

A pragmatic approach. Paul Carus wrote that his magazines *The Open Court* and *The Monist* "although apparently very theoretical, have very practical aims." And on another occasion, "If the values of our abstract ideas are not ultimately founded upon the reality of positive facts, they are like bills or drafts for the payment of which there is no money in the bank."

This is pragmatism with a small p; Blouke's grandfather was dead against William James's folksy philosophy of pragmatism with the capital P. "I would deem it a misfortune," Carus wrote in 1908, "if his philosophy would ever exercise a determining and permanent influence upon the national life of our country . . . [if that were to happen,] we would all exercise the utmost mutual tolerance, for we would grant the privilege to everyone to regard his thoughts as true—true to him and true at least at the time. We would draw the line only when we meet with people who have the impudence to believe in the objectivity, the permanence, the reliability of their truth, and demand consistency in all statements of truth." Paul Carus rejected this exaltation of the sentimental and subjective over an agreed standard common to all. Of course his grandson has constantly found himself at loggerheads with the highly influential 'progressive' education movement, whose origins are often traced back to James and his disciple Dewey. Blouke has been especially concerned to encourage measures that would increase the accountability of educational institutions. And many defenders of the progressive view of education have opposed or deprecated objective measurement of their institutions' outputs.

Internationalism and rootedness. When Edward Hegeler founded *The Open Court* magazine in 1887, one of its goals—as close to his heart as the Religion of Science and indeed inseparable from it—was to transplant European thought, especially German thought, to America. His descendents have followed in that path, maintaining roots on both sides of the Atlantic, as well as adding some across the Pacific. This has been reflected most recently in the international content of the Open Court readers and of the Carus magazines, including *Cricket, Muse*, and others. It goes back to Paul Carus's willingness to support Buddhist missionaries in this country around the turn of the century, and his eleven years' work with Daisetz Teitaro Suzuki. As a cameo of American culture at its best, you could hardly improve on Suzuki's account of his labor with Carus in translating the *Tao Te Ching*. "In order to translate passages from Lao-Tzu," Suzuki recalled sixty years later, "I had to explain to Dr. Carus the feeling behind each Chinese term. But being himself a German writing in English, he translated these Chinese ideas into abstract conceptual terms. If only I had been more literarily equipped then—" A young Japanese and a middle-aged German, huddled together painstakingly struggling to render an ancient Chinese text into English!

Along with these three major strands of continuity—engineering, practical orientation, internationalism—are a host of lesser ones. Paul Carus was an inveterate networker all his life, as Blouke has been. Both started their projects in the very building where the conference here documented was held—Open Court Publishing Company in 1887, textbook publishing in 1962. Both espouse an attitude Paul Carus called 'meliorism', neither optimism nor pessimism, but not resignation either. "Let the world be bad!" wrote Paul Carus early in his career. "Our duty is to work with steady labor for its improvement." Both Paul and Blouke carried on a vast correspondence, frequently enclosing books and articles for the recipient. Both were known for their diligence and persistence, as was Edward Hegeler. "Having set out to do a thing," recalled Hegeler's business partner, "he had the most unyielding determination, the equal of which I have never seen."

If you network and correspond enough, you will inevitably hook up with the occasional crank, and this, too, is part of the continuing thread. One of the crankiest people, in every sense, that

Paul Carus took up with (after having beat him out for the Open Court job) was an impecunious, irritable former academic who had been defrocked and ostracized for alleged sexual impropriety, who lived in a decaying farmhouse in Pennsylvania, and wrote nearly incomprehensible prose advocating a philosophy Paul Carus found implausible. They broke off more than once, but still Carus published more of his writings in his lifetime than anyone else. His name was Charles Sanders Peirce, and he is now often regarded as America's answer to Plato and Kant in the history of world philosophy.

Ernst Mach was by no means as obscure as Peirce, but he was an independent-minded outsider to the world of nineteenth-century physics and philosophy. Encouraged by Edward Hegeler, Paul Carus published five of Mach's books and many additional articles. One book, the *Popular Scientific Lectures*, was first collected and published in English and appeared only later in its original German. Mach told Carus that the English translations "are much more important to me than the German editions," not least because they sold better. Over the years, the two men corresponded on subjects ranging from colored eyeglasses to political philosophy to Buddhism and religion, and Mach dedicated his last book to Paul Carus. Eventually no less a personage than V.I. Lenin, in his book-length tirade against Mach (and Mach's then-numerous Russian followers), characterized Paul Carus as "a leader of a gang of American literary rascals who are engaged in doping the people with religious opium."

Blouke has yet to receive a personal thunderbolt from a future revolutionary leader, but synthetic phonics was a cranky idea when Blouke took it up and made it the basis of a reading program in 1962; there was so little published on the subject that he chose to work with a teacher from Tiskilwa, Illinois to put it into teachable shape for the first Open Court reading program. Meanwhile, mountains of empirical research in the past two decades have shown that Blouke was right.

Even closer to the heart of Open Court publishing in the liberal arts, the ideas of maintaining intellectual standards and cultural upgrading were marginal if not cranky at the time. The ideas in the pathbreaking (though widely reviled) book Carl Bereiter co-authored in 1967, *Teaching Disadvantaged Children in the*

Preschool—that such children lack "the knowledge that middle-class children possess" and need to acquire it fast, by direct teaching—were definitely not in the cultural mainstream of the 1960s, as those of us who were in that mainstream can testify. (Nor are they much more popular even now.) Fortunately, these contrarian ideas encouraged Blouke to bring Carl Bereiter into the Open Court Editorial Advisory Board in the late 1960s, and from there into the author team first of Open Court's reading program, and then of its elementary math program. This volume celebrates, then, not only Blouke Carus, and a long continuity within the Carus family, but also a working relationship between him and Carl Bereiter that began thirty years ago and continues into the present.

References

Bereiter, C. 1997. Situated Cognition and How to Overcome It. In D. Kirshner and J.A. Whitson, eds., *Situated Cognition: Social, Semiotic, and Psychological Perspectives* (Hillsdale, NJ: Erlbaum), pp. 281–300.

———. 2002. *Education and Mind in the Knowledge Age*. Mahwah, NJ: Erlbaum.

Bereiter C. and M. Scardamalia. 1983. Schooling and the Growth of Intentional Cognition: Helping Children Take Charge of Their Own Minds. In Z. Lamm, ed., *Zeramim hadashim be-hinukh* (New Trends in Education) (Tel-Aviv: Yahdev), pp. 73–100.

———. 1996. Rethinking Learning. In D.R. Olson and N. Torrance, eds., *Handbook of Education and Human Development: New Models of Learning, Teaching, and Schooling* (Cambridge, MA: Blackwell), pp. 485–513.

2
Liberal Education in a Knowledge Society

Carl Bereiter

Two of the most important influences on educational planning today are what for want of an established name I will call the futuristic business literature and the work coming out of cognitive science, broadly defined. There are, of course, many other influences, often from groups with a concern for some particular subject or aspect of schooling. But the two I have named are especially sweeping in their implications for educational change, each, in quite different ways, suggesting a reconceptualization of what schooling should be about. Yet each of these stops short of answering the question, 'What should it mean to be an educated person in the twenty-first century?'

That is the kind of question that has motivated the development of liberal education and its periodic transformations. The rise of the natural sciences led to the most profound transformation of liberal education. There were fears that it might not survive the transformation but it did, and no one would any longer conceive of an educated person who was ignorant of science. Now we are facing the possibility of a more radical transformation, one that does not involve so much the incorporation of new disciplines as a change in the way all disciplines are approached. Rumblings of such a transformation have been occurring throughout the past century,

11

but the two new influences, along with the technologies they draw upon, may finally make it happen. Will it mean the end of liberal education (assuming it is not already dead) or will liberal education re-emerge, strengthened through its renovation? I think liberal education can be renewed, but it will take a careful synthesis of new ideas and enduring principles.

Liberal education is essentially enculturation. It is more than the handing on of a body of knowledge and wisdom, although that is a large part of it. That is the part that liberal education has in common with enculturation in all societies. What makes liberal education distinctive—what makes it 'liberal'—is its cosmopolitanism. Liberal education initiates the young into a culture that transcends the particularities of their social and ethnic backgrounds. A major concern of many advocates of liberal education is that cosmopolitanism itself is coming under attack. Although I share that concern, I shall not dwell on it here. It has been more than adequately discussed. Instead, I will assume in the ensuing discussion that cosmopolitanism of some kind is an agreed-upon end of education. The liberal tradition, the new wave of economic globalization, and recent advances in the learning sciences all point in this direction. But how is such cosmopolitanism to be achieved when cultures are colliding and undergoing rapid, perhaps catastrophic change, when knowledge is expanding more rapidly than anyone can keep up with, and when the process of enculturation itself is subject to radical innovation? That is the question I raise for discussion here.

The discussion begins by drawing out the contrasting educational implications of the futuristic business literature and of cognitive learning research—the one emphasizing skills and personal qualities, the other emphasizing knowledge. Merging the two into lists of educational objectives, as is now common, does not begin to resolve underlying differences. The resolution I propose depends upon taking seriously the idea of a knowledge society, a society organized around the production of knowledge in the same sense that an agrarian society is organized around agricultural production and an industrial society is organized around manufacture. My proposal is that the school should be a productive part of that society, a workshop for the generation of knowledge. Transforming schools into workshops for the production of knowledge mobilizes those skills and personal qualities valued by business futurists, putting them to work toward ends that are consistent with contemporary conceptions of learning and with the objectives of a modernized liberal education.

Two Views of Education for the Twenty-First Century

By the 'futuristic business literature' I refer to that flood of publications from organizational theorists, management consultants, economists, futurologists, and diverse social scientists that take as a backdrop the rapid rate of technological change, the rise of Asia-Pacific economies, digitization, globalization, outsourcing, the shift from a manufacturing-based to a knowledge-based economy, and the need for constant innovation. This literature covers a great range in quality of ideas, which raises the twin dangers that policy makers may be influenced most by the lowest-level and easiest to grasp ideas and that discriminating people will reject the whole literature, thereby ignoring ideas that provide a basis for well-reasoned new educational policies.

Some low-end educational ideas are that technology will revolutionize everything, that we don't need schools anymore, and that there is no use mastering any body of knowledge because it will soon be obsolete. The high-end educational ideas mainly flow from a recognition of the ascendant importance of knowledge: knowledge as a third factor in production, along with capital and labor; learning as the means for organizations to gain a competitive edge; finally, the idea of a social transformation going on that is as extreme as the nineteenth-century shift from an agrarian to an industrial society—the shift to a knowledge society.

When it comes to formulating curriculum guidelines, however, the low-end and the high-end ideas seem to point in the same direction. They point to a set of personal qualities that must be cultivated if the education system is to produce people who can thrive in and contribute to the new order: imagination and creativity, ability to work in groups, communication skills, information-finding skills, problem solving abilities, technological literacy, and above all a continual readiness to learn. It is difficult to fault these, and they are now appearing conspicuously in curriculum guidelines and standards. But are they sufficient, and do they point educational planning in the right direction? That they are not the only answer becomes evident if we consider these questions from the perspective of cognitive learning research.

Because the term 'cognitive learning research' is sometimes seriously misinterpreted, I need to make a brief digression. When I was little my mother used to listen to a soap opera in which the commercials repeatedly extolled the gentle virtues of Ivory Snow in contrast to "harsh granulated soap." As an impressionable child I accordingly developed an intense dislike for that ugly-sounding substance. It therefore came as a shock when I learned later that Ivory Snow was also granulated soap. (Granulated simply means that the soap comes in particles rather than as a cake.) The only discriminative force was in the word 'harsh'. Cognitive science seems to be attracting the same undeserved scorn as granulated soap. Every new theory that makes a place for emotion, embodiment, sociality, or culture is contrasted with 'conventional cognitive science' or 'cognitive science based on the computer metaphor', and so many educators and social scientists have got the idea that cognitive science is some ugly, sterile, mechanistic undertaking intent on reducing minds to computer programs. But those new theories are granulated soap too.

Cognitive science embraces an increasing range of approaches, addressing an increasing range of issues. It gains its strength from disciplined pursuit of the question, 'How does it work?' Cognitive learning research shares this wide-open character. There is no established 'cognitive approach' in education. Yet, for all its diversity, when the work of cognitive educational researchers is put alongside the futuristic business literature, the kinds of prescriptions for education in the twenty-first century suggested by these two bodies of work are seen to differ profoundly. The emphasis of the business literature is on process outcomes, on turning out students who function in such-and-such ways. The current emphasis in cognitive learning research is on content, on turning out students with a genuine understanding of science, mathematics, and other school subjects.

Educational reformers inspired by the futuristic business literature commonly minimize the value of content mastery. For instance, an announcement of Stanford University's "Just-In-Time

Learning on Internet" project confidently proclaims, "Traditional text books and traditional teaching methods requiring weeks of study are being made obsolete by the information explosion." The project leaders suggest that publishers might abandon their traditional bookish ways and start charging customers on a "pay-per-question" basis (White and Korner 1995).

Are cognitive learning researchers, then, simply out of touch with the digital age? On the contrary, it seems that most of the business writers—along with many educators, unfortunately—are out of touch with progress in the understanding of learning. In the 1970s, cognitive learning research was where the futuristic literature is now, emphasizing cognitive strategies and learning-to-learn. For a combination of reasons, the emphasis has since shifted dramatically toward content learning. First there was the research on reading, which demonstrated that the overriding determinant of what one will get out of reading is what one already knows about the topic (Anderson and Pearson 1984). Then there was the accumulation of research on expertise, which showed that in all kinds of areas, practical as well as intellectual, expertise depends more on deep knowledge of one's domain, its problems and tools, than it does on general mental abilities (Chi and Glaser 1988). Perhaps most surprising was the research on misconceptions, which added up to the conclusion that students are passing through the schools having failed to grasp most of the ideas that constitute modern knowledge. Schools, it appears, are turning out graduates with pre-Newtonian conceptions of physics, pre-Darwinian conceptions of biology, and pre-Smithian conceptions of economics (Wandersee, Mintzes, and Novak 1994). This ought at least to give some pause to futurists who imagine students at home in a postmodern world of quanta and dynamic systems.[1] Finally, however, the emphasis on content has been buoyed by the successes of new educational

---

1. Any notion that students should be able to leap directly from premodern to postmodern understanding of the natural world ought to be abandoned. The misconceptions research indicates that students' failure to grasp key notions such as acceleration, natural selection, and market reflects a failure to grasp the relatively simple systemic relations that constitute a Newtonian or Darwinian or Smithian theory. That students might be able to grasp the more complex systemic relations that constitute contemporary theories seems therefore a mere pipe dream.

efforts aimed at learning with understanding. Once students start to get deeply into the pursuit of understanding, they begin to show spontaneously all the traits that the futuristic business literature urges: imagination, collaboration, problem-solving, communicative skill, and readiness to go on learning.

A commonsense response to the differing implications of futuristic business literature and cognitive learning research would be, 'Let's have both'. Why not teach both the general skills and dispositions urged by the former and the deep content knowledge stressed by the latter? In fact, that is what curriculum guidelines and standards are tending increasingly to propose (cf. New Standards 1995). Attractive as this eclectic solution may be, its effect is to drain away the energy that might have produced something new and exciting out of the interaction of these two new forces.

A New Culture for Learning

The futuristic business literature does convey a revolutionary vision, but it is not to be found in the paragraphs on education. Those are, for the most part, a mixture of technological euphoria and run-of-the-mill school-bashing. The revolutionary vision has to do with knowledge-based organizations—ones whose competitive advantage depends on cultivation and use of the organization's knowledge resources. Because those knowledge resources are generated out of (and to a large extent reside in) the work of everyone in the organization, maximizing them requires designing the organization so as to make everyone a contributor. That is the revolutionary part: abandoning bureaucratic structures in which a worker's responsibility is defined by routine tasks and where non-routine problems are referred to a higher level, replacing them by mission-oriented team structures in which problems are solved and new knowledge is generated within the working groups. That vision has much in common with a new vision of education taking shape within cognitive learning research. The two together, I believe, joined with the enduring vision of a liberal education, do give us an idea of what education for the twenty-first century should be.

Early cognitive learning research was not only focused on cognitive strategies, it was also focused on the individual learner. Along with a shift toward content came a shift from trying to inculcate learning strategies in the individual student to trying to create classroom cultures that support inquiry and the pursuit of deeper understanding. Educational historians will probably give credit for this shift to a revival of Vygotsky's socio-cultural theory of development and to the theory of situated cognition, which came out of anthropology. These ideas found a ready audience, however, among cognitive learning researchers who had spent the previous decade trying to improve learning by teaching individual cognitive strategies. It was not that the strategies did not work or that they were too hard to teach. The results were often quite impressive in the short run. You could get children to think harder and better about what they were reading and writing and about the problems they were trying to solve, but the effects tended to dissipate as they went on with regular classroom life. We seemed to be teaching a level of mental activity beyond anything required in normal schooling.

It became evident, therefore, that any general upgrading of students' intellectual abilities and dispositions would require changing the prevailing culture of the classroom. Ordinary classroom life is organized around activities (Doyle 1986). This is true across the whole spectrum ranging from tightly controlled classrooms where the main activity is filling in workbook pages to child-centered classrooms where the activities are self-chosen and often self-initiated projects. The new challenge has become to reorganize classroom life around the pursuit of knowledge.

The shift from focus on individual cognitive strategies to classroom culture is clearly delineated in the influential work of Ann Brown. In the 1970s her research dealt with teaching memory strategies to mildly retarded children (Brown 1978). By the 1980s individual strategy instruction had evolved into 'reciprocal teaching' (Palincsar and Brown 1984), in which children were organized into what might be characterized as rather highly structured support groups for reading comprehension. Reciprocal teaching then became assimilated into the more comprehensive 'communities of learners' (Brown and Campione 1990) in which the students became researchers and teachers of one another. Similar if not so clearly demarcated shifts occurred among many of the other cognitive learning researchers who had started out working with individual cognitive strategies.

The cultural shift that is implied in the new cognitive approaches remains poorly understood in the educational community, however—the shift, that is, from classroom life organized around activities to classroom life organized around the pursuit of knowledge. Instead, reciprocal teaching, communities of learners, and other transformations of classroom culture are merely perceived as new activities to replace or supplement old ones. The hottest innovations going in schooling today are 'project-based learning' and 'multiple intelligences'. The first is an old idea from the progressive education era brought back to life by new electronic media. The second is based on a theory of intelligence (Gardner 1983) that has stimulated the invention of all kinds of new activities. New and more educative activities may indeed improve learning, but they short-circuit efforts to bring about the cultural shift that seems essential if schools are to play the role in knowledge development that cognitive research indicates they should.

In order to take hold, I believe, this cultural shift must assume a more revolutionary form. Otherwise it will be continually reduced to 'hands-on learning', 'learner-centered education', or some other refurbishment of progressive education. Here is where the ideas about organizational transformation and knowledge work, prominent in the business literature, may be of service.[2] What I shall propose is that schools be reconstituted along the lines of other organizations whose function is to produce knowledge.

Learning goes on in all organizations, but only some organizations have the function of producing knowledge. The learning that goes on in any organization, whether it is a shoe factory or a research laboratory, is internal to individual minds and to the developing practices of work groups and of the organization as a whole. The excitement over the idea of a 'learning organization' reflects a growing appreciation of the value of this learning. It increases the competence of the organization to perform its func-

---

2. The business literature is having some influence at the level of school administration. There are school systems endeavoring to adopt Total Quality Management, for instance. (See the special issue of *Educational Leadership*, November 1992, devoted to TQM.) But that is on an entirely different plane from the classroom-level transformation I am talking about.

tions; in these intensely competitive times, learning is one way for an organization to gain a competitive edge. Accordingly, we see efforts to promote learning that range from formal courses in company-run schools to coffee bars where employees may hang out and exchange instructive stories about their work (Wenger 1995).

In addition, however, and quite apart from this internal betterment that we call learning, some organizations have the job of producing knowledge. These include university research centers, independent laboratories, market research and opinion research companies, and research and design departments within larger organizations. Unfortunately, in the current learning organization lingo, this knowledge production is called learning, too, thus obscuring an important distinction.[3] Of course, learning goes on in these knowledge-producing organizations as in all others— learning that develops the competence of the organization to do its work. But the work of the organization is not learning, it is producing knowledge. We accordingly refer to these as knowledge-building organizations (Bereiter and Scardamalia 1996; Scardamalia and Bereiter 1999; Scardamalia, Bereiter, and Lamon 1994). A research laboratory is a knowledge-building organization. A shoe factory is not, although it may contain a research group that is.[4] Schools today are not knowledge-building organizations. I am proposing that they become so. That is a radical cultural shift.

The school becomes a workshop for the production of knowledge. The students are workers. They are learners, too, of course; and because of the nature of their work they may be expected to learn a great deal. But learning is not their job. Their job is producing knowledge. It is meaningful work, because what they are producing is something for their own use, and so their work has

---

3. Senge (1996), evidently sensing that a distinction is needed, has introduced a contrast between 'adaptive learning' and 'generative learning', the latter being learning that creates novelty. This is a help, but things become even clearer if we recognize that knowledge creation is not learning at all, even though—like all intentional activity—it results in learning for those engaged in it.

4. I have read, however, that Nike does not actually manufacture shoes. They design shoes and contract out their manufacture. Thus, it would appear, Nike is in fact in the knowledge-producing business, with its knowledge being translated by others into physical objects.

that quality, so rare in the industrial age, that comes with building one's own house or raising one's own food.

Many educators would endorse this proposal in the belief that it is what they are already doing. Yet very little of so-called 'constructivist' pedagogy that I have observed or read about is actually concerned with the production of knowledge. Instead, it is concerned with the carrying out of projects that use knowledge but have some other objective than its production. Students may plan a trip to Mars or the building of a station on the moon, they may draw up an environmental or a business plan, or they may play a game or even create a game. At their best, such projects may generate a considerable amount of learning, but it is important to realize the difference between them and authentic knowledge creation.

This difference is dramatized in an experiment by Yarnall and Kafai (1996). I will dwell on this experiment because, by providing a sharp contrast, it serves to clarify what is meant by engaging students in the production of knowledge as distinct from engaging them in knowledge-related projects. Yarnall and Kafai adopted an approach called 'Learning Science Through Design'. In the course of studying ocean habitats, elementary school students were set to work creating educational computer games related to the ocean theme. In their report, Yarnall and Kafai lump this approach together with Community of Learners (Brown and Campione 1994) and CSILE (Scardamalia and Bereiter 1994) as 'project-based' approaches. While that is an accurate categorization, it reflects the common weakness in elementary education for elevating a procedural characteristic to the status of a pedagogical philosophy. The authors then proceed to distinguish Learning Science through Design from the other two approaches in that it is less structured and awards students a higher level of "creative control over the production of an artifact."

Evidently the students did throw themselves energetically into creating the computer games; they collaborated, consulted experts, and discussed programming problems. So if the purpose was to teach software design and programming, the project would have to be considered a success. But what about 'Learning Science through Design'? In 20 out of the 20 games the task the designers set for players was to answer quiz-type questions. Some of the games were explicitly modeled on quiz shows. Most, it appears, used the ocean theme as context for the quiz questions (if you don't answer the question correctly a grouper bites you, for instance). A computer bulletin board was used for discussion, but, the authors report, the discussions were about game design and programming, not about oceans. Incredibly, the one science question posted was rejected by the teacher, who told the student not to expect others to do his research for him! The authors are candid in concluding that 'Learning Science through Design' in this instance failed "to create a consistent context for a deeper level of subject inquiry," and they suggest that in the future their method might need "to structure the electronic exchanges around content more along the lines described by both Scardamalia and her colleagues in the CSILE project and Brown and her colleagues in the COL environment." This sounds like a minor modification in procedure, however, whereas doing so successfully—that is, getting students truly engaged with problems of marine biology instead of being solely concerned with software design—would involve a shift in focus so radical that the game-building activity might no longer be relevant.

I have seen students in a Community of Learners classroom intensely engaged with the problem of how male sea otters are able to mark off a territory of ocean as their own—a problem that was not handed to them but that they hit upon themselves as an anomaly in information they had assembled. The same sort of thing occurred in a CSILE classroom when a group studying the Arctic biome could not reconcile the reasons they were given for why trees do not grow in the Arctic with information other groups were providing about trees growing in deserts and in tropical rainforests.

The issue here is not only the learning of science content. It is also learning about knowledge: learning that it is more than stuff sitting in textbooks to be used for answering quiz questions. Even more, it is a matter of gaining experience of what I take to be the essence of life in a knowledge-building organization: the experience of producing knowledge of real value to someone.

This is not to rule out games, imaginary trips to Mars, and other often cleverly designed activities occupying that category now fittingly named 'edutainment'. But the extreme prominence given to them in modern pedagogy suggests to me an underlying belief that students have to be lured into learning, that they cannot be expected to pursue knowledge in its own right. No one says this openly, however, for belief in children's natural curiosity as the driving force in learning is one of the pillars of child-centered education. What I do hear, however, is something even less savory. When I show educators examples of students' genuine, sustained efforts to construct real knowledge, someone almost always remarks, 'That's fine for students who are motivated, but what about . . . ?' and there follows one of those shrugs or evasive mumbles that are meant to convey that we all know what kind of kids we are talking about although it is no longer safe to label them.

The unrealistic part of the child-centered faith is the belief that each child's natural curiosity should be sufficient to sustain knowledge-seeking six or more hours a day for twelve or more years. Those of us who are trying to change classroom culture are not banking on that. Rather, the expectation is that if the production of usable knowledge gets established as the classroom's collective task, then ordinary motives of conformity and citizenship will suffice to keep students engaged when curiosity flags. There may be situations where establishing the classroom as a knowledge production workshop proves impossible, but it is certainly a more attainable objective than keeping the curiosity of 30 individual students constantly aroused.

Knowledge Construction in the Classroom

The idea of schools as workshops for the construction of knowledge wins ready assent from educators. The difficulty is in getting them to see that this is anything different from students planning space missions: It is all 'project-based learning' or playing at being scientists. In discussing adult organizations earlier, it was easy to distinguish learning from knowledge building. Everyone learns, and progressive organizations do much to promote learning, but learning is not what people are employed for. Creating or adding value to knowledge, by contrast, is the purpose of an increasing number of jobs. Learning is the reason we send children to school, however, and knowledge building is only going to be valued insofar as students learn from doing it. But that does not make the distinction between learning and knowledge building any the less important. Students currently engage in all kinds of schoolwork, from doing sheets of arithmetic exercises to producing elaborate multimedia presentations, most of which is far removed from any kind of work that goes on in a knowledge society. A simple way to put my proposal, therefore, is as follows: Since students need to do some kind of work in order to learn, why not let that work be the construction of knowledge? The reason we need a distinction between learning and knowledge building is in order for a question like that to make sense.

One major prejudice must be overcome if knowledge building, as real productive work similar to what goes on in industrial laboratories and university research centers, is to find a foothold in educational policy. This is the prejudice that bestows credit only on the first person to come forth with an idea. Although this may be a perfectly reasonable principle in patent law, when generalized it virtually denies the possibility of children's being real creators of knowledge; for rarely if ever will a child produce knowledge that is new to the world. But originality is always relative to context. If it should turn out that there are intelligent beings on another planet and that everything scientists on earth have discovered is already old hat to them, would that mean that Newton and Darwin were not scientists after all?

Furthermore, an original theory or explanation is only one kind of knowledge product, albeit an exceptionally important one. Other worthwhile products of knowledge building are interpretations of theories, criticisms, translations of them into simpler terms, analyses of their implications or applications in some context of interest, descriptions of phenomema which the theory does or does not explain, experimental demonstrations, simulations, and historical accounts. Many adults pursue respectable careers producing knowledge of these kinds, often demonstrating creativity and depth of insight in the process. There is no reason to deny students credit when they do likewise.

A student in a CSILE class enters a note asking what keeps gravity from leaving the earth. Later another student reports that she has read that gravity is a force between things and therefore not something contained within things. Several students seize on this as making sense of the idea they have heard that gravity is everywhere. As we adults read these notes we conclude that a genuine advance in knowledge has occurred, helped along as much by the first student's naive question as by the second student's important finding. We do not know how much has been *learned*—that is, how much individual students in the class will carry away from this episode. Undoubtedly it will vary. What we do know is that knowledge has been produced, not of news-making or prize-winning calibre, but as important to the intellectual world that the students live in as the discoveries of a leading-edge university research team are to the intellectual world they live in. That is really all we need to allow in order to accept knowledge building by students as genuine productive work rather than merely a learning activity.

Students in any kind of classroom ought to be able to respond informatively to the question, 'What have you learned?' As many parents have found, this is often a difficult question for young people. But in the kind of knowledge-building classroom I am advocating, students should also be able to answer an even more challenging question: 'What advances in knowledge has your class made?' Answering such a question requires not only an awareness of one's own mental state but also an awareness of that abstraction known as 'the state of knowledge' in a community. The answer would of course overlap in content with answers to 'What have you learned?' but it would take quite a different form. It might go like this: 'Well, we've been working on systems of the body and we started out with one group studying the eye and another group studying the brain. But pretty soon we realized that to understand how we see we had to work on how the brain and the eye are connected. We have a pretty good idea now of how information gets from objects to the retina and from the retina to the brain, but we don't understand what happens after that—like, how you know what you're looking at. Some kids don't think that's a problem, but I do . . . We've also been working on the Aztecs and the Incas and those other groups. We've collected lots of information, but we're just starting to put it together to understand what their civilizations were like. It's hard, you know, because they didn't think about things the way we do . . .'

The preceding example combines remarks made by various students when asked to tell about their class's work. I suggest it is very similar to what one might get on dropping in on a university research group and asking how their work was going. The knowledge that the students have constructed is of course of a different order, but their unsolved problems are indeed unsolved in the world at large. They can legitimately claim membership in the communities of people who are working on such problems. They are, in short, doing real knowledge building, not playing pretend.

Over the span of the school years, the job of students in the knowledge workshop is to construct an understanding of the whole world. That was the job Aristotle undertook, only today's students may go at it with more help and with improved tools and resources. The achievement of such a unified and comprehensive understanding has traditionally been the highest aim of liberal education. However, in the past it has been seen as largely a matter of gaining possession of an *existing* understanding of the known world, such as Aristotle's or those of the medieval *Summae* or later the enlightenment project of Diderot's *Encyclopédie*. There were, of course, students who went beyond these fixed understandings to construct knowledge of their own, but in doing so they went well beyond the expectations of the curriculum and perhaps even beyond its allowable limits. The proposal to make knowledge building the principal activity in schooling would mean enlarging liberal education so as to encompass both the grasping of what others have already understood and the sustained, collective effort to extend the boundaries of what is known.

Enculturation into World 3

In the preceding section I suggested that knowledge building could be thought of as simply another kind of schoolwork, a kind especially appropriate to students in a knowledge society. But there is much more to it than that. Multiculturalists, Marxist critics, and advocates of liberal education are alike in regarding schooling as a form of enculturation. To answer the question 'What should it mean to be an educated person in the twenty-first century?' we have to consider what kind of culture is foreseen and how schooling should relate to it. There is much more to this issue than I can begin to address. The uncertainties of prediction and the alarming nature of many trends in contemporary culture are daunting.

One social prediction seems much less risky than others, however, and that is the expectation of a continuing rise in the importance of knowledge and knowledge work. The only way this prediction could prove wrong would be if knowledge and technology stopped advancing, and barring worldwide suppression that could not occur. We do not know what the social consequences will be for employment, equity, quality of life, and so on—no matter how confidently pundits may extrapolate current trends. What we can say is that knowledge will be an increasingly salient part of the environment. You will not know your way around in tomorrow's world unless you know your way around knowledge.

A statement like the preceding can, however, mean next to nothing in a discussion of educational policy. To many people these days it will mean knowing your way around on the Internet, knowing how to do searches for Worldwide Web documents. The Web does, in fact, nicely epitomize a world overrun with knowledge; and so I am amazed to keep encountering writers on the Web proclaiming the centrality of information search skills as an educational objective for the knowledge age. The skills needed to do Web searches can be learned in a few hours (less, if you know a bit of Boolean algebra). But years of subject-matter learning must come to the fore if you are to avoid retrieving thousands of documents none of which contains the information you were hoping to find. Knowing your way around the Worldwide Web really means being on familiar terms with world knowledge in its manifold aspects. The more you know the greater your chance of learning something new. That is the real excitement of the new knowledge resources, yet it seems scarcely to be appreciated at all by the information media enthusiasts presuming to lead education into the knowledge age. If it were appreciated, it would go some way toward re-establishing the importance of liberal education.

The trouble, I believe, lies in a folk psychology which conceives of the mind as a storehouse of items of information, along with a set of mental abilities and skills for working with those items.[5] With this conception, it is very difficult to think of knowledge as the principal basis for finding or acquiring new knowledge, just as it is difficult to think of knowledge production as distinct from learning.

---

5   A still influential work in curriculum planning, Bloom's *Taxonomy of Educational Objectives*, makes this view of knowledge explicit: "[T]hink of knowledge as something filed or stored in the mind. The task for the individual in each knowledge test situation is to find the appropriate signals and cues in the problem which will most effectively bring out whatever knowledge is filed or stored" (Bloom 1956, p. 29).

We need a broader conception of knowledge. We must be able to treat it as a part of the world—along with computers, CD players, backpacks, and street people—that students become enculturated into. Without that, I fear, schooling will remain lodged in an earlier and more primitive age, no matter how many computers line the walls, and will little prepare students for the world that exists on the other side of the modem.

Working out a vision for education in a knowledge society minimally requires taking account of knowledge in two quite distinct senses: first, knowledge as something that people acquire and that becomes a part of them; second, knowledge as something that they work with and that in some sense takes on a life of its own. The knowledge-building classroom, as I have been characterizing it, embodies this dual conception of knowledge. It thus presents a miniature of the knowledge society into which students are to become enculturated.

Common sense of course recognizes this dual character of knowledge. When we talk about a child 'knowing (or not knowing) the Pythagorean theorem' we simultaneously refer to knowledge as an attribute of the child's mental state and to the Pythagorean theorem as a piece of knowledge in its own right—as something created by a mathematician in ancient times and surviving to this day as a worthwhile thing-to-be-known. But in order to carry on a serious discussion about knowledge in education, we need distinguishing labels. Karl Popper has provided some, which can be quite useful so long as we are careful not to encumber them with excess meaning. The labels come from his metaphor of three worlds. World 1, the physical world, need not concern us at this point. The important distinction is between Worlds 2 and 3. World 2 is the subjective world, comprising the knowledge in people's heads. (Without doing violence to Popper's concept, we can expand World 2 to include situated knowledge as well—knowledge that is implicit in the practices of communities and not assignable to individual minds.) World 3 is, roughly speaking, the world of ideas. It consists of immaterial knowledge objects that can be discussed, modified, replaced, and so on.[6] The Pythagorean theorem is an object in

---

6. Note that this is different from Plato's world of ideas, which pre-exist human understanding and are eternal. World 3 is wholly a human construction and is undergoing continual renovation.

World 3. The child's knowledge of the Pythagorean theorem is part of the child's World 2. The distinction thus coincides with the distinction I have been making between knowledge building and learning. Knowledge building is work carried out to produce changes in World 3. Learning consists of changes in World 2.

From an educational standpoint, what is especially attractive about the World 3 idea is that it encompasses both the traditional idea of a fund of accumulated knowledge that is passed on to the young and the more dynamic idea of knowledge advancing through people's creative efforts. We may think of World 3 as a workspace in which there are knowledge objects in various stages of development. Some are finished to the extent that no one bothers to tinker with them anymore. Some, like phlogiston theory, are of no current value and are preserved for historical interest only. Others are under current development and are the subjects of research, criticism, controversy, repair operations, and novel conjecture. The Pythagorean theorem is one of the finished objects of World 3. But when students produce explanations of the theorem or intuitive proofs or examples of application, these are World 3 objects as well and the activity that produces them is work in World 3, just as was the work of Pythagoras. This conception of World 3 as a realm of activity stretches Popper's concept, but not very much. He said at one point (1972, p. 156), "I suggest that one day we will have to revolutionize psychology by looking at the human mind as an organ for interacting with the objects of the third world; for understanding them, contributing to them, participating in them; and for bringing them to bear on the first world." This seems an apt description of mind in the knowledge age. Translating it into an educational prescription leads naturally to thinking of World 3 as a workspace and of education as providing entrée to it.

Accordingly, we may define the role of schools in the knowledge age as follows: It is *to enculturate students into World 3.* Enculturation into World 3 entails much more than mastering a body of established knowledge. Indeed, it leaves open such questions as what constitutes established knowledge and what needs to be mastered and in what ways. It implies, rather, that those perennial curriculum issues should be considered within the context of students' active participation in the world where such issues matter. Enculturation into any world means becoming familiar with what is there, learning how to act, becoming involved in what is going on, and generally coming to feel at home in it. At a deeper level, enculturation implies that artifacts and activities will come to have a *meaning* for the newcomer that is consistent with the meaning they have for others in that world. This does not mean that one becomes the same as everyone else, but it does mean that the world is no longer exotic, bewildering, or forbidding.

My favorite line expressing enculturation into World 3 appeared in a computer-based dialogue among elementary school students inquiring into problems of genetics: "Mendel worked on Karen's problem." Captured in these five words is the sense of a shared knowledge-building enterprise, continuity with the past, and the conception of a World 3 object (in this case, a formulated problem) that persists over time and space and that various people may work on in different ways. In short, a whole epistemology is represented here, an epistemology sophisticated enough for the knowledge age and something far beyond what educators speak of as 'co-operative learning', 'problem-based learning', 'constructivist learning', or (groan) 'learner-centered education'. It is knowledge-centered education; and Mendel gets into the picture, not as a dead white male with the authority of the scientific establishment behind him but as someone with a contribution to make to a current knowledge problem.

For Popper, as a philosopher of science, World 3 consisted primarily of discussible propositions or declarative knowledge—theories, conjectures, problem formulations, historical accounts, interpretations, proofs, criticisms, and the like. However, he saw these as cultural objects existing in a larger world that includes other cultural objects such as poems, sonatas, folktales, food recipes, rituals, and monuments. Liberal education is enculturation into this larger world of cultural objects. World 3 is and always has been an important part of the world for liberal education. What I am proposing is that World 3—especially in its constructive, creative aspect—needs to become a larger part, if liberal education is to rise to the challenges of the knowledge age.

The world of cultural objects is quite different for a liberally educated Indonesian, for instance, from what it is for a liberally educated Italian. To be sure, both would probably score better on a test of cultural literacy than would the average American student for whom it was designed; but in the art, literature, music, and history with which they are intimately familiar, there will be profound differences. These differences are valuable; cultures are kept alive by people who cherish and live on intimate terms with the objects of their cultures, and this is much of what gives richness to life. Nothing I say should be thought to deny these time-honored values. But it is important to recognize that things are different with the objects of World 3. Multiculturalists to the contrary, there are not culture-specific sciences, mathematics, literary or historical theories.[7] There are cultural differences, just as there are individual differences, in how people think about these things; but they are not differences that preclude constructive criticism and collaborative knowledge building. Or if they are, then something is wrong that education needs to set right.

The boundaries of World 3 are approximately the boundaries of what can be profitably argued about in general terms.[8] Liberal education, I am suggesting, has the dual task of expanding those boundaries and of equipping students to engage in the argument. Not that arguing is all one does with World 3 objects; there is finding implications and applications, explaining, comparing, revising, and so on. But if a proposition is not arguable it is generally not amenable to these other operations either, and if people do not understand a World 3 object well enough to argue constructively about it they are probably not competent to do much else with it.

Liberal education today is embroiled in serious controversy about *what* cultural objects, representing *whose* culture, are to figure in the curriculum. This is an important controversy, accentuated by the increasing cultural divisions to be found within modern societies. But the largest cultural divide, cutting across the whole world with great consequence, is that which separates people who

---

7. Part of the multiculturalist-postmodernist argument, however, is to reject a distinction between science and myth (cf. Rorty 1991). But myths do not put forth arguable propositions, and no one would even think of disputing, much less believing some other culture's creation myths, for instance. Science and scholarship, in contrast, do put forth propositions that are open to challenge by anyone anywhere and it is thus that World 3 transcends cultural boundaries.

8. The qualifier 'in general terms' is needed because most of what people argue about, of course, in everyday life are particular cases, and these are not World 3 objects.

are at home in World 3 from those who are not. Any decision about enculturation that excludes students from enculturation into a cosmopolitan World 3 is a serious denial of children's rights to education. Exclusion from World 3 could come in the form of an educational program so intent on preserving indigenous culture or ethnic pride that it relegates World 3 to the status of a foreign culture. This is what is happening when educators start referring to 'Eurocentric science', for instance. Or exclusion could take the form of an educational program so child-centered or so intent on learning objectives that there is no participation in any larger intellectual world.

Much of what is going on in education seems to be exclusionary in one or more of these ways. Worse than that, it seems that the education system itself is on the wrong side of the cultural divide, ill-disposed to treat knowledge as a focus of productive work. Better models of schooling are available, models that are compatible with the needs of a knowledge-based economy, with the best of cognitive learning research, and with enduring values of liberal education. But those models cannot simply be taken up as variations on project-based learning or whatever new method comes to the fore. In order to move to the other side of the divide, in order to find their place in a knowledge society, schools must undergo a much more radical transformation. Only by becoming knowledge-building organizations themselves, I believe, can schools hope to provide students with a way into the life of a knowledge society.

References

Anderson, R.C. and P.D. Pearson. 1984. A Schema-theoretic View of Basic Processes in Reading Comprehension. In P.D. Pearson, ed., *Handbook of Reading Research* (New York: Longman), pp. 255–292.

Bereiter, C. and M. Scardamalia. 1996. Rethinking Learning. In D.R. Olson and. N. Torrance, eds., *Handbook of Education and Human Development: New Models of Learning, Teaching, and Schooling* (Cambridge, MA: Blackwell), pp. 485–513.

Bloom, B.S., ed. 1956. *Taxonomy of Educational Objectives: Handbook 1. Cognitive Domain.* New York: David McKay.

Brown, A.L. 1978. Knowing When, Where, and How to Remember: A Problem of Metacognition. In R. Glaser, ed., *Advances in Instructional Psychology* (Hillsdale, NJ: Erlbaum), pp. 77–165.

Brown, A.L. and J.C. Campione. 1990. Communities of Learning and Thinking, or A Context by Any Other Name. *Contributions to Human Development* 21, 108–126.

———. 1994. Guided Discovery in a Community of Learners. In K. McGilley, ed., *Classroom Lessons: Integrating Cognitive Theory and Classroom Practice* (Cambridge, MA: MIT Press), pp. 229–270.

Chi, M.T.H., R. Glaser, and M. Farr, ed. 1988. *The Nature of Expertise.* Hillsdale, NJ: Erlbaum.

Doyle, W. 1986. Classroom Organization and Management. In M.C. Wittrock, ed., *Handbook of Research on Teaching* (New York: Macmillan), pp. 392–431.

Drucker, P. 1993. *Post-Capitalist Society.* New York: HarperBusiness.

Gardner, H. 1983. *Frames of Mind: The Theory of Multiple Intelligences.* New York: Basic Books.

Palincsar, A.S. and A.L. Brown. 1984. Reciprocal Teaching of Comprehension-fostering and Comprehension-monitoring Activities. *Cognition and Instruction* 1, 117–175.

Popper, K.R. 1972. *Objective Knowledge: An Evolutionary Approach.* Oxford: Clarendon.

Popper, K.R. and J.C. Eccles. 1977. *The Self and Its Brain.* Berlin: Springer-Verlag.

Rorty, R. 1991. *Objectivity, Relativism, and Truth: Philosophical Papers, Vol. 1.* Cambridge: Cambridge University Press.

Scardamalia, M. and C. Bereiter. 1994. Computer Support for Knowledge-building Communities. *Journal of the Learning Sciences* 3(3), 265–283.

———. 1999. Schools as Knowledge-building Organizations. In D. Keating and C. Hertzman, eds., *Today's Children, Tomorrow's Society* (New York: Guildford), pp. 274–289.

Scardamalia, M., C. Bereiter, and M. Lamon. 1994. The CSILE Project: Trying to Bring the Classroom into World 3. In K. McGilley, ed., *Classroom Lessons: Integrating Cognitive Theory and Classroom Practice* (Cambridge, MA: MIT Press), pp. 201–228.

Wandersee, J., J. Mintzes, and J. Novak. 1994. Research on Alternative Conceptions in Science. In D. Gabel, eds., *Handbook of Research on Science Teaching and Learning* (New York: Macmillan), pp. 177–210.

Wenger, E. 1995. *Communities of Practice.* New York: Cambridge University Press.

White, G. and G. Korner. 1995. *Just in Time Learning on the Internet.* Stanford University, Center for the Study of Learning and Instruction. (WWW page, http://www-csli.stanford.edu/csli/projects/interface9495-jitl.html.)

Yarnall, L. and Y. Kafai. April 1996. Issues in Project-based Science Activities: Children's Constructions of Ocean Software Games. Paper presented at the annual meeting of the American Educational Research Association, New York. (WWW page, http://www.gse.ucla.edu/kafai/Paper_Kafai%2FYarnall.html).

3

Educational Objectives in Advanced Countries: Some Economic Considerations

J.S.S. Edwards and S.C. Ogilvie

One of the two main influences on education planning today, Carl Bereiter remarks at the beginning of his paper on 'Liberal Education in a Knowledge Society' (Chapter 2 in this volume), is a set of economic views on what should be the educational objectives of advanced countries at the beginning of the twenty-first century. Bereiter's paper combines these economic concerns with recent work in cognitive science, in order to make recommendations for education planning.

This is a laudable objective, and one generally neglected by members of both disciplines. Economists tend to focus on whether economic agents are more (or less) educated, but to ignore the technologies by which educated economic agents are produced. And, as history suggests, for centuries educators (and more recently cognitive scientists) have tended largely to ignore the economic relevance of what schools taught and how they taught it. Bringing together economists' assessments of the objectives of education with cognitive scientists' findings about how to achieve these objectives is therefore an important task.

What should be the economic objectives of education in advanced countries? This might seem to be a straightforward question with quite simple answers. Certainly, the 'futuristic business literature' which Bereiter identifies as a major influence on current education planning proffers extremely simple answers to this question. In our view, however, the answer is not that simple. The main aim of this paper is to examine what current thinking in economics actually suggests about what should be the economic objectives of education in advanced countries today. We conclude that economic research implies rather different priorities for education than those suggested by the futuristic business literature. This in turn, we suggest, presents different challenges to cognitive science and education planning.

We begin by looking at education as a way of making people better producers, since this is the approach to educational objectives adopted both by the futuristic business literature and by most economists until recently. If improving people's production skills is the priority, what does the economic evidence suggest should be our main educational objectives? What implications does this have for the 'liberal education' tradition?

We then go on to ask whether it is right to define economic objectives for education solely in terms of making people better producers. Economic agents are consumers as well as producers, and recent work in economics suggests that education may play an equally or more important role as a way of improving people's skills as consumers—consumers of both material goods and political and cultural ideas.

Finally, we briefly addresses Bereiter's argument that the best way to achieve both content mastery and knowledge skills is to enculturate children into 'World 3'—the world of ideas. World 3, we argue, is a big place and resources for education are limited. As economists, we ask whether some regions of World 3 are more productive areas to enculturate children into than others.

I. Production Skills: What Does Economics Suggest Should Be the Educational Objectives of Advanced Countries Today?

Let us begin by examining education as a way for people to invest in improving their skills as producers. From this perspective, what should be the economic objectives of education in advanced countries today? It might appear that persuasive answers to this question have already been advanced in the 'futuristic business literature'. Both education planners in the United States and politicians during recent election campaigns in Britain have clearly been influenced by such answers. As summarized by Bereiter in his paper, and as reflected in publications such as Thomas A. Stewart's book, *Intellectual Capital* (Stewart 1997), the futuristic business literature advances the following general argument. In the last 30 years, they say, the nature of economic activity in advanced countries has changed fundamentally.[1] Whereas economies used to be oriented around producing physical output—agricultural commodities in agrarian societies, manufactured goods in industrial societies—now they are organized around producing knowledge.[2] This has given rise to a so-called 'knowledge society', which presents new and unprecedented challenges to education provision.[3] The sources of these unprecedented challenges are "the rapid rate of technological change, the rise of Asia Pacific economies, digitization, globalization, outsourcing, the shift from a manufacturing-based to a knowledge-based economy, and the need for constant

----

1. On the timing of this transformation into "a new, knowledge-based economy," as having taken place over the past three decades, see for instance Stewart 1997, p. 3.

2. Carl Bereiter, in 'Liberal Education in a Knowledge Society', summarizes this literature by referring to the importance of "taking seriously the idea of a knowledge society, a society organized around the production of knowledge in the same sense than an agrarian society is organized around agricultural production and an industrial society is organized around manufacture" (p. 12). Stewart (1997), p. 3, writes about how "knowledge has become the most important component of business activity." An early expositor of this point of view appears to have been Pope John Paul II (widely known for his profound views on economics), who wrote in his 1991 encyclical *Centesimus Annus* that "Whereas at one time the decisive factor of production was the land, and later capital . . . today the decisive factor is increasingly man himself, that is, his knowledge" (quoted in Stewart 1997, p. 12).

3. Bereiter, 'Liberal Education in a Knowledge Society', p. 13: "the ascendant importance of knowledge: knowledge as a third factor in production, along with capital and labor; learning as the means for organizations to gain a competitive edge; . . . the idea of a social transformation going on that is as extreme as the nineteenth-century shift from an agrarian to an industrial society—the shift to a knowlege society." Stewart (1997), p. 5, acknowledges that "knowledge has always been important," but continues that "knowledge is more important than ever before . . . because we are in the midst of an economic revolution that is creating the Information Age."

innovation."[4] Consequently, these challenges are not merely a temporary problem, but are permanent trends which are going to intensify over the foreseeable future.[5] To respond to these challenges, the argument goes, workers in the 'knowledge society' have to possess new skills: "imagination and creativity, ability to work in groups, communication skills, information-finding skills, problem-solving abilities, technological literacy, and above all a continual readiness to learn."[6] Yet, the futuristic business literature implies, workers are not currently getting the optimal quantity and quality of these skills from the education system. According to the futuristic business thinkers, this is a problem not just for a small minority of unemployable people, but for every single future worker and manager. That is, education systems in advanced countries are failing almost all their 'customers', and must be revolutionized in order adequately to serve the revolutionized nature of economic activity in the 'knowledge society'.

This story sounds so plausible that it has entered the working vocabulary of businessmen, politicians, planners, journalists, and ordinary people. It has almost become part of common sense. But viewed from the point of view of economics, the 'futuristic business literature' is, to put it bluntly, all but worthless: it amounts to little more than a collection of slogans, with next to nothing by way of theoretical or empirical basis. This may sound deeply disappointing. What the economic objectives of education should be

---

4. Bereiter, 'Liberal Education in a Knowledge Society', p. 13. Stewart refers to "large, unruly forces: globalization, which has opened enormous new markets and, a necessary corollary, enormous numbers of new competitors; the spread of information technology . . .; the dismantling of the many-tiered corporate hierarchy . . . a new Information Age economy" (1997, p. 6); later he summarizes these transformations as being four in number: "globalization, computerization, economic disintermediation, and intangibilization" (p. 7).

5. Stewart 1997, p. 6, argues that these changes are a revolution in the strict dictionary sense of the word: 'a sudden, radical, or complete change ... a basic reorientation'. In his view (p. 6), 'the changes surrounding us are not mere trends but the workings of large, unruly forces', i.e. they are not going to be reversed. Later (p. 10), Stewart refers to the 'Information Revolution's reinvention of business, economic life, and society' and claims that 'this new event will transfigure and disfigure all it touches'.

6. Bereiter, 'Liberal Education in a Knowledge Society', p. 13. Stewart writes that "success in a knowledge-based economy depends on new skills and new kinds of organizations and management" (1997, p. 17).

is an important question. It can't simply be ignored. This paper argues that it doesn't have to be ignored. Educators should indeed pay attention to economic objectives, but these objectives need to be identified more carefully, analyzed more logically, and supported with much firmer empirical findings. In this paper, we survey developments over the past generation in the labor-market experiences of more educated and less educated people in advanced countries. These findings, we suggest, imply rather different challenges for cognitive scientists and education planners in rich western economies at the beginning of the twenty-first century.

Before we begin, we need to be clear about some basic features of the following analysis, which are characteristic of economists' approaches to discussing education. The first is that economists tend to focus on the role of education in economic success, as measured, for example, by the higher wages received by more educated workers. This is not to deny that education yields other benefits to individuals, by, say, enhancing the quality of their lives, or to society, by producing better citizens; indeed, we will direct our attention to such questions in the next section of our paper. These other benefits, however, are typically not the subject of economic analyses of education.

The second characteristic feature is that economic analyses of education do not consider the details of the educational process— that is, they stay out of the realms of cognitive science and educational psychology, the field of expertise of many of the contributors to this volume. For economists, better-educated individuals are individuals who have completed more years of formal education: typically, economists have nothing to say about whether a given number of years of formal education results in better-educated individuals if these years are organized in one way rather than another.

With these preliminaries out of the way, let us turn next to the meaning of a 'knowledge society'. We are frankly rather sceptical about this term as it is defined in the futuristic business literature. As far as we can determine, this literature has conflated at least four different sets of arguments into the single, vague, catch-all slogan of a 'knowledge society'. Definition 1 claims that a 'knowledge society' is, in Bereiter's summary, "a society organized around the production of knowledge in the same sense that an agrarian society is organized around agricultural production and an industrial society is organized around manufacture."[7] Definition 2 claims that advanced countries are 'knowledge societies' in that technological change is much more important for economic growth than ever before.[8] Definition 3 argues that advanced countries are 'knowledge societies' in the sense that economic success is now determined by the ability of individuals and firms to accumulate and transform information in such a way as to produce and market goods efficiently and flexibly, something which has never before been the case.[9] Definition 4 is that advanced countries are 'knowledge societies' in the sense that without the ability to understand and transform knowledge (in other words, without high levels of education) it is hard for individuals to find decent jobs in such societies.[10]

Not only does the slogan 'knowledge society' conflate four very distinct sets of arguments, but for several of these arguments there is very little hard economic evidence. Advanced countries today are not knowledge societies in the sense of Definition 2, that technological change plays a greater role than ever before. The pace of technological change has certainly been rapid in the recent past, but it is not clear that it has been faster recently than in the more distant past, nor that its contribution to economic growth has been relatively more important recently.[11]

Nor are present-day advanced countries knowledge societies in the sense of Definition 3, that economic success is for the first time in history dependent on the ability of firms to process information effectively. In 1995, Nick von Tunzelmann carried out a thorough

7. Bereiter, 'Liberal Education in a Knowledge Society', p. 12.
8. Stewart 1997, pp. 6–7, 12–14, 21–22, 76, 79–106.
9. Stewart 1997, p. ix: "Information and knowledge are the thermonuclear competitive weapons of our time. Knowledge is more valuable and more powerful than natural resources, big factories, or fat bankrolls. In industry after industry, success comes to the companies that have the best information or wield it most effectively . . ."
10. Stewart 1997: "We are all knowledge workers now, working for knowledge companies" (p. xiv); "the skills individuals and companies need to succeed in their new environment, the knowledge economy are, in many cases, different from the ones they are used to" (p. xii).
11. See Collins and Bosworth 1996, Table 7 and pp. 185–86.

survey of what economic historians now know about the process of industrialization over the past 250 years in Britain, continental Europe, the United States, the U.S.S.R., Japan, and the NICs (Von Tunzelmann 1995). According to von Tunzelmann, a major factor contributing to successful industrialization in all these countries since 1750 has been "the knowledge base accumulated over time by the producing unit, i.e. the firm."[12] That is, successful economies have been 'knowledge societies' for a very long time. At least since the first industrial revolution, which began in Britain around 1750, and possibly already during the English and Dutch agricultural revolutions of the sixteenth and seventeenth centuries, the production and efficient use of knowledge has been an essential component of economic success. In this sense, every successful economy in history has been a knowledge society, and economic history provides no empirical basis for arguing that the economic contribution of knowledge today is higher than it has been in other rapidly growing economies over the past several centuries.

It is also difficult to marshall any economic evidence to sustain Definition 1, according to which a 'knowledge society' is "a society organized around the production of knowledge" (in Bereiter's summary) or (in Thomas Stewart's formulation) one in which "knowledge and information . . . have become the economy's . . . most important products."[13] A more convincing characterization of the advanced economies at present is that they are organized around the production of services—in the U.S.A., for example, more than 70 percent of workers are currently employed in services.[14] This observation seems to us to lead to a more useful interpretation of

---

12. Von Tunzelmann 1995, p. 4. Von Tunzelmann draws a distinction between 'information' (the sum total of messages generated in the world, which is in principle marketable) and 'knowledge' (which is not marketable because it is embodied in the highly various learning processes of individuals and firms). The fact that knowledge is not marketable, von Tunzelmann argues, is why firms exist: they have advantages over both individuals and markets in accessing, accumulating, combining and transforming knowledge from diverse sources for particular production purposes (p. 5).

13. Bereiter, 'Liberal Education in a Knowledge Society', p. 12; Stewart 1997, p. x.

14. In 1992, services accounted for 72.5 percent of total employment in the U.S.A., and 62 percent in the (then) European Community countries (OECD 1994), Table 1.1).

the sense in which advanced economies as a whole constitute a 'knowledge society', once it is recognized that service sector jobs are increasingly likely to be in highly-skilled areas, such as teaching, financial services or information technology, rather than in unskilled areas.[15]

This in turn provides some support for the only sense of 'knowledge society' for which there is much hard economic evidence at all. This is Definition 4, according to which a 'knowledge society' is one in which workers and managers who have higher levels of education are likely to enjoy higher economic returns. Even this definition of a 'knowledge society' should be subjected to closer empirical scrutiny, however, since many of the statements made about it in the futuristic business literature are not justified by the facts, and consequently the educational objectives derived from it are also largely unjustified.

Let us begin this closer empirical scrutiny by examining developments in labor markets in the advanced economies over the past 15 or 20 years. In particular, let us focus on the extent to which there has been growing inequality between skilled, well-educated workers and unskilled, less-educated ones.[16] Since the late 1970s, unskilled, less-educated workers in advanced economies have experienced a significant worsening of their position in the labor market compared to that of skilled, well-educated workers. Perhaps the best-known aspect of this growing inequality concerns earnings. In the U.S.A., the ratio of the average earnings of males aged 25–64 with less than full secondary education to the average earnings of males in the same age group with university degrees fell by 21 percent over the period 1979–92. In the U.K. the corresponding change (for males aged 25–59 over the period 1979–91) was a 17 percent fall.[17] In the U.S.A. these changes have meant a significant fall in real earnings for less-educated workers over the period, while in the U.K. the changes have involved only a very slight fall in real earnings.

---

15. In both the U.S.A. and the E.C., finance and business services was the area of services employment which experienced the fastest rate of growth over 1979–92 (OECD, Table 1.3).

16. In what follows we will not be maintaining any distinction between 'skilled' and 'educated', but rather using these terms synonymously.

17. Glyn 1995, Table 7.

The growing inequality in the earnings of less- and well-edu-cated workers is not, however, observed in other advanced economies to anything like the same extent as in the U.K. and the U.S.A. In many other countries, particularly continental European ones, there has not been any increase in the inequality of earnings between less- and well-educated workers since the late 1970s. What has happened has been an increase in the inequality of employ-ment between these groups. Relative to well-educated workers, less well-educated workers in Germany, Italy, and Belgium have experi-enced a greater increase in the incidence of unemployment if they are actively participating in the labor market, and also a greater increase in withdrawal from the labor market.[18] It should be noted, however, that the increased inequality in earnings between less- and well-educated workers in the U.S.A. and the U.K. has not pre-vented less-educated workers in these countries from experiencing as much increase in inequality of employment as their counterparts in continental Europe. Less-educated workers in the U.K. and the U.S.A. have experienced a markedly larger deterioration of their labor-market position than less-educated workers in other advanced countries.

This deterioration of the relative labor-market position of the less-educated has taken place in the context of their diminishing numerical importance in the labor force throughout advanced economies.[19] It cannot, therefore, be explained as a result of an increased supply of less-educated labor—that is, counter to the claims of the futuristic business literature, education systems in advanced economies do not appear to be systematically failing to educate a majority of their students to the changing demands of the economy. Instead, the observed increase in the share of well-edu-cated workers in the employed labor force together with an improvement in their relative labor market position appears to be

18. Glyn 1995, Table 7.
19. The proportion of the labor force with degrees increased throughout OECD countries in the 1980s, often by about 50 percent (OECD 1994). In the U.K., 6 per-cent of the employed labor force in 1979 had a degree or higher qualification, 44 percent had an intermediate qualification, and 50 percent had no qualifications. The corresponding figures for 1991 were 8 percent, 55 percent and 37 percent respectively (Machin 1996, Table 8).

the result of a shift in the demand for labor away from less-educated workers to well-educated ones, to which a significant proportion of people have responded by securing more education for themselves.[20]

Two main reasons have been adduced for this shift in demand toward more educated workers: increased international trade, and technical change biased in favour of high-skilled labor. These two reasons are often lumped together, with significantly more stress being laid on international trade—the specter of 'globalization' so frequently invoked not just by the futuristic business literature but by politicians and conspiracy theorists of a variety of persuasions. But these two causes of the shift in labor demand toward more educated workers—globalization and technical change—are conceptually distinct. Retaining this distinction is very important: these two factors have had quantitatively very different effects on labor demand; they have differing probabilities of continuing into the foreseeable future; and they have quite distinct policy implications.

The international trade argument—economic 'globalization'—is the one on which most emphasis is customarily placed. In its simplest version, it argues that less-developed economies, with relatively low wages, are increasingly able to export labor-intensive goods to advanced economies. This competition from low-wage economies makes production of these goods in advanced economies unprofitable, since producing such goods uses a substantial amount of unskilled, but relatively high-wage, labor. The result is some combination of falling relative wages and rising relative unemployment for unskilled workers in the advanced economies. The skill-biased technical change argument is rather different. It simply states that, for unexplained reasons, technical change over the recent past has systematically been biased against unskilled workers and in favour of high-skilled workers. The two arguments are not, of course, mutually exclusive—both factors may

---

20. For instance, 15 years ago only 2 out of 3 American adults were high-school graduates, compared to 4 out of 5 today. In 1980, 20 percent of American men had spent at least 4 years in college; by 1994 it had risen to 25 percent. Among American women, 13 percent had spent at least 4 years in college in 1980, compared to 20 percent by 1994. The same pattern can be seen in other advanced economies: in 1993 German university enrollment surpassed enrollment in the vocational apprenticeship system for the first time. See Stewart 1997, p. 47.

have been significant. For education planning, it is important to establish how significant each of these factors has been.

The relative importance of increased trade and skill-biased technical change in explaining the shift in the demand for labor away from unskilled towards skilled workers is ultimately an empirical matter. The available evidence suggests that skill-biased technical change has been the more important factor. The World Bank points out that in 1992 imports of manufactures from developing economies were only about 2 percent of advanced economies' GDP.[21] Even though these imports were labor-intensive, the direct effect on employment in advanced economies must have been small. Factor content calculations suggest that trade with developing economies since the mid-1970s has reduced the demand for unskilled workers in advanced economies by 2 to 5 percent of the unskilled labor force (1 to 3 percent of total employment). This evidence implies that the effects of trade have not been large enough to account for the observed fall in the demand for unskilled labor.

In addition, there is also evidence specifically supporting the view that the main reason for the shift in labor demand toward more educated workers has been skill-biased technical change (Machin 1996). If trade were the major reason for the fall in unskilled labor demand, then most of the fall in the employment share of unskilled workers should be accounted for by falls in employment in those industries which are subject to competition in the form of imports from low-wage economies. To the extent that the relative wages of unskilled labor decline as a result of international trade, unskilled labor should then be replacing skilled labor within industries which are not subject to competition from low-wage economies. However, the evidence shows that the majority of the decrease in the proportion of unskilled labor is not due to decreases in particular unskilled-labor-intensive industries, but has occurred within all industries. This is inconsistent with the trade explanation. Furthermore, the increases in the proportion of skilled workers which have occurred in all industries are positively correlated with indicators of technical change: the fastest increases in the use of skilled workers during the 1980s have occurred in industries which are more technologically advanced.

---

21. World Bank 1995, p. 56.

Skill-biased technical change, therefore, appears to be the major reason for the worsening of the labor market position of less-educated workers in advanced economies, although trade considerations have played some part. Increased competition from low-wage economies may also have been one reason for the bias in technical change against unskilled labor. Despite these qualifications, the available evidence is not consistent with the view that 'globalization', in so far as this means increased trade with low-wage economies, is the major factor underlying the deterioration in the relative labor market position of the less-educated in advanced economies.

What interpretation can be given to the meaning of a 'knowledge society' in the light of this review of labor-market developments in advanced economies? As we have argued above, most of the features glued together into the unwieldy conglomerate term 'knowledge society' are nothing like as new and unprecedented as is often claimed. However, advanced economies have become more extreme examples of 'knowledge societies' in so far as the labor-market returns to being well-educated have increased significantly in recent decades. Individuals with little education are now in a relatively worse labor-market position than they were thirty years ago, especially in the U.K. and the U.S.A.

However, these developments in the recent past are simply accentuations of factors that were already present, factors that can be observed in poor countries as well as advanced ones. Indeed, in some ways, education has a greater impact on people's well-being in poor economies than in advanced economies, since in poor economies education levels are significant predictors not just of wage rates, but of farm productivity, child mortality, family morbidity (illness levels), fertility rates, female nutritional status, and many other non-pecuniary measures of economic well-being.[22] In poor and rich economies alike, on average, individuals with higher levels of education have better labor-market opportunities than do

---

22. From the vast literature on the effects of education in less-developed economies, see especially: World Bank 1984, pp. 69–70, 76–77, 82–84; Birdsall 1988, pp. 514–16; Behrman and Wolfe 1984; Kanbargi and Kulkarni 1986; Kanbargi and Kulkarni 1991, pp. 125–163; Schultz 1988, pp. 585–614; Behrman and Deolalikar 1988, pp. 660–674; Psacharopoulos 1984; Jamison and Lau 1982.

individuals with lower levels of education, and this has been true for a long time. The changes in the labor-market position of the less- and the well-educated that have occurred in advanced economies since the late 1970s have very starkly emphasized that more educated people have better opportunities than less educated ones. Our own view is that advanced economies have been 'knowledge societies' for some considerable time, in that the better-educated members of these societies have consistently had better labor-market opportunities.

What implications does this interpretation of a 'knowledge society' have for educational objectives in advanced countries? In order to answer this question, let us begin by noting that the education system can contribute little to alleviating the problems currently being experienced by less-educated workers in advanced economies, except by the provision of specific training to enhance their skills, which may be one policy option. A second point to note is that there is no obvious reason to assume that the deterioration in the labor-market position of the less-educated over the past 15–20 years will continue. Since this deterioration is primarily the result of skill-biased technical change, and since the reasons for this bias in the direction of technical change are not understood, it is quite possible that the relative labor market position of the less-educated will improve in the future if the nature of technical change alters. However, competition from low-wage economies is likely to continue in the future, and this will have some effect in reinforcing the decline in labor-market opportunities for the less-educated, although its effects should not be overstated.

The main educational objective for advanced countries should, in our view, be to improve the attainments of children at the bottom of the distribution of educational achievement. Justification for this objective can be given either specifically in terms of recent developments in advanced-country labor markets, or more generally in terms of the desire for greater equality in labor market outcomes for individuals. There are some reasons to think that this objective is particularly pressing for the U.K. and the U.S.A. As we have seen, the less-educated in these countries have experienced an especially severe worsening of their labor-market opportunities in recent years. Furthermore, the U.K. and U.S.A. appear to be the two advanced countries with the greatest dispersion of educational attainments. A larger proportion of young people in these countries participate in higher education than in most other advanced countries, while at the same time there are greater deficiencies in basic skills such as literacy and numeracy in the U.K. and U.S.A. than in most other advanced countries.[23] The performance of U.K. and U.S.A. children in internationally co-ordinated mathematics tests also shows a wider distribution of performance than in most other advanced countries, as the table below indicates.

TABLE 3.1

Scores of 13-year-olds in International Mathematics Tests, 1990

	England	France	Italy	Switzerland	U.S.A.
Average	59.5	64.2	64.0	70.8	55.3
Highest decile	89.3	89.3	88.0	93.3	82.7
Lowest decile	32.0	37.3	36.5	50.7	29.3

Source: Prais 1993, Table 3

When considering what can be done to achieve this educational objective, it is important to ask why individuals have not already responded to the incentives for improved educational attainments. In fact, a large proportion of individuals *have* responded to these incentives, as is shown by the much larger proportion of adults finishing school or attending college in America and other advanced economies today than was the case even 15 years ago (Stewart 1997, p. 47). However, it is clear that a disturbingly large minority of individuals are *not* responding to the incentives created by the fact that more education leads to higher paychecks, and it is important for economists to ask why.

---

23. The U.K. Department for Education and Employment *Skills Audit* (1996) assessed the educational achievements of the U.K., the U.S.A., France, Germany, and Singapore. In terms of the percentage of the population with a first degree, the U.S.A. ranked first and the U.K. second out of the five countries. However, in terms of the literacy of adults (an assessment based on the opinions of multinational companies) the U.K. ranked only fifth, while in terms of the numeracy of adults (also based on multinationals' opinions), the U.S.A. and the U.K. ranked equal fourth.

It could be argued that the amount of education an individual should acquire can be determined by a simple weighing of benefits against costs. The benefits are calculated by the individual in terms of the returns he or she gets from more education, in the form of higher earnings or a greater likelihood of being able to get a job. The costs are calculated in terms of the effort and disutility (boredom, frustration) required to obtain particular qualifications, and earnings foregone while continuing to acquire education. From this point of view, the fact that some individuals choose to acquire only a minimum level of education could be interpreted as the result of a calculation on the part of these individuals that the costs to them of acquiring more education exceeded the benefits. If this argument were correct, the case for trying to improve the educational attainments of the less-educated would be weak.

There are various reasons why the argument just given is not correct. First, the decision to acquire better education involves incurring significant current costs in the expectation of future returns. It is not easy for individuals to borrow against higher future earnings in order to finance the education that might get them these future earnings, so individuals with low family incomes, or limited assets, may not be able to afford the level of education they would wish to acquire. This problem should not be over-emphasized, since various forms of public support for financing education exist in almost all countries, but it does provide one reason why less-educated individuals may have ended up with an inappropriately low level of education.

A second reason for doubting that individuals with low educational attainments have rationally chosen to acquire this low level of education is the likelihood that the benefits of education are not accurately perceived by all individuals. We clearly do not expect children to appreciate fully the benefits of education which must be set off against the costs of acquiring it (in terms of effort): parents are expected to act on their children's behalf in this respect. But parents with little education themselves, who may have had poor experiences with the educational system, are also likely to underestimate the value of education. This problem may be particularly serious in the very early stages of education: to the extent that educational achievements in secondary school and subsequently require as a necessary condition successful primary education, it is very important to try to make education for very young children enjoyable (low-cost in terms of effort), in order for it to be effective.

A third reason, related to the previous one, concerns the nature of education as a good. Many parents, and their children, know very little about what sort of education is being received. Most people have very limited experience of different forms of education, and they are very dependent on the information provided by teachers at schools and colleges in order to judge whether their children are receiving the appropriate form of education, and whether it is worth acquiring more education. It is no criticism of teachers or parents to say that in a situation where a child's performance at school depends on the parents' attitude to education, and the information about education provided by teachers, it is very likely that by the age of 16 many children will find themselves with a level of education which cannot be said to have been the outcome of a rational choice.

Low educational attainments may also not reflect individuals' rational choices because of imperfections in the institutions which supply education. In most advanced economies, the dominant supplier of education is the public education system, which generally enjoys something close to a monopoly position. It is widely recognized that there are localities in which the public education system fails to provide an adequate quality of education. Even where alternative suppliers exist, as a rule they are only accessible to the better-off. Less well-off children, even if they or their parents would rationally choose a higher level of educational attainment, may not be able to obtain it because it is not supplied by the monopoly producer, whether for economic or for political reasons. The inability to obtain an adequate quality of elementary education from monopolistic suppliers may in turn prevent children from being able to take advantage of (or even gain access to) secondary or post-secondary education. Where this is the case, children's low attainment in post-elementary education cannot be regarded as an outcome of rational choice, but rather of constrained access to supply.

The arguments above suggest that the objective of improving the educational attainments of average- and below-average school-leavers in advanced countries remains a sensible one. How to achieve this objective is a complex and difficult question, as will be clear from what has been said in this paper. Achievement of this objective requires more than just developments in the educational systems of advanced countries, but such developments are certainly necessary if the objective is to be achieved. Carl Bereiter's paper reports the results of work in cognitive science which is relevant for improving the way children learn, but it is disappointing to us in that it appears to treat children in general as having homogeneous requirements for improved methods of learning and acquiring education. The analysis in this paper suggests that a more differentiated approach to education in advanced countries is required. To put it bluntly, there are relatively few problems of any significance in the education that is received by high achievers in these countries, but there are serious problems in that received by low achievers, particularly in the U.K. and the U.S.A. From an economist's point of view, in allocating resources to pursue the educational objectives advanced in Bereiter's paper, it would be most important to focus on improving the educational experience of low achievers.

Indeed, from a historical point of view the major difference between educational objectives in present-day 'knowledge societies' and in past ones may reside precisely in this question of how widely and equally dispersed education is across the whole population. The main difference between past and present-day 'knowledge societies' may not be the importance of knowledge, but rather the fact that in past 'knowledge societies', only a minority of economic agents transformed knowledge, while the remainder of the population did routine tasks because there were no machines to do them. Consequently, these societies could get by with education systems focused only on a small elite group. Nowadays in advanced economies a much larger proportion of people have to be able to transform knowledge, and this poses new challenges to educators. The distinctively new feature of present-day societies, compared to past ones, is not the economic importance of knowledge transformation, but rather the economic importance of transmitting knowledge-transforming skills to the entire population—not just the most intelligent, or those who have already been enculturated to World 3 in middle- and upper-class families. If this is true, the unprecedented challenge faced by educators in advanced countries today is not that knowledge transformation has become important for the first time in history, but rather than for the first time in history it has become essential to lower the costs of education for social groups which in earlier eras remained uneducated.

We are aware that some may find difficulties with our conclusion that the economic evidence shows no obvious problems of any significance in the education received by high and medium achievers. 'How do economists know,' a businessman may object, 'that the supply of human capital in our economy is sufficient for the demand? Think how much better I could do in my business if my electrical engineers could add, or my production line people could read the instructions on the machines they use every day. All you're saying is that I can stay in business given the current level of education of my employees. But you have no evidence that my firm wouldn't be substantially more profitable if education were improved—not just for the lowest achievers (whom I am not employing anyway), but across the board. Certainly I, for one, could produce more at lower cost.'

One response to this would to say, 'All right, if education is so important to you, are you willing to pay higher wages to get it? Otherwise, you're basically saying you'd like to be able to purchase a better grade of *any* input—bauxite, for instance—at the same price as the present low grade ore you currently purchase—in other words, you'd like a subsidy to your production costs.' A recent survey of businesses' expenditures on employee training suggest that there is a sense in which businessmen who complain about low levels of worker skills are not willing to put their money where their mouths are. Recent studies show that in the U.K. there has been little change since 1985 in the amount of off-the-job training or the percentage of workers partipating in it, that spending on training has fallen since 1993, that half of British businessmen preferred to poach trained workers from other firms rather than train their existing employees, and that half of British companies fail to spend their annual training budgets. The article concludes that "When push comes to shove, British bosses—like many of their peers in other countries—are dubious about the merits of training" (*Economist* 1997, p. 104). If this is the attitude of businessmen to spending money on *training*, which is oriented specifically to their firms' needs, one can only conclude that their attitude to spending money on *education*, directed at inculcating general skills such as arithmetic and reading, would be even more restrained.

A more differentiated response to the employer's point might agree that it does seem unreasonable that an employee should have spent 16 years in full-time education, should clearly have been intelligent enough to get a university degree in, say, electrical engineering, and yet not be able to write a coherent report or add up without a calculator, skills we think of as ones people should be able to learn in grade school. This surely does suggest a failure in the education system, even for medium and high achievers. The economist would respond that one would expect the higher salaries earnable by electrical engineers who can write compared to those who cannot write gradually to feed through to more people equipping themselves with this combination of skills. But we have already seen the factors which may mean this takes place slowly or insufficiently: firstly, education is a long-term decision; secondly, individuals do not necessarily accurately perceive the benefits of higher training; and thirdly, parents and children are dependent on what the education system serves out to them, and the education system itself may be poorly informed about the economic returns to certain skills, or have no incentive to provide these skills even if it is aware of their returns to individuals. This means that there may indeed be some role for improved education provision as a way of providing that electrical engineer with a higher level of skills with the same 16 years of education input, and thus of providing his employer with a higher level of skills in his employee at the same wage cost. The same imperfections in the education market which lead the lowest achievers in the U.S. and the U.K. to get inappropriately low levels of education may also to some extent be affecting medium and high achievers. It may be this which prompts the concerns of employers about the skills shortage, and the persuasiveness of the futuristic business literature in claiming that the education system is failing almost all of its 'customers'.

It is therefore *possible* that education failures are taking place among medium and high achievers as well as low achievers. However, there is *clear empirical evidence* that education failures are taking place among the low achievers, and that these failures are quantitatively quite significant. In our view, therefore, the main priority, especially in the U.S. and the U.K., must remain to address the education problems of low achieving learners. We are aware that this has long been a major focus of some cognitive scientists—

including contributors to this volume. However, we are concerned that taking on board the futuristic business literature, which implies that the education system is equally failing *all* students, may diffuse the efforts which cognitive scientists and education planners ought to continue to focus unrelentingly on *low-achieving* students.

A further implication of our discussion would be as follows. Insofar as a significant minority of low-achieving children are not investing in an optimal quantity of education because they do not have an accurate perception of the benefits, and insofar as this misperception of the benefits is particularly acute among very young children, then this would imply that a particularly important priority for cognitive scientists and educators is to reduce the costs of obtaining an education for very young children. This means that the most serious priority may not be to teach the 'imagination and creativity, ability to work in groups, communication skills, information-finding skills, problem-solving abilities, and technological literacy' stressed by the futuristic business literature. To us, these seem to be skills more appropriate for rather older pupils, who have already overcome the early barriers to learning. The main problem may be to devise pedagogical approaches which lower the cost to disadvantaged 4-, 5-, and 6-year-olds of obtaining the very basic skills of numeracy, literacy, and enculturation into World 3 which will be necessary for them to participate productively in learning more complex skills such as imagination, creativity, group-work, information-finding, and technology in later school years.

To sum up, it seems to us that the futuristic business literature is identifying educational objectives which are more relevant to medium- and high-achieving students who are already securing levels of education which equip them reasonably well for a knowledge society. The economic literature we have surveyed in this paper, by contrast, would identify a major educational objective as being to devise ways of enabling low-achieving students to walk, before teaching high-achieving students how to run. Ideally, of course, we would all like the education system to serve both objectives. However, the economic findings we have surveyed in this paper suggest that the real failure of the education systems of advanced countries today is disproportionately concentrated within a relatively small group of children who cannot afford the current costs of an education (in terms of personal effort and disutility). As a consequence, these children are currently destined to adult lifetimes of very low wages and very high unemployment, and it seems probable that they will pass on their perceptions of the relative costs and benefits of education to their own children. This is costly not only for such individuals, but for us all, and for generations of disadvantaged children to come. In summary, from the point of view of production, the economic evidence is very clear about what our major educational objective should be: the single thing most worth doing is to raise the education levels of the least educated.

What implications do the economic considerations discussed so far have for the liberal education tradition? Liberal education is defined as consisting of those arts and sciences which are 'liberal' rather than 'mechanical' or 'servile'—that is, those disciplines and activities which are "directed to general intellectual enlargement and refinement; not narrowly restricted to the requirements of technical or professional training."[24] In our view, the economic findings surveyed so far suggest a generally positive but rather narrow role for liberal education. Most formal education in advanced countries still corresponds more or less to this definition of a liberal education (it is oriented toward general intellectual enlargement rather than vocational training), and the economic findings show indisputably that those children with more years of formal education have much better employment opportunities than those who have less. It is unclear precisely what characteristics of education make people more effective as producers, but it is clear that something about it does so. If Bereiter is right, it may be that it is because the liberal education tradition focuses on enculturation into a cosmopolitan 'World 3', and such enculturation is the most effective way of teaching the skills people subsequently use to be efficient producers. If this is true, then liberal education can be

---

24. *Compact Oxford English Dictionary*, p. 967, (p. 881, col. 3). The first quoted use of the term in English was in 1375. Its use over the last six centuries reflects lively debate about which disciplines and activities are included in a liberal education, but the criterion has continued to be the distinction between the 'liberal' (those 'arts' and 'sciences' considered 'worthy of a free man') and the 'servile' or 'mechanical' (those disciplines oriented toward technical or professional training).

assigned a role as a sort of handmaiden to the acquisition of economically useful skills. From this perspective, economic considerations would assign a positive but somewhat 'mechanical and servile' role to liberal education.

II. Education as a Way of Training Effective Consumers

But is this all an economist would say in support of a liberal education? In our view, even from a strictly economic perspective, this is an unnecessarily limited assessment of the role of a liberal education. This assessment results from a common tendency, by economists and businessmen alike, to focus on education exclusively as a way of training people to be good *producers*. In the remainder of this paper, we suggest that this exclusive emphasis on production has led to the neglect of an equally important educational objective, namely to enhance people's skills as *consumers*. This is particularly important in advanced countries, where markets offer an extremely wide choice of material and cultural goods, and impose correspondingly wide demands on consumers' ability to evaluate their choices. We suggest that widening the focus to regard education as encompassing consumption as well as production skills poses interesting new challenges for cognitive research and for education planning, and assigns a less 'servile' and 'mechanical' role to 'liberal education'.

Our point of departure is the fact that although economic research suggests that education is generally good for production, there is very little evidence about what precisely it is about education that is good. Indeed, given this lack of evidence, it is at least theoretically possible that if education is viewed solely as a way of making people good producers, a substantial increase in the vocational component of education at the expense of a corresponding decrease in the liberal component could be justified as an educational objective. A case could be made that an education more directly targeted toward professional skills would have advantages over one 'directed to general intellectual enlargement and refinement'.

Intuitively, however, most of us—even the most hard-nosed economist among us—would oppose this idea. But on what grounds? One might simply invoke moral absolutes and assert that the knowledge of elite culture embodied in a 'liberal education' has an absolute worth which justifies forcing children to allocate resources to it. But in our view there may be a more analytical reason for supporting the idea of a liberal education, one which derives support from some very recent currents in the economic analysis of how people form their preferences and consumption habits.

Advanced countries today are often described, in uncomplimentary terms, as 'consumer societies'. One of the most widely decried aspects of 'consumer society' is the tendency of uneducated consumers to prefer goods that require little investment to consume: they prefer television to novels, Jackie Collins to Jane Austen, Stallone movies to avant-garde French cinema, Madonna to Beethoven, astrology to astronomy, futuristic business literature to economics journals, and generally pop culture to elite culture. One doesn't have to be a snob or a socialist—one doesn't have to disrespect popular tastes, or believe that choices should be taken out of people's hands—to think that people are often making low-quality decisions, perhaps simply for lack of better training. On the other hand, there are also people who choose to consume elite culture, not because they think such culture is morally 'better' (although they may hold this view) but because they enjoy it more.

Traditionally, economists have had very little to say about how people form preferences. Most of modern economics proceeds on the assumption that preferences are given, that they are relatively stable, and that their main determinants are basic biological needs: food, drink, shelter, and recreation. But it's quite obvious that in advanced economies the average person's choice of consumption doesn't have much to do with these basic needs. Instead, it appears to depend on childhood experiences, social interactions, and cultural influences. Recently some economists—notable among them Gary Becker, in his recent book *Accounting for Tastes*—have begun to try to develop more analytical ways of understanding how people form their preferences and why they get into the habit of consuming particular things.[25]

---

25. Becker 1996, p. 3.

The point of departure is something economists term an individual's 'discount rate', the amount by which he or she discounts future over present happiness.[26] Traditionally, economics assumed that discount rates, although they differed among individuals, were constant and fixed for each individual.[27] Empirically, however, discount rates not only vary systematically according to people's personal characteristics (such as age, income and education), but also change over time for the same individual.[28]

To explain why this might be the case, economists such as Becker postulate that a person's discount rate—how much that person takes future satisfaction into account in current decisions—depends on his or her ability to imagine what future satisfactions will be like. This ability is determined partly by inheritance, but also partly by the individual's choices, in particular the choice to spend resources (time, effort, goods) in producing 'imagination capital' that helps the person better appreciate what future satisfactions will be like.[29] More concretely, economic studies exist which suggest that education, parental training, addiction to drugs, and religion all affect people's ability to imagine and appreciate the future, and thus affect how much they discount future over present consumption.[30]

How much 'imagination capital' people have will in turn affect which goods they prefer to consume. If you have a lot of imagination capital, you will place greater weight on future consequences of current choices. This will make you more likely to do things which increase your future happiness, even at the cost of current happiness. You will be less likely to become addicted to harmful substances. You'll be more likely to take exercise or turn up to work

---

26. A discount rate is the proportional amount by which the additional future consumption required to compensate an individual for a unit decrease in current consumption exceeds 1, when the individual is consuming equal amounts of current and future consumption.

27. It has even been argued recently that the ability to anticipate future utilities has a strong biological component; see Rogers 1994.

28. Becker 1996, pp. 10–11.

29. Becker and Mulligan 1997.

30. See, for instance, Becker 1996, pp. 3–23, 118–138; Akabayashi 1995, cited in Becker 1996, p. 11.

on time. And you will more likely at least to try forms of consumption with higher initial costs but potentially high future returns (such as listening to Beethoven or learning to play a musical instrument yourself) instead of sticking to Madonna.

Here's where a second aspect of the new economic analysis of preferences comes in: the economic analysis of habit formation. Economists have analyzed the behaviour of people who engage in habitual or addictive activities—not just 'harmful' habits such as tobacco addiction or gambling, but 'beneficial' habits such as saving money, staying with your spouse, or listening to Beethoven.[31] And they have found that although clearly in some habits purely chemical and medical addiction plays a role, in almost all habits— including chemical addictions—so too does something called 'reinforcement'. 'Reinforcement' means that an increase in current consumption of a good will tend to raise demand for the consumption of that good in the future. In economic terminology, past and present consumption of tobacco (or Beethoven) are complements—the more you consume it now, the more you will consume it in future. This is true to some extent for many goods, but it applies more to certain goods than to others.

The economic analysis of preference formation and consumption habits is still in its infancy. However, if its early results are to be relied on, they would imply a whole new set of economic objectives for education. They would imply that education be viewed not only, or even primarily, as an investment in human capital in the sense of *production* capital (which is the sense in which the term 'human capital' is invariably used). Rather, education should also be viewed as in investment in human *consumption* capital.[32] Education is an activity which, economic studies suggest, tends to lower people's discount rates, that is to increase the weight they place on future compared to present consumption. This in turn makes them more willing to engage in forms of consumption which

31. Stigler and Becker 1977; Becker and Murphy 1988; Becker, Grossman, and Murphy 1991; Becker, Grossman, and Murphy 1994; Becker 1992; Becker 1996, pp. 8–10.

32. Becker 1996, pp. 4–5, puts this point quite forcefully: "Although the human capital literature has focused on education, on-the-job training, and other activities that raise earnings, capital that directly influences consumption and utilities [is] sometimes even more important."

have beneficial rather than harmful future consequences.[33] Once a person has begun a certain beneficial (or harmful) consumption habit, he or she is likely to continue doing so because of 'reinforcement', the complementarity between present and future consumption, the fact that once you learn how to generate satisfaction from a particular activity you will be more productive at generating satisfaction from that activity in future, and therefore be more likely to engage in it.

From this point of view, we can arrive at a conclusion about educational objectives that is much more favorable to traditional ideas of 'liberal education', and also to Bereiter's idea of making World 3 more central to it. It can be argued that, historically, ideals of liberal education have always been geared to consumption rather than production. In antiquity, they focussed on making the educated individual a better person, not so much in the sense of being more useful to society, but in the sense of enabling him or her to lead a better life, to make consumption decisions with longer time-horizons, and not simply to choose on the basis of immediate pay-off. In more recent times, especially in democratic societies, there has been an added emphasis on making the individual a more intelligent *political* consumer, one who is better able to judge political and social proposals, not just on their immediate pay-off but on their long-term consequences.

Regarding education as a way of making people better consumers as well as producers suggests a number of additional educational objectives. For one thing, it may be the case that the minority of children whom the education system is failing (to the extent that this is reflected in their low education levels, low wages and high unemployment in later life) are those for whom discount rates are, for some reason, particularly high. One reason a child may have a high rate of discounting future over present benefits may be family background and pre-school experiences. Once it is recognized that discount rates vary, one objective for the very early years of education might be to overcome the problem of high discount rates for those children who suffer from them.

---

33. Becker 1996, pp. 11, 63, 82–83; Farrell and Fuchs 1982; Chaloupka 1991; Townsend 1987.

One way of approaching the problem of high discount rates has already been discussed. This is to make education less costly (in terms of boredom or frustration), so that highly-discounted expected future benefits may still have a chance of outweighing these costs. But this is only a palliative, not a solution. The problem of a high rate of discounting future over present benefits will still dog that child into the future and limit his or her capacity to invest in education and many other beneficial activities throughout life.

A more fundamental approach to the possibility that a substantial minority of children come into school with much higher discount rates than the rest, rendering them less able to learn even at similar levels of native intelligence, would be to devise pedagogical approaches which might lower these children's discount rates. This approach would not focus so much on making education low-cost, but on making education a higher-return activity, by equipping children with the 'imagination capital' which would enable them to value future benefits more highly relative to current ones.

As mentioned above, analyses of forms of consumption such as smoking, with low present costs and high future ones, show that, holding other measurable variables constant, higher levels of education are associated with lower rates of discounting the future over the present. Economists have concluded from this that education tends to lower an individual's discount rate. But they don't know why. In our view, it is even possible that there is in fact no causal link between education and discount rates. The empirical findings may simply reflect a selection bias: individuals who inherently have low discount rates are more likely both to educate themselves and to refrain from forms of consumption with high future costs. But it is also possible that education itself plays a role in reducing discount rates. Perhaps cognitive scientists may be able to establish if this is the case and why it might be so. If it does turn out to be the case, they might even suggest ways in which children who enter school with high discount rates can be assisted to achieve lower ones.

The analysis of how people form consumption habits also has a further potential implication for educational objectives. Economic analyses suggest that human beings have a strong tendency to form habits; as Gary Becker puts it, "Habit helps economize on the cost of searching for information, and of applying the information to a new situation . . . And most people get mental and physical comfort and reassurance in continuity to do what they did in the past."[34] Habits can be either beneficial (turning up to work on time, practicing the piano, reading informative or stimulating books) or harmful (using certain drugs, gambling, over-eating). Once a habit is formed, it appears to be self-sustaining, because of 'reinforcement', the existence of high complementarities between present and future consumption of the particular good involved. Moreover, both theory and empirical findings suggest that young people have a greater tendency to form new habits than do older people.[35]

These findings imply that a possible objective for education is to ensure that children, while they are still very young and open to forming new habits, experience beneficial forms of consumption which may then become habitual through reinforcement. Economists observe empirically that some forms of consumption are much more habit-forming than others, and describe them as being goods with higher complementarities between past and future levels of consumption. But economists don't know why some goods have this habit-forming characteristic. Cognitive scientists may be able to isolate precisely what *kind* of learning experiences do have this habit-forming reinforcement characteristic and which don't. If such habit-formation is important, then cognitive science may be able to tell us which parts of the world of liberal education are likely to be more or less beneficially habit-forming for children of particular backgrounds, sexes, and ages.

III. Scarce Resources and Competing Ends: Are Some Parts of World 3 More Important than Others?

Viewing education as investment in consumption will also help us in the all-important question left open by Bereiter's proposal, which is the one with which we should like to conclude our paper. This is the question of what precise skills and knowledge should be made central to education. Human knowledge is very large, if not infinitely so. Yet the resources, not just of money but of time and

---

34. Becker 1996, p. 122.
35. Becker 1996, pp. 31–33, 59–60, 81–83.

effort, which can be allocated to learning it are inevitably limited, even in the most generously funded education system. Education planners, parents, teachers, and students need some guide to those areas to which these limited resources may be most productively allocated. Bereiter goes part of the way toward providing an answer when he concludes that enculturating children into World 3—the world of ideas—is the best way of enabling them to find out for themselves the knowledge and skills they will need when they come to work as adults in a 'knowledge society'. However, World 3 itself is a very big place and the question which automatically arises in an economist's mind is the following: in the view of cognitive science, are all parts of World 3 equally productive ends to which to allocate scarce resources in education?

Bereiter's proposal implies that this question doesn't matter: that learning *anything* about the topography of World 3 is more important than a detailed knowledge of particular regions of it. But is this true? Are not some regions of World 3 more productive places to begin, if one wants to learn about the other regions of this world? To extend the metaphor, aren't there—on the one hand—mountain tops from which one can see wide lands to be discovered, advantageous ports, and navigable rivers; and—on the other hand—trackless forests and arid deserts? Is it not possible that one of the reasons old-fashioned 'rote learning' began to be so widely criticized in the 1960s was that it focussed too much on areas of World 3 which appear trackless and arid to all but a small elite of highly intelligent (or already enculturated middle-class) learners?

The new economics of preference formation and consumption habits would suggest that, if one views education as an investment in human *consumption* capital as well as human production capital, then one over-riding consideration—practically never raised in educational debates—will be to make sure that all children, or as many as possible, undergo the experience of consuming something that requires a considerable investment. If this consumption object is also to be part of a cosmopolitan World 3, in Bereiter's vision of it, we have narrowed things down a good deal. But here we should like to stop, and invite discussion from people who specialize in the other side of the question: the technologies with which educational objectives can be achieved.

References

Akabayashi, H. 1995. The Role of Incentives in the Function and Formation of Family Background: Theory and Evidence. Unpublished memorandum, University of Chicago.

Becker, Gary S. 1996. *Accounting for Tastes*. Cambridge, MA: Harvard University Press.

———. 1992. Habits, Addictions, and Traditions. *Kyklos* 45, 327–345.

Becker, Gary S., M. Grossman, and K.M. Murphy. 1991. Rational Addiction and the Effect of Price on Consumption. *American Economic Review* 81, 237–241.

———. An Empirical Analysis of Cigarette Addiction. *American Economic Review* 84, 396–418.

Becker, Gary S. and C.B. Mulligan. 1997. The Endogenous Determination of Time Preference. *Quarterly Journal of Economics* 112, 729–758.

Becker, Gary S. and K.M. Murphy. 1988. A Theory of Rational Addiction. *Journal of Political Economy* 96, 675–700.

Behrman, J. and B.L. Wolfe. 1984. The Socioeconomic Impact of Schooling in a Developing Country. *Review of Economics and Statistics* 66.

Behrman, Jere R. and Anil B. Deolalikar. 1988. Health and Nutrition. In Chenery and Srinivasan 1988, Vol. 1, pp. 633–711.

Birdsall, Nancy. 1988. Economic Approaches to Growth. In Chenery and Srinivasan 1988, Vol. 1, pp. 477–542.

Chaloupka, F. 1991. Rational Addictive Behavior and Cigarette Smoking. *Journal of Political Economy* 99, 722–742

Chenery, H. and T.N. Srinivasan, eds. 1988. *Handbook of Development Economics*. Amsterdam: North Holland.

Collins, Susan M. and Barry P. Bosworth. 1996. Economic Growth in East Asia: Accumulation versus Assimilation. *Brookings Papers on Economic Activity* 2, pp. 185–207.

Department for Education and Employment. 1996. *The Skills Audit: A Report from an Interdepartmental Group*. London: HMSO.

The Economist. 1997. The Margaret Thatcher of Training. *The Economist* (17th May).

Farrell, P. and V.R. Fuchs. 1982. Schooling and Health: The Cigarette Connection. *Journal of Health Economics* 1, 217–230.

Glyn, Andrew. 1995. The Assessment: Unemployment and Inequality. *Oxford Review of Economic Policy* 11, pp. 1–25.

Jamison, T. and L.J. Lau. 1982. *Farmer Education and Farm Efficiency*. Baltimore: Johns Hopkins University Press.

Kanbargi, R. and T. Kulkani. 1986. Child Labour and Schooling in South India. In J. Stoeckel and A.K. Jain, eds., *Fertility in Asia: Assessing the Impact of Development Projects* (London: Pinter, 1986), pp. 110–134.

———. 1991. Child Work, Schooling, and Fertility in Rural Karnataka, India. In R. Kanbargi, ed., *Child Labour in the Indian Subcontinent: Dimensions and Implications* (New Delhi: Sage), pp. 125–163.

Machin, Stephen. 1996. Wage Inequality in the U.K. *Oxford Review of Economic Policy* 12, 47–64.

OECD. 1994. *The OECD Jobs Study*. Paris: Organization for Economic Co-operation and Development.

Prais, S.J. 1993. Economic Performance and Education: The Nature of Britain's Deficiencies. Keynes Lecture in Economics. *Proceeding of the British Academy* 84, 131–120.

Psacharapoulos, G. 1984. The Contribution of Education to Economic Growth. In J.W. Kendrick, ed., *International Comparisons of Productivity and Causes of the Slowdown* (Cambridge, MA: Ballinger), pp. 325–360.

Rogers, A.R. 1994. Evolution of Time Preference by Natural Selection. *American Economic Review* 84, 460–481.

Schultz, T. Paul. 1988. Education Investments and Returns. In Chenery and Srinivasan 1988, Vol. 1, pp. 544–630.

Stewart, Thomas A. 1997. *Intellectual Capital: The New Wealth of Organizations*. New York: Doubleday.

Stigler, G.J. and G.S. Becker. 1977. De Gustibus Non Est Disputandum. *American Economic Review* 67, 76–90.

Townsend, J.L. 1987. Cigarette Tax, Economic Welfare, and Social Class Patterns of Smoking. *Applied Economics* 19, 355–365

Von Tunzelmann, G.N. 1995. *Technology and Industrial Progress: The Foundations of Economic Growth*. Aldershot: Elgar.

World Bank. 1984. *World Development Report 1984: Population Change and Economic Development*. Oxford: Oxford University Press.

———. 1995. *World Development Report 1995*. Oxford: Oxford University Press.

4

Collective Cognitive Responsibility for the Advancement of Knowledge

Marlene Scardamalia

If there is any consensus about what education in a knowledge society should be like, it is to be found in a cluster of terms that pervade the oral and printed discourse on this issue—including especially the 'futuristic business literature' that Bereiter cites in his target article: *lifelong learning, flexibility, creativity, higher-order thinking skills, collaboration, distributed expertise, learning organizations, innovation, technological literacy*. At times these appear to be empty buzzwords, but they may also be thought of as attempts to give expression to a central intuition that has yet to be formulated in terms that are clear enough to be very useful in generating designs and policies. In this chapter I attempt to extract a main idea from these vague terms and show how it can be applied to generate a kind of education that really does address new challenges in a new way.

A central idea is *collective cognitive responsibility*. Although this concept does not capture everything suggested in the foregoing list of terms, it captures much that they have in common and something more. Let us first expand upon the idea in the context of adult work and then apply it in the context of education.

Collective Cognitive Responsibility in the Workplace

Expert medical teams, flight crews, and sports teams have begun to serve as models for the kinds of groups that are expected to carry on much of the higher-level work in knowledge-based enterprises. Expert teams exhibit continual learning, flexibility, good thinking, and collaboration; but they also exhibit other characteristics of a more distinctive nature. Although each member of the team may have particular expertise and particular duties, the team members are also able to take over for one another on a moment-to-moment basis. This provides a flexibility that enables the group effort to succeed despite unexpected complications. Along with the capability is a commitment on the part of each member to do whatever is necessary to make the team effort succeed. Expert teams have been around for a long time. The whaling crews that Melville described in *Moby-Dick* exemplify what I have been describing. And, of course, expert sports teams exhibit just the combination of distinctive roles and skills on one hand and resourceful co-operation on the other that go to make up collective responsibility. What is new is that expert teams are becoming the paradigms for working groups of all kinds, replacing the bureaucratic and assembly line paradigms, in which roles are fixed and the way to handle the unexpected is to refer it to a higher level in the organization.

Collective responsibility, then, refers to the condition in which responsibility for the success of a group effort is distributed across all the members rather than being concentrated in the leader. Collective *cognitive* responsibility involves an added dimension. In modern enterprises there is usually a cognitive dimension in addition to the more tangible and practical aspects. This is obviously the case in research groups and other groups directly concerned with knowledge production, but it is also the case in enterprises where knowledge production is subordinate to other goals. The members of an expert surgical team, for example, will ideally share responsibility not only for carrying out the surgical procedure; they also take collective responsibility for understanding what is happening, for staying cognitively on top of events as they unfold. In a well-functioning office, the staff will not only keep records and appointments in order and get required work out on time; they will also take responsibility for knowing what needs to be known and for insuring that others know what needs to be known. This is what is meant by collective cognitive responsibility.

In discussions with business people, I find that they instantly recognize cognitive responsibility as a problem, even though they have not previously thought of it in those terms. They recognize that their employees may be carrying out overt tasks with a high level of responsibility, but that things keep going wrong or projects deteriorate because problems are either not being recognized or are thought to be someone else's responsibility. The calendars, to-do lists, and project management software designed to keep people organized and on task provide little help in this regard. They may include cognitive items—'Decide . . . ', 'Look into . . . ', 'Plan . . . '—but these have the effect of limiting cognitive responsibility to particular people and of obscuring the continual living with problems and ideas that is part of the work life of an expert team. The irony is that in our so-called knowledge society, many people who are ostensibly doing knowledge work remain primarily engaged with material things, while the kind of knowledge processing that should be constantly going on in the background is slighted or left to management. Cognitive responsibility, it appears, is harder to maintain than responsibility for tangible outcomes.

The Withholding of Cognitive Responsibility in Schools

Schools present an especially interesting case with regard to cognitive responsibility. Cognitive objectives figure prominently in the reasons why schools exist. However it was the absence of collective cognitive responsibility as a goal for the teaching enterprise that led us to identify what we have elsewhere called the Teacher A model (Bereiter and Scardamalia 1987).

In the Teacher A model, learning is a by-product of doing schoolwork. The students' job is to do assigned work, in the case of a traditional classroom, or to carry out self-directed projects and activities, in the case of the more modern classroom. The teachers' job is to plan and supervise the schoolwork, and they often do this well enough that the classroom presents a picture of happy, busy, hard-working students. Students are evaluated on the quality of their work and judged as working up to, below, or (among those labeled over-achievers) beyond their capacity. There may be evaluations of learning, often externally imposed. But for students falling short in such evaluations, the remedy is additional school-work. One diagnostic sign pointing to a Teacher A is an insatiable demand for exercise sheets. In the most extreme examples of Teacher A behavior, there is no such thing as *cognitive* responsibility, either on the part of the teacher or of the students. All the focus is on tasks and activities.

In the Teacher B model, the teacher assumes cognitive responsibility, but the students are not expected to do so. Most of instructional theory and design are aimed at some version of this model, and there are many variations, ranging from direct instruction to guided discovery. In a model B classroom, the teacher has cognitive objectives, both long-range and immediate, judges where the students are with respect to them, and gears actions to the attainment of those objectives. The students may be made aware of the objectives and encouraged to pursue them as well, but their actual *responsibility* is limited to overt tasks and activities, much like the students in a Teacher A classroom.

It should not be surprising, therefore, if the students themselves have a Teacher A, task-centered conception of learning, regardless of whether their teachers adhere to Model A or B. In studies of students' implicit theories of learning, this appears to be overwhelmingly the case, at least among elementary school students (Bereiter and Scardamalia, 1989). Participants were asked to suppose that they had an extra hour a week in which to learn anything they wished. The focus of the interview was on what they would do in order to learn, how long they thought it would take, how they would know if they had learned, what difficulties they anticipated, and how they would deal with them. Even young students indicated appropriate things they would do in order to learn—reading and asking questions if the purpose was to acquire factual knowledge, observing and practicing if the purpose was to acquire a skill. But with few exceptions they had no realistic idea of how long learning would take, and had no idea of how to cope with difficulties except by doing more of what they proposed to do. Their implicit theory, as we made it out, was that learning follows naturally from carrying out learning activities and completing tasks, one after another, and that is all there is to it—exactly the model we attribute to Teacher A. In only a few elementary school students did we see even a glimmer of what is common in the educated adults we interviewed, an awareness that learning can be problematic and may require strategic moves to bring it about.

Students have little idea of the strategic activity involved in learning if all such strategic activity has been carried out by their teachers and without their knowledge. There are indications that even among university students, many of them only have explicit strategies for memorization, lacking strategies for learning with understanding (Biggs 1979). The Teacher C model, as we defined it, is distinguished by an effort to turn strategic cognitive activity over to the students. Many teachers would avow that this is what they are trying to do—to make students responsible for their own learning. However, in parallel interviews with teachers, we found that this often means performing tasks in a responsible manner—a Teacher A view of responsibility. For teachers to move from endorsing the Teacher C model to the point where they actually practice it is evidently a significant learning accomplishment in its own right, requiring a good deal of coaching, reflective practice, and mutual support (Anderson and Roit 1993). It represents overcoming a career-long habituation to being the sole engineer of the learning process, however that is conceived.

I must emphasize that these remarks are not limited to teachers who pursue a didactic approach. The Teacher A and B models may be readily observed in classrooms conducted according to principles of informal, hands-on, child-centered, open education. The controls exercised by teachers in such classrooms may be less obvious, but they even more closely fit the term 'engineer.' Lillian Weber, in her influential book, *The English Infant School and Informal Education* (1971), quoted approvingly from a National Froebel Foundation handbook, which asserted that in an informal classroom

> the teacher actually has a more active directing part to play than on any planned instructional programme through which pupils are processed in an almost routine way. But the part to be played is of course a very different kind. It is based on not *imposing* anything on children, but on so closely co-operating with their native interests and drives that whatever they are led to do is felt as something that comes out of themselves. (Quoted in Weber 1971, p. 109)

Weber called this 'implementing' rather than 'directing'; but it is clearly not a matter of turning responsibility over to the children. If it is successful, the children are only aware of doing what they want, even though they have been subtly led to it by the teacher.

Collective Cognitive Responsibility in the Classroom

Why won't teachers turn higher levels of cognitive responsibility over to students? Answers may be sought in the need to maintain a position of authority and in disbelief in the capacity of students to shoulder such responsibility. But prior to these is a concrete fact of life: the ratio of one teacher to 30 or so students. This condition not only favors a centralized management structure; it also severely constrains the kind of discourse that can go on. As analysts of classroom discourse have observed, classroom exchanges are usually both initiated and terminated by the teacher (Sinclair and Coulthard 1975). A typical exchange will start with the teacher asking a question, followed by a response from a student, and terminated by a remark by the teacher, often followed immediately by the initiation of a new exchange; such as 'Right. And what did the British do then?' With such a discourse structure, it should not be surprising that all the higher-level control of the discourse is exercised by the teacher. The students are cast into a perpetually reactive and receptive role.

Not much can be done to turn more responsibility over to the students unless the structure of classroom discourse is changed. Small group work has been the principal way of breaking the pattern in which all communication is mediated through the teacher. It can be quite productive (Barnes 1977; Wells, Chang, and Maher 1990), and it involves a substantial transfer of responsibility to the students. However, it also has its drawbacks. It may prove unmanageable unless the groups have definite and limited tasks, but this reduces the cognitive responsibility exercised by the students. Without the leavening influence of the teacher, there is a tendency for small group discussion to be dominated by the more outspoken students. Knowledge generated in small groups tends to be ephemeral, there being no recording of it and no teacher to serve as the corporate memory; and what is produced in one group is not readily available to others.

It was these seemingly intractable problems of discourse structure that first led me to investigate the possibilities of technology to change it. The first prototype of CSILE (Computer-Supported Intentional Learning Environments) was implemented in 1983 in an undergraduate Developmental Psychology course of over 300 students at York University. In years preceding the introduction of CSILE, I regularly asked students to write summaries of my lectures, as part of course requirements. These summaries provided a fascinating landscape of ideas that students brought to, and took from my lectures. Once I recovered from the shock of reading summaries that I thought could not possibly follow from my lecture, I began to see how these diverse interpretations provided a powerful teaching tool. However, reviewing and finding points of convergence and divergence in all of these summaries was a demanding and time-consuming activity for me. CSILE was first used to shift this responsibility to the students, by having them enter their ideas into a communal space where they could read each other's entries and engage in reflective activity. Prior to the introduction of the technology I could find no time-efficient means of turning this responsibility over to them. Experiments with CSILE led us to view cognitive responsibility as a social-cultural challenge, requiring a great deal more than individual intentional effort.

With the rapid growth of the Internet, many schools are moving to incorporate network communication into their educational activities. Most of these uses, however, make no fundamental change in the structure of classroom discourse or in the allocation of cognitive responsibility. In some cases the Internet merely provides a library of resources to be used in producing reports or other documents. In other cases joint research or design projects are organized among widely separated schools. Students may, for instance, contribute information on weather, plant life, or dialect in their respective localities, and then work to synthesize this information and draw generalizations from it. Such projects are rich in cognitive possibilities, but the higher-level cognitive work of goal-setting, planning, and monitoring will not be done by the students. Often it is not done by the teachers either, but by some central body that administers the project.[1] In model projects that we have seen,

---

1. The Ministry of Education in British Columbia maintains a Web page devoted to cross-school projects, some of which are evidently administered by a branch of the Ministry. See http://www.etc.bc.ca/tdebhome/projects.html.

the students' activity is so highly structured for them in advance that it may amount to filling in cells in a spreadsheet, the rows and columns of which have been specified by the project organizers.

Schools also use e-mail, conferencing, or listserve applications that function as communication media, but generally not in ways that play a transformative role. Although communication with geographically distant classrooms has been enthusiastically endorsed by teachers, reports suggest that these play rather limited 'getting acquainted' roles. Discussions over the Internet show low levels of participation and a lack of continuity and moreover typically require a good deal of teacher direction (Guzdial 1997; Hewitt and Scardamalia 1998).

In the design of CSILE we were not directly concerned with these special-purpose applications of network technology. Instead, we aimed at altering the day-to-day discourse patterns, so that students would assume what we called in one article "higher levels of agency" (Scardamalia and Bereiter 1991). We looked to networked computers as offering the possibility of a decentralized structure for the flow of information. CSILE linked students to a communal database created by the students themselves through the notes and comments that they contributed to it (Scardamalia et al. 1989).

Description of CSILE/Knowledge Forum

CSILE—the second-generation of which is called Knowledge Forum® (http://www.Knowledge Forum.com)—is an asynchronous discourse medium, which means that participants do not have to be engaged at the same time, as they do in an oral discussion or in a telephone conversation. In this way it is like e-mail. But, unlike e-mail, it does not consist of person-to-person messages. Instead, it consists of contributions to a community knowledge base, which resides on a server and is accessible to everyone in the network. Thus, the knowledge represented by notes in the database is preserved and continually available for search, retrieval, comment, reference, and revision. Various specific supports for knowledge building are provided, and keep being enhanced in successive versions of the software.

Knowledge Forum aims for fidelity to the ways work with ideas is carried out in the real world. Ideas are, of course, central to high-level knowledge work of all kinds. Research, scholarship, and invention indeed lose their character unless everything that is done directly or indirectly derives from and feeds into the further development of ideas. Ideas are seldom treated in isolation. They are systemically interconnected—one idea subsumes, contradicts, constrains, or otherwise relates to a number of others. To gain understanding is to explore these interconnections, and to drill deeper while *rising-above*, to gain broader perspective. Successful knowledge building, we may say, exhibits *deep embedding*, both as regards the embedding of ideas in larger conceptual structures and the embedding of ideas in the practices of the knowledge building community. Participants share responsibility for community knowledge, in addition to individual achievement.

Knowledge Forum in its current stage of development permits a depth of embedding that goes well beyond what is possible with other forms of so-called knowledgeware, such as the threaded discourse systems common on the Web. A simple Knowledge Forum note may be thought of as the embodiment of a single idea; but the note is identified with a problem and with 'scaffolds', which give the note a role in more extended work with ideas such as theory refinement, evidence gathering, argumentation, literary interpretation, and so forth. Furthermore, every note has a place in one or more views. The views themselves are graphical representations of higher-level conceptual structures and are constructed by participants to give greater meaning to the notes they contain. Students, teachers, and telementors or tele-experts (experts invited to join the online discourse) share responsibility for ensuring that these views do justice to the notes and at the same time represent their best collective understanding. Views help to establish a high standard for knowledge work. Participants know that what is represented in these view reflects the collective best of the community. Views may also be used to enter official curriculum frameworks. Students then link their notes to goal statements, to determine the extent to which their efforts meet or supersede the goals that ministries and departments of education have for them. Notes can live in multiple views (a curriculum-standards view, a previously constructed student-generated view, a view created by a tele-expert, and so forth). Participants are encouraged to create increasingly high-level 'rise-above' views that point to other views, or 'rise-above' notes, which subsume other notes. They can annotate or 'build on' or quote someone else's note. Quotes result in automatic links being established between the notes, along with bibliographic cross-references. In short, Knowledge Forum supports deep embeddedness: with notes and views serving to embed ideas in increasingly demanding contexts, going deeper into the content while at the same time situating these ideas in views that provide an integrative context for them. This deep embeddedness is what brings ideas to the center of their work, and in turn enables collective cognitive responsibility.

These capabilities only become effective, of course, if the social practices of the classroom make use of them. Thus there has developed along with the technology a knowledge building pedagogy, where the embeddedness idea comes to pervade the very culture of the classroom. I will later characterize this pedagogy by a set of distinctive attributes and illustrate these with examples. The overarching principle, however, is to foster collective cognitive responsibility. The first challenge is to progressively turn over to students the responsibility of using notes and views to create a valuable shared knowledge resource for their community.

The second challenge is ensuring that ideas always remain the focus of this responsibility, that the activities and the mechanics never obscure the goals that give meaning and purpose to their tasks. This represents the largest single challenge to efforts to make knowledge building a reality in schools. All the traditions of schooling—both the traditions of teacher-directed instruction and the traditions of child-centered activity methods—are arraigned against it. These traditions, in turn, are grounded in the social reality of one teacher having to manage 20 to 40 children. These combine to make activities, not ideas, the center of classroom life. Changing this, so that ideas move to the center and activities become subordinate, represents a dramatic shift (Scardamalia 1997). The classroom may still look much the same, just as the heavens still look the same to one who has undergone the Copernican switch, but everything is understood differently and it becomes possible to move into new levels of work with ideas that could not even have been imagined before.

In summary, the challenge addressed by Knowledge Forum and knowledge building pedagogy is *to engage students in the collabora-*

tive solution of knowledge problems, in such a way that responsibil-
ity for the success of the effort is shared by the students and teacher
instead of being borne by the teacher alone.

Grasping the Idea of Idea-Centered Education

Like the Copernican Revolution, the change from an activity-cen-
tered to an idea-centered view of education has an all-or-none character (Scardamalia 1999). There is a real sense in which you either
get it or you don't. However, there is this added difficulty with the
educational change: most modern teachers believe they already put
ideas at the center. Teaching for understanding and 'constructivism'—the idea that learners construct their own knowledge—are
widely proclaimed and they seem to be saying what I have been
saying only in different words. They are, of course, related to
knowledge building. Knowledge building is a way of teaching for
understanding and, as Bereiter (2002) makes clear, it is constructivist. But it is also radically different from most of what goes on in
the name of teaching for understanding and constructivism.
Because of the slipperiness of words, the difference is difficult to
convey, although teachers are very much aware of the difference
once they have made the transition.

To clarify what is distinctive about knowledge building and the
technology that supports it, I have listed in Table 4.1 twelve ideas
that in combination set a knowledge building classroom off as profoundly different from even the best of traditional and modern
classrooms. Table 4.1 also suggests the close links between knowledge building practices and technology, which in combination help
to produce these shifts. Fortunately, the interconnectedness of
these ideas means that implementing one tends to unlock the others. Although in principle you could have the practices without the
technology, we have found the technology to be important not only
for practical reasons—to overcome the objective obstacles created
by classroom conditions—but also for conceptual reasons. The
core ideas of knowledge building often come across as abstract and
fanciful until people see them embodied in the technology. The
combined practices and technology also help align participants and
their environment so that knowledge advancement: 1. is in the

social fabric of the organization; 2. is enhanced through primacy given to creative work with ideas; and 3. represents sustained work at the frontiers of understanding (Scardamalia 2000; 2001). This culture captures the natural human tendency to play creatively with ideas, and expands it to the unnatural human capacity to exceed the boundaries of what is known and knowable—to exceed expectations rather than settle into routines. Creating a shared intellectual resource and a rallying point for community work helps to provide an alternative to tasks, lessons, projects and other expert-designed motivators of work, replacing them with a system of interactions around ideas that leads to the continual improvement of these ideas. Tasks and projects are completed, but they are not reduced to routine or sufficing strategies that obscure the broader goals that gave meaning to them in the first place.

TABLE 4.1
Socio-Cognitive and Technological Determinants of
Knowledge Building

REAL IDEAS, AUTHENTIC PROBLEMS

Socio-cognitive dynamics: Knowledge problems arise from efforts to understand the world. Ideas produced or appropriated are as real as things touched and felt. Problems are ones that learners really care about—usually very different from textbook problems and puzzles.

Technological dynamics: *Knowledge Forum* creates a culture for creative work with ideas. Notes and views serve as direct reflections of the core work of the organization and of the ideas of its creators.

IMPROVABLE IDEAS

Socio-cognitive dynamics: All ideas are treated as improvable. Participants work continuously to improve the quality, coherence, and utility of ideas. For such work to prosper, the culture must be one of psychological safety, so that people feel safe in taking risks—revealing ignorance, voicing half-baked notions, giving and receiving criticism.

Technological dynamics: *Knowledge Forum* supports recursion in all aspects of its design—there is always a higher level, there is always opportunity to revise. Background operations reflect change: continual improvement, revision, theory refinement.

IDEA DIVERSITY

Socio-cognitive dynamics: Idea diversity is essential to the development of knowledge advancement, just as biodiversity is essential to the success of an ecosystem. To understand an idea is to understand the ideas that surround it, including those that stand in contrast to it. Idea diversity creates a rich environment for ideas to evolve into new and more refined forms.

Technological dynamics: Bulletin boards, discussion forums, and so forth, provide opportunities for diversity of ideas but they only weakly support interaction of ideas. In *Knowledge Forum*, facilities for linking ideas and for bringing different combinations of ideas together in different notes and views promote the interaction that makes productive use of diversity.

RISE ABOVE

Socio-cognitive dynamics: Creative knowledge building entails working toward more inclusive principles and higher-level formulations of problems. It means learning to work with diversity, complexity and messiness, and out of that achieve new syntheses. By moving to higher planes of understanding knowledge builders transcend trivialities and oversimplifications and move beyond current best practices.

Technological dynamics: In expert knowledge building teams, as in *Knowledge Forum*, conditions to which people adapt change as a result of the successes of other people in the environment. Adapting means adapting to a progressive set of conditions that keep raising the bar. Rise-above notes and views support unlimited embedding of ideas in increasingly advanced structures, and support emergent rather than fixed goals.

EPISTEMIC AGENCY

Socio-cognitive dynamics: Participants set forth their ideas and negotiate a fit between personal ideas and ideas of others, using contrasts to spark and sustain knowledge advancement rather than depending on others to chart that course for them. They deal with problems of goals, motivation, evaluation, and long-range planning that are normally left to teachers or managers.

Technological dynamics: *Knowledge Forum* provides support for theory construction and refinement and for viewing ideas in the

(continued)

context of related but different ideas. Scaffolds for high-level knowledge processes are reflected in the use and variety of epistemological terms (such as conjecture, wonder, hypothesize, and so forth), and in the corresponding growth in conceptual content.

COMMUNITY KNOWLEDGE, COLLECTIVE RESPONSIBILITY

Socio-cognitive dynamics: Contributions to shared, top-level goals of the organization are prized and rewarded as much as individual achievements. Team members produce ideas of value to others and share responsibility for the overall advancement of knowledge in the community.

Technological dynamics: *Knowledge Forum*'s open, collaborative workspace holds conceptual artifacts that are contributed by community members. Community membership is defined in terms of reading and building-on the notes of others, ensuring that views are informative and helpful for the community, linking views in ways that demonstrate view interrelationships. More generally, effectiveness of the community is gauged by the extent to which all participants share responsibility for the highest levels of the organization's knowledge work.

DEMOCRATIZING KNOWLEDGE

Socio-cognitive dynamics: All participants are legitimate contributors to the shared goals of the community; all take pride in knowledge advances achieved by the group. The diversity and divisional differences represented in any organization do not lead to separations along knowledge have/have-not or innovator/non-innovator lines. All are empowered to engage in knowledge innovation.

Technological dynamics: There is a way into the central knowledge space for all participants; analytic tools allow participants to assess evenness of contributions and other indicators of the extent to which all members do their part in a joint enterprise.

SYMMETRIC KNOWLEDGE ADVANCEMENT

Socio-cognitive dynamics: Expertise is distributed within and between communities. Symmetry in knowledge advancement results from knowledge exchange and from the fact that to give knowledge is to get knowledge.

Technological dynamics: *Knowledge Forum* supports virtual visits and the co-construction of views across teams, both within and between communities. Extended communities serve to embed ideas in increasingly broad social contexts. Symmetry in knowledge work is directly reflected in the flow and reworking of information across views and databases of different teams and communities.

PERVASIVE KNOWLEDGE BUILDING

Socio-cognitive dynamics: Knowledge building is not confined to particular occasions or subjects but pervades mental life—in and out of school.

Technological dynamics: *Knowledge Forum* encourages knowledge building as the central and guiding force of the community's mission, not as an add-on. Contributions to collective resources reflect all aspects of knowledge work

CONSTRUCTIVE USES OF AUTHORITATIVE SOURCES

Socio-cognitive dynamics: To know a discipline is to be in touch with the present state and growing edge of knowledge in the field. This requires respect and understanding of authoritative sources, combined with a critical stance toward them.

Technological dynamics: *Knowledge Forum* encourages participants to use authoritative sources, along with other information sources, as data for their own knowledge building and idea-improving processes. Participants are encouraged to contribute new information to central resources, to reference and build-on authoritative sources; bibliographies are generated automatically from referenced resources.

KNOWLEDGE BUILDING DISCOURSE

Socio-cognitive dynamics: The discourse of knowledge building communities results in more than the sharing of knowledge; the knowledge itself is refined and transformed through the discursive practices of the community—practices that have the advancement of knowledge as their explicit goal.

Technological dynamics: *Knowledge Forum* supports rich inter-textual and inter-team notes and views and emergent rather than predetermined goals and workspaces. Revision, reference, and anno-

(continued)

tation further encourage participants to identify shared problems and gaps in understanding and to advance understanding beyond the level of the most knowledgeable individual.

EMBEDDED AND TRANSFORMATIVE ASSESSMENT

Socio-cognitive dynamics: Assessment is part of the effort to advance knowledge—it is used to identify problems as the work proceeds and is embedded in the day-to-day workings of the organization.The community engages in its own internal assessment, which is both more fine-tuned and rigorous than external assessment, and serves to ensure that the community's work will exceed the expectations of external assessors

Technological dynamics: Standards and benchmarks are objects of discourse in *Knowledge Forum*, to be annotated, built on, and risen above. Increases in literacy, twenty-first-century skills, and productivity are by-products of mainline knowledge work, and advance in parallel.

To illustrate the ideas summarized in Table 4.1, I narrate four examples from actual classrooms. They illustrate both knowledge-building pedagogy and the role that *Knowledge Forum* plays in it. I hope they will also convey a sense of the whole that Table 4.1 cannot convey—a sense of the spirit of classroom communities in which ideas are at the center, knowledge building is the job, and collective cognitive responsibility is nurtured over the course of the elementary school years. For ease of reference, I use italics to refer to the specific ideas elaborated in Table 4.1.

1. GRADE 1 SCIENCE: ADAPTATION, CYCLES, AND ENERGY

The starting point for knowledge-building in *Knowledge Forum* is a *view*. Figure 4.1 shows a view co-constructed by a Grade 1 teacher, her students, and a teacher-researcher to launch a year-long study of the topics that provincial guidelines specified for Grade 1 science. A view may contain *notes* or pointers to other views.

In this case, as a top-level organizer, the view contains only pointers to other views. In Figure 4.2, we follow one of these pointers, the one in the Fall view that points to work on leaves. Here there are a number of notes authored by the children. As the note

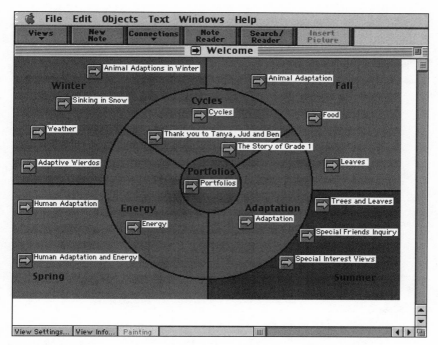

FIGURE 4.1
Top-level 'Welcome' view titled Adaptation, Cycles, and Energy, with pointers to related views.

titles indicate, they do not contain miscellaneous information about leaves but instead focus on a problem that the students themselves had come up with (*real ideas, authentic problems*): What causes leaves to change color in the fall?

Figure 4.3 shows one of the notes, which hypothesizes that plugs develop that prevent sap from getting to the leaves, causing the chlorophyll to die. Some other theories, illustrating the principle of *idea diversity*, are

"Fall—I think the chlorophyll goes into the tree to keep warm for the winter."

"I think leaves change color because when the leaf falls down I think that the chlorophyll goes to the outside of the leaf so it leaks off the leaf."

"Because it's too cold for the chlorophyll to make food for the tree."

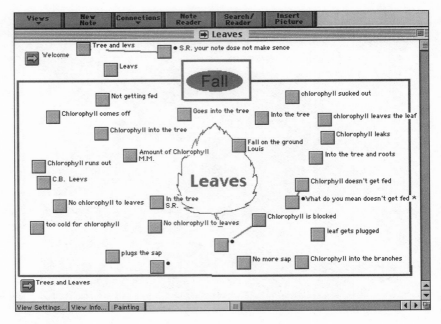

FIGURE 4.2
The 'Leaves' sub-view follows a pointer from the 'Welcome' View (Figure 4.1). Children's notes focus on the problem: What causes leaves to change color in the fall?

What we cannot see here, but what the teacher reports in the virtual tour of her knowledge base,[2] is an account of a field trip the students took to a maple-tree farm to see how maple syrup is made. One child, watching the sap flow from the tree, noted that her theory regarding chlorophyll must be wrong, because the sap that she saw was not green. Others raised many other issues about what they saw, and how the flow of sap gave them new ideas about the internal structure of a tree, and the relation of its internal structure to their theories. What was impressive, as the teacher reports, is that the work in Knowledge Forum and the visit to the maple-syrup farm were not closely related in time. She was surprised and delighted that a relationship was discovered, as she had

---

2. The virtual tour, which describes these events in the teacher's own words and voice is available at (http://ikit.org/virtualsuite/visits).

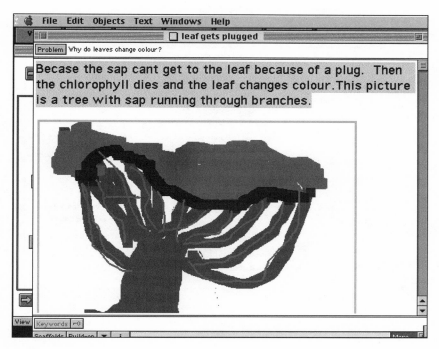

FIGURE 4.3
'Leaf gets plugged' theory note from the 'Leaves' view (Figure 4.2). Shows student's hypothesis explaining why leaves change color.

not anticipated it herself. This juxtaposition of theory and relevant evidence suggests *epistemic agency*: Personally held beliefs are viewed in relation to ideas suggested by others and by everyday phenomena. We also know, from the teacher's account, that the students became actively engaged in other efforts to test their theories, through self-invented experiments. For instance, they collected leaves and placed them in the freezer in the basement of the school. This was their way of testing the time and degree of color change they might see with the leaves. As the above accounts suggest, their theories seemed real enough to them that they carried them to the playground, took them along with them to the field trip, and reportedly to the dinner table. The transportability of these ideas, I propose, follows from their articulation and availability in a communal space where they became an object for inquiry by everyone.

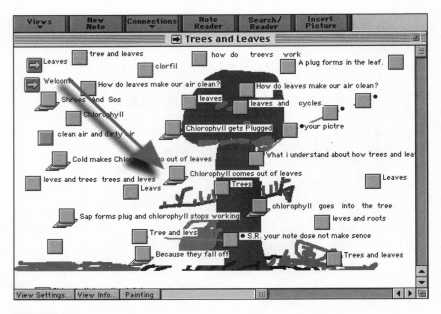

FIGURE 4.4
'Trees and Leaves' view contains rise-above notes.

We see evidence of the extended life of these ideas in a subsequent view (Figure 4.4). This view contains several notes of a special kind called *'rise-above'* notes. These notes are the result of the students and teacher working together to collect into one common note similar theoretical accounts. One rise-above note reads, "These notes share the idea that the sap gets plugged and that is why the leaves change color." Students who felt that accurately characterized their theory then dragged and dropped their notes into the rise-above note, removing them from the screen but making them still available through the rise-above. Thus we see the *rise-above* principle in action. As suggested by the various text and graphics notes that the students wrote, there was a way in for everyone—a common discourse space to aid the *democratization of knowledge. Pervasive knowledge building* is reflected in the extensibility of their work with ideas in many contexts, both in school and out, and across diverse knowledge media. *Community knowledge, collective responsibility* is evident in their work with one another. *Symmetric knowledge advancement* is suggested by the teacher's report that she gained a deeper understanding of photosynthesis and of why plants turn different colors in the fall through her involvement in the students' inquiries.

GRADE 3. LITERATURE STUDIES

Notes in Knowledge Forum have customizable scaffolds to support high level knowledge processes. Figure 4.5 illustrates a 'theory building' scaffold that we have used to encourage young students to engage in Theory Building while they write their notes.

The Grade 3 students edited this scaffold, saving the first 'My theory' support, adding a new support titled 'Did you know?,' and deleting the rest. 'Did you know?' was their favorite scaffold support, and could be found in almost all of their writings on the Harry Potter novel they were reading. *"Did you know* Quidditch is a game that you play on broomsticks?" *"Did you know* if you catch the Snitch your team gets 150 points and the game is over?" *"Did you know* J.K. moved twice from her home? In her school on the first day they had a test!" After the students produced this first round of notes the teacher introduced them to the contrast between 'knowledge telling' and 'knowledge transforming' discourse, as set out in educational literature (Bereiter and Scardamalia 1993). One

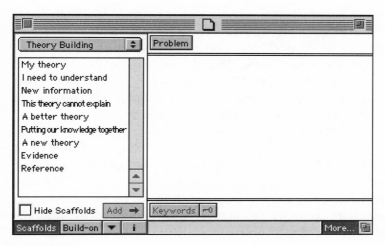

FIGURE 4.5
Note with the 'Theory Building' scaffold.

child had an insight: perhaps *'Did you know?'* was their favorite scaffold support because it was easy to use. This child suggested that *'Did you know?'* supported knowledge telling, and that their notes were just repeating information from the text. Others argued that they were doing more than knowledge telling—that they were learning to find key information in texts. Regardless of their different interpretations, they collectively decided to revise the scaffold, to bring back more of the original items, and to add some new supports. There was a corresponding shift in their Knowledge Forum notes, from recording information taken from the text to interpretive accounts, frequently scaffolded through the *evidence* support. This brief episode demonstrates their ability to distinguish knowledge telling from *knowledge building discourse*, and to purposefully shift to the latter. It also demonstrates their ability to exert *epistemic agency* in the design of their environment, to *democratize knowledge* through provision of supports designed to encourage all participants to engage in increasingly demanding knowledge work, and to make *constructive use of authoritative sources* regarding the distinction between knowledge telling and knowledge transforming discourse.

GRADE 4: 'OUR LIGHT LEARNINGS'

We now move ahead to a Grade 4 classroom and to the final stages of an extended inquiry into problems having to do with light. Although the inquiry dealt with issues that commonly figure in the study of light in elementary science classes, it is worth noting that, in keeping with *real ideas, authentic problems*, the study was launched in this case by questions about lighting that arose from the class's attending a performance of a Shakespeare play.

Figure 4.6, like Figure 4.1, represents a view-of-views. In this case, however, the views are actually depicted, in the form of miniatures of views actually constructed by the students in each of six areas of inquiry—angles and reflections, sources of light, and so on. Following the pointer to any of those views would take you to a view that contains the actual notes produced by students in their work in that problem area. Students helped maintain each view, determining what was and was not appropriate to appear on it, looking to the arrangement of notes on the view, and

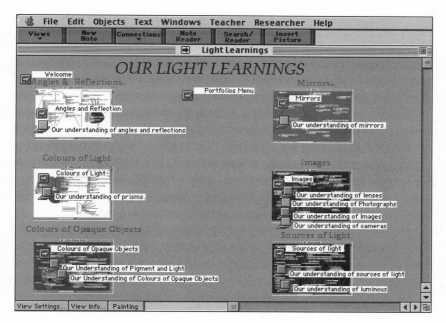

FIGURE 4.6
'Light Learnings' 'view-of-views', Grade 4 classroom.

so on. Thus they took collective cognitive responsibility for view construction.

The notes attached to the 'Our Light Learnings' view are all *rise-above* notes. Whereas in Grade 1 such notes were produced by the teacher and the students were responsible only for deciding whether their own notes belonged in a particular rise-above, in Grade 4 'rising above' became a major responsibility of the students. Figure 4.7 shows one of the resulting notes and Figure 4.8 shows the first part of another, longer rise-above note. The similar structure of the two notes is due to Knowledge Forum's customizable scaffolds that were in this case designed to fit this particular task of producing a note that integrates 'Our theory', 'Our evidence', 'Putting our knowledge together', and 'What we still need to understand'. The numbers in small boxes are links to supportive notes in other views, which are also referenced at the bottom of the rise-above note. Referencing occurs automatically whenever one note or a portion of a note is copied into another, and the

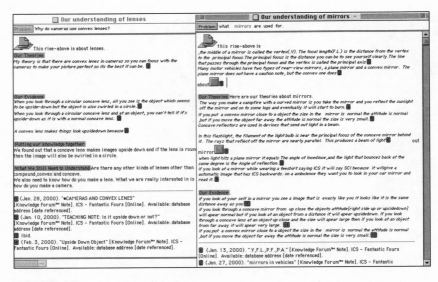

FIGURE 4.7
Two rise-above notes from the 'Our Light Learnings' view.

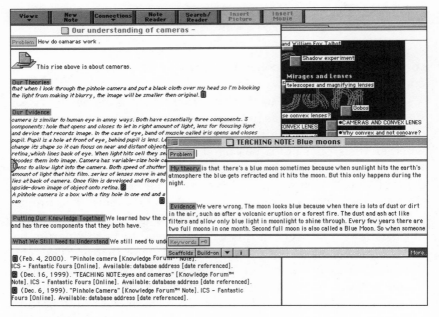

FIGURE 4.8
Two different rise-above notes from the 'Images' view.

copied material appears as a quote. Thus students cite each other, they do not copy their ideas and claim them as their own. The result is, depending on how you look at it, a richly interconnected hypertext document or a review article with ample references. In any case, it graphically represents *community knowledge, collective responsibility* brought about through *knowledge building discourse*, and *idea diversity.*

GRADE 5/6. ISLANDS, EVOLUTION, AND BIODIVERSITY

A number of advances in collective cognitive responsibility are evident in the grade 5/6 class. These students explored problems related to islands, evolution, and biodiversity. While the Grade 1 teacher was the primary designer of the top-level curriculum view, the Grade 6 students took greater responsibility for the top-level as well as local views. They organized their work around curriculum objectives, and divided up responsibilities, as reflected in a set of linked views that coordinated their work. For example, they divided up the island problem space so that some students conducted research on different island types (Coral Atoll, Volcanic, Sedimentary, Continental); others on locations (Hawaii, Galapagos, Java, Madagascar, Iceland); and others on issues regarding the formation and inhabitants of islands (species, how to create an island, the earth's layers). The depth of their inquiry was reflected in their efforts to learn from each other and in their portfolios (personal views with select contributions from the database, annotated to provide a reflective overview). For example, here is one student's portfolio summary note: *"This (*referring to a note selected for the portfolio) *is my theory of evolution. This* (another selected note) *is Jason's note that sparked a huge debate. The debate was at first about whether my theory or Alexa's theory of evolution was right, but eventually it became about whether science is always right, and the validity of resources* (three portfolio notes were selected that focus on the validity of resources). *These notes are about whether science is always right, and whether how old it is affects how correct it is."* There is clear demonstration of *constructive use of authoritative sources.* Additionally, committees of students were responsible for maintaining views, and videotapes of discussions among view managers indicate that *collective cognitive responsibility* and *embedded* *and transformative assessment* were taken very seriously by students, as they dealt with the tension between ensuring that their view contained contributions to knowledge and being fair to their classmates. An analysis of the work in this classroom demonstrates important shifts from learning to knowledge building, along all of the dimensions indicated in Table 4.1.

The teacher's role in all four of these examples is largely that of helping students shoulder their responsibilities and advancing knowledge along with them. It is noteworthy that three of the four examples are from teachers' first-year efforts with knowledge building and Knowledge Forum. I attribute the quick uptake to various factors: 1. the school philosophy is in keeping with this work, and the principal fosters community engagement and stewardship; 2. two other teachers in the school had been engaged in the two preceding years, with impressive results and models to offer to new teachers; 3. research grants allowed us to hire one of the two experienced teachers, to work directly with the three new teachers in a teacher-researcher capacity. All of these teachers and the principal are exciting colleagues, working within a laboratory school setting that prizes teacher-research arrangements.[3] Thus this faster-than-usual (Blumenfeld et al. 2000) uptake of new ideas and school-based innovation is attributable to multiple factors, which surely extend beyond those I have listed.

One of the enabling factors, as the examples suggest, is the technology itself. It is what enables cognitive responsibility to be distributed. Hewitt (1996) has traced the changes that took place in one classroom over three years as the focus was shifted from personal knowledge accumulation to the collaborative solution of knowledge problems. One of the interesting markers of this shift was an increase in the number of epistemological terms occurring in students' notes. Hakkarainen (1995) studied a number of CSILE discussions on science topics to ascertain the extent to which they conform to canons of scientific inquiry. His conclusion, buttressed

---

3. The school is the Institute for Child Study of the University of Toronto (ICS). ICS participants are Patti MacDonald (Grade 1), Mary Jane Moreau, (Grade 3), Richard Messina (Grade 4), Bev Caswell (Grades 5-6), Richard Reeve (teacher-researcher), and Elizabeth Morley (Principal). The project researcher is Mary Lamon.

by independent judgments from two philosophers of science, is that the students collectively exhibit a high level of what may properly be called scientific thinking. Other in-progress research indicates that reading other students' notes is predictive of later achievement on advanced placement tests (Power 2000). If that is correct, it suggests that awareness of diverse ideas helps one clarify and think through scientific ideas. Other research indicates that students who explicate their naive conceptions are more likely to make contributions to knowledge advancement—and these advances are more related to articulating their ideas than to their scholastic achievement test scores (Van Aalst 1999). These findings suggest that articulating ideas and bringing misconceptions out in the open—generally, dealing with *idea diversity*—provides an effective context for knowledge advancement.

Expanding Possibilities

Although the laboratory school from which the preceding examples were taken plays a key role in advancing the pedagogical and technological frontier, other important innovative work is going on in at least 12 countries, in grades 1 to university, including inner-city schools, and in health care settings, public-service organizations, small businesses, and other settings. We have now begun to create virtual visits (http://ikit.org/virtualsuite/visits) that allow members of this worldwide community to visit each other electronically. Could such efforts eventually provide a reasonable substitute for live visits to knowledge building classrooms? Will they foster knowledge building practices for newcomers? It is impossible to know at this early stage. There is another development that suggests new possibilities. Underlying these environments are analytic tools that allow us to examine students' individual and collective contributions (text and graphic notes and views in Knowledge Forum). These analytic tools provide detailed accounts of development that can be made available to teachers (and potentially to students) immediately, and these results can also be fed directly back into the process of continual improvement. Thus the goal of *embedded, and transformative assessment* is becoming increasingly possible and exciting.

If we distinguish knowledge building from learning, then a legitimate concern is with what individual children learn from taking part in knowledge building activities. Assessments are reassuring about general levels of academic achievement (Scardamalia et al. 1992; Scardamalia, Bereiter, and Lamon 1994): Compared to non-CSILE controls, CSILE students did significantly better in language and reading and show no deficit in other areas. Their literacy advantage grows with additional years using CSILE/Knowledge Forum, and they show advantages in graphical literacy (Scardamalia et al. 1994). The students also show more sophisticated understandings about knowledge and learning (Scardamalia et al. 1994). That is as close as we currently come to documenting what I am here suggesting is the major advantage students in a knowledge-building classroom can carry with them into a knowledge society: ability and willingness to take on responsibility for the collective solution of knowledge problems.

Barriers to Adoption

Although most educators who visit a knowledge-building classroom are impressed, many of them to a high degree, there are a number of concerns that stand in the way of wholehearted commitment to the idea of knowledge building. The first, and most insidious—because it seldom comes out in the open—is the belief that most children lack the motivation and ability to do the things the educator has just witnessed. This shows up first as a suggestion that the children and the teacher, or both, are exceptional. In practice it shows up as a tendency to overstructure and overmanage activity, with the result that some of the essential characteristics of knowledge building are sacrificed—particularly, authentic problems, epistemic agency, and cognitive responsibility.

A second, and surprisingly widespread, concern is that students will learn something wrong. This concern crops up even among educators who are well aware of the extensive research indicating how profound is the mislearning that normally occurs in schooling. Research carried out in CSILE classrooms indicates that the spread of misconceptions and false information is minimal, and is easily exceeded by the amount of correction of misinformation and misunderstanding that go on. This is not to claim that the students are immune to the misconceptions that pervade society. But knowledge building work in a medium like Knowledge Forum brings them out in the open, whereas they usually remain hidden in conventional school work, and the process of idea improvement, if sustained, can be relied on to overcome many of them.

A third concern arises from a belief that can be summarized as 'Learn first, produce later'. This belief is common throughout the education world and underlies much educational practice, especially in liberal education. It is devastating to the approach I have been describing, because it implies that creative work with ideas can come only after a long period of absorbing knowledge that has already become established. This belief is implicit in such terms as 'basic education' and 'foundations'. And, of course, the belief has considerable substance. Many kinds of human performance presuppose prior learning; we would not want to entrust airline piloting or thoracic surgery to on-the-job learning, even though we recognize that such skills reach a high level only through practice.

Picasso is often held up as an exemplar of the 'learn first' approach. Although he was an extraordinary innovator, he devoted his early years to assiduously mastering classical styles and techniques. But it is important to note that he learned by producing art works—derivative ones, to be sure, but we may presume that like most art students he was simultaneously striving to produce works of artistic merit and to learn. According to self-reports, students in the knowledge-building classes we work with also have this dual motivation. They are consciously trying to learn but at the same time they are trying to produce theories, ideas, and other objects of scientific or scholarly merit. In this chapter I have emphasized producing ideas—knowledge building; in another paper, included as an appendix to this book, Bereiter and I deal with intentional learning.

Although we have never witnessed knowledge building unaccompanied by learning, we have witnessed a great deal of learning that was never converted to knowledge building. We continually advise teachers against assigning a portion of the day to 'learning' and a different portion to 'knowledge building'. Such a division weakens both, whereas they ought naturally to reinforce and boost each other. Even on into their late careers, knowledge builders ought to be simultaneously engaged in advancing the frontiers of knowledge and in personal learning. That is what a non-trivial conception of 'lifelong learning' ought to comprise. I have been arguing that this combination of knowledge building and learning can start in early childhood.

Even after conceptual barriers have been removed, and even with the strongest technological supports, instituting a knowledge building classroom remains a challenge. It entails creating a culture in the classroom that is not a miniature of the surrounding culture but rather is a model of what that surrounding culture might become—a culture in which the creation and improvement of ideas pervades social life. One of the most successful teachers reported that it usually took him from September to January or February each year, to get his grade 5–6 class functioning well as a knowledge-building community. This was true even though, because of the split-grade structure, a number of the students each year were carry-overs from the year before. Once the community was functioning, however, new students entering the class could join it with relative ease. That was because the other students could help with the enculturation. We have seen some evidence that when a school-wide culture of knowledge building is established, the year-to-year problems of culture-building diminish and instead there is an upward progression where each year the culture advances beyond where it was before. Then you have a genuine knowledge building culture, with its own dynamic of continual advancement. That, I maintain, is what schools must become if they are to play their part in the Knowledge Age.[4]

References

Anderson, V. and M. Roit. 1993. Planning and Implementing Collaborative Strategy Instruction for Delayed Readers in Grades 6–10. *Elementary School Journal* 94 (2), 121–137.

---

4. The author wishes to acknowledge the generous support of Bell Canada, the Ontario Ministry of Education, the Social Sciences and Humanities Research Council of Canada, and the TeleLearning Network of Centres of Excellence. I am indebted to the students and teachers who contributed their time and talents to this project, and to the entire CSILE/Knowledge Forum team, without whose contributions the work reported here would not have been possible. I am also grateful to Carl Bereiter and André Carus for their thoughtful input to this manuscript.

Barnes, D. 1977. *Communication and Learning in Small Groups*. London: Penguin.

Bereiter, C. 2002. Liberal Education in a Knowledge Society. Chapter 2 in this volume.

Bereiter, C. and M. Scardamalia. 1987. An Attainable Version of High Literacy: Approaches to Teaching Higher-Order Skills in Reading and Writing. *Curriculum Inquiry* 17 (1), 19–30.

———. 1989. Intentional Learning As A Goal of Instruction. In Lauren B. Resnick, ed., *Knowing, Learning, and Instruction: Essays in Honor of Robert Glaser* (Hillsdale, NJ: Erlbaum), pp. 361–392.

———. 1993. *Surpassing Ourselves: An Inquiry into the Nature and Implications of Expertise*. Chicago: Open Court.

Biggs, J.B. 1979. Individual Differences in Study Processes and the Quality of Learning Outcomes. *Higher Education* 8, 381–394.

Blumenfeld, P., B.J. Fishman, J. Krajcik, R.W. Marx, and E. Soloway. 2000. Creating Usable Innovations in Systemic Reform: Scaling Up Technology-Embedded Project-Based Science in Urban Schools. *Educational Psychologist* 35(3), 149–164.

Guzdial, M. 1997. Information Ecology of Collaborations in Educational Settings: Influence of Tool. In R. Hall, N. Miyake, and N. Enyedy, eds., *CSCL '97* (Toronto: CSCL), pp. 83–90.

Hakkarainen, K. 1995. *Collaborative Inquiry in the Computer-Supported Intentional Learning Environments*. Paper presented at the European Association for Research on Learning and Instruction, Nijmegen, Netherlands.

Hewitt, J. 1996. Progress toward a Knowledge-Building Community. Unpublished doctoral dissertation, University of Toronto.

Hewitt, J. and M. Scardamalia. 1998. Design Principles for the Support of Distributed Processes. *Educational Psychology Review* 10 (1), 75–96. http://csile.oise.utoronto.ca/abstracts/distributed/

Power, D. November 2000. Global Partnerships: Telelearning for Sustaining Rural Communities: The Changing Role of Small Schools in Knowledge Societies? K. Stevens (Chair). Symposium conducted at the Telelearning 2000 5th Annual Conference, Toronto.

Scardamalia, M. April 1997. The Knowledge Society Challenge. Presentation conducted at the Colloquium Series, Harvard University. Retrieved 23rd January 2002 from http://kf.oise.utoronto.ca/ms/ideas. html

———. 1999. Moving Ideas to the Center. In L. Harasim, ed., *Wisdom and Wizardry: Celebrating the Pioneers of Online Education* (Vancouver: Telelearning), pp. 14–15.

————. 2000. Can Schools Enter a Knowledge Society? In M. Selinger and J. Wynn, eds., *Educational Technology and the Impact on Teaching and Learning* (Abingdon, RM), pp. 5–10.

————. 2001. Getting Real about 21st-century Education. *Journal of Educational Change* 2, 171–76.

Scardamalia, M., and C. Bereiter. 1991. Higher Levels of Agency for Children in Knowledge-Building: A Challenge for the Design of New Knowledge Media. *Journal of the Learning Sciences* 1(1), 37–68.

Scardamalia, M., C. Bereiter, C. Brett, P.J. Burtis, C. Calhoun, and N. Smith Lea. 1992. Educational Applications of a Networked Communal Database. *Interactive Learning Environments* 2(1), 45–71.

Scardamalia, M, C. Bereiter, and M. Lamon. 1994. The CSILE Project: Trying to Bring the Classroom into World 3. In K. McGilley, ed., *Classroom Lessons: Integrating Cognitive Theory and Classroom Practice* (Cambridge, MA: MIT Press), pp. 201–228.

Scardamalia, M., C. Bereiter, R.S. McLean, J. Swallow, and E. Woodruff. 1989. Computer-Supported Intentional Learning Environments. *Journal of Educational Computing Research* 5(1), 51–68.

Sinclair, J. McH. and J.M. Coulthard. 1975. *Towards an Analysis of Discourse: The English Used by Teachers and Pupils*. London: Oxford University Press

van Aalst, J.C.W. 1999. Learning, Knowledge Building, and Subject Matter Knowledge in School Science. Unpublished doctoral dissertation, University of Toronto.

Weber, L. 1971. *The English Infant School and Informal Education*. Englewood Cliffs, NJ: Prentice-Hall.

Wells, G., G.L. Chang, and A. Maher. 1990. Creating Classroom Communities of Literate Thinkers. In S. Sharan, ed., *Co-operative Learning: Theory and Research* (New York: Praeger), pp. 95–121.

5

Higher Education at a 'Post-Modern' Crossroads: Reflections on One Person's Experience

James Miller

Carl Bereiter in his paper on 'Liberal Education in a Knowledge Society' raises a great many interesting questions, but one of the most interesting is raised by the title itself: how—if at all—does an education that is properly called 'liberal' fit in with the needs of a so-called 'knowledge society'?

In approaching this question, I will be speaking as a frank amateur. Unlike Carl Bereiter and his colleagues Marlene Scardamalia and Gordon Wells, I know very little about current debates among cognitive psychologists and educational theorists. I will therefore be drawing primarily on my own experience—as a teacher, and as a journalist. I will eventually say something about what I have learned by teaching at the Graduate Faculty of the New School for Social Research, in New York City. But I will start with my experience writing an essay, published in 1997, about recent books on the university for *Lingua Franca*, a monthly "review of academic life."

The piece for *Lingua Franca* began rather simply, as an assignment to review a book called *The University in Ruins*, by a man named Bill Readings. Before his untimely death in a plane crash, Readings was a professor of English in Montreal (and a protégée of Jean-Francois Lyotard, the French theorist of our 'post-modern' condition).

As it happens, Readings had written a very provocative book. But it was also a book that left me feeling profoundly ambivalent. On the one hand, the historical passages in his book piqued my interest in certain classical nineteenth-century accounts of higher education and its proper aims. On the other hand, I found myself disagreeing willy-nilly with Readings's own conclusion, that these classical aims, in our own society, were now irrelevant.

On Readings's telling of the story, the modern ideal of a liberal education was most powerfully embodied in the curriculum designed for the University of Berlin by the great German linguist and philosopher, Wilhelm von Humboldt. Instituted in the first decades of the nineteenth century, and widely imitated thereafter, Humboldt's curriculum was not only meant to promote scientific inquiry, but also to build among its students a sense of integrated personal character. The challenge was to help students organize the multiplicity of known facts into a coherent whole. Central to Humboldt's curriculum, and unifying its sense of cultural mission, was an understanding of philosophy as the rigorous practice of critique. If educated properly, a student would not only become acquainted with selected contents of various specialized fields of positive knowledge, but also learn (in Humboldt's words) "the formal art of the use of mental powers, the process of judgment." (Or, as Carl Bereiter puts it in his paper, a properly liberal education has the task of "equipping students to engage in the argument," to criticize and revise productively the ideas they inherit.)

I will confess that I have always felt an affinity for something like this vision—and so, I think, did Bill Readings. The tone of his book, however, is dismayed and in some ways defeated. Striking a pose of tough-minded realism, and writing as a declared theorist of our 'post-modern' situation, Readings argues that Humboldt's ideal is irrelevant, because largely pointless to the production of usefully specialized knowledge in our own post-industrial, highly globalized society.

Readings therefore takes the title of his own book with utter seriousness: the University, in his view, really *is* in ruins. Instead of Humboldt's cohesive vision of combining critical judgment with an understanding of a shared general culture, we now have universities that prefer to pursue what is often called, simply if elliptically, 'Excellence'. At this conference, for example, we have heard

Gordon Wells describe the goal of knowledge as the building of "excellent products."

But as Bill Readings remarks, in my view quite rightly, "excellence" is a notion that has general applicability "in direct relation to its emptiness."

Why is excellence an empty idea? Consider a typical piece of academic (and bureaucratic) prose, cited by Readings: it appears in a publication of the Office of Research and University Graduate Studies at Indiana University: "Excellence of the proposed scholarship is the major criterion employed in the evaluation procedure."

Superficially, this statement is unassailable. The objection to it runs as follows: by treating 'excellence' as if it were a self-evident common denominator of good research in all fields, the statement begs the question of what counts as 'good' in each field. But this in fact varies widely. Along with the proliferation of academic specialities and sub-specialities has come a proliferation of different standards of judgment: professional philosophers, for example, are often liable to find risible the work of colleagues in literary theory, who are nevertheless highly esteemed within their own discipline. The empty notion of 'excellence' thus masks sharp disagreements over the value of different programs of research, particularly in the humanities and social sciences. Whenever disagreements threaten to erupt, the academic response for the past generation has been to avert conflict by proudly proclaiming the appearance of new 'paradigms', and then recognizing new disciplines and new sub-fields, and sometimes establishing entirely new departments, each with its own insular yet indubitably high standards of 'excellence'.

Yet for just this reason, as Readings persuasively shows, the rhetoric of excellence fits remarkably well with the needs of both the university and of modern American society. Excellence, besides being an empty pseudo-principle, serves a very positive function: if nothing else, it allows an uneasy peace to prevail between otherwise bitterly hostile groups of scholars and researchers. It facilitates the peaceful coexistence of the arts and sciences, it legitimates innovative programs for women and blacks and gays, and it also paves the way for interdisciplinary programs, something close to my own heart, since I am one of those odd academic ducks with a bona fide interdisciplinary Ph.D. (in History of Ideas, from Brandeis).

In effect, the empty rhetoric of excellence thus makes it easier to pursue intellectual 'diversity'—a sometimes worthy goal, and in this day and age, the holy grail of a great many higher educators.

In retrospect, to speak only of myself, I am sure that I personally reaped the benefits of this late-blooming academic commitment to intellectual diversity. In 1976, I got my first job at the University of Texas in a political science department. In obtaining this job, I was the beneficiary of the creation of a new sub-sub-field within the long-recognized sub-field of political theory. The department's old guard I found to be a complacent crew of behaviorists and comparativists and conservative political theorists, primarily united by their staunch anti-Communism. Pressed by the swelling ranks of graduate students interested in critical theory and neo-Marxism, however, they had reluctantly capitulated to the student demand to diversify their course offerings, and specifically to hire someone, *anyone*—this turned out to be me—who took Marxism seriously. Within a decade, there were a lot of people like me. We had our own scholarly meetings, we had our own journals, we had our own jargon with nifty terms like alienation and hegemony and reification—we had, in short, everything we needed to produce our own new paradigm! And, of course, within our own circumscribed field of research, we had our own very high standards of 'excellence'.

There is only one small problem with this otherwise cheerful story about the rise of a new academic paradigm. As niche sub-fields in the academy have proliferated (like niche markets in the economy as a whole), it has become tempting to surrender in the face of fragmentation, giving up on one of Humboldt's classical goals—namely helping students to organize the multiplicity of facts they know into a coherent picture embedded within a larger cultural whole. At the same time, the vacuous pursuit of 'excellence' has offered a warrant for abdicating the independent exercise of critical judgment—and that, remember, was the sacred aim of a liberal education, in Humboldt's view.

Administrators today understandably shy away from intellectual turf wars by granting new fiefdoms. Professors, especially in larger departments, just as understandably give up trying to read each other's research, avoiding hard judgments by mechanically counting the number of publications in refereed journals, letting a crude and often meaningless statistic specify the commonly accepted threshold of 'excellence'.

As a result, in higher education today, in an unwitting parody of laissez-faire economics, almost anything goes, so long as it satisfies a relevant constituency.

If the Department of Defense wants to exploit the resources of the physics department to build a better bomb, let them, so long as the government gives the school a lucrative grant.

If professors demand to teach gender roles in the oeuvre of Madonna, let them, so long as students are willing to take such courses. (In the modern academy, such 'cutting-edge' innovation is, as often as not, a supply-side phenomenon.)

If students want to study computer programming, let them, so long as they pony up the money to take such courses.

As Readings puts it, with acid accuracy, "henceforth the question of the University is only the question of relative value-for-money." In this brave new world of post-modern learning, students are *consumers*—of precisely *what*, one can never be certain.

Enough, for now, about Bill Readings. His analysis is obviously polemical, and like any good diatribe, it is peppered with hyperbole. My own ambivalent reaction to Readings led me to spend a year developing a much longer essay that ended up reviewing a number of books, besides Readings, that I found of interest. These books ranged widely. I read optimistic treatises by liberals, in particular *The Opening of the American Mind*, an almost painfully earnest new book by the American historian Lawrence Levine. But I also went back and read closely the notorious conservative jeremiad that had provoked Levine's book, namely *The Closing of the American Mind* by Allan Bloom.

My problem in writing the piece was simple. Despite being a man of the left, with an interest in philosophers like Michel Foucault and in social movements like the New Left and in cultural phenomena like rock 'n' roll, all anathematized by the likes of Allan Bloom, I found myself in fundamental sympathy, neither with the academic new left nor with liberal optimists like Lawrence Levine, but rather with the pessimists, be they conservative curmudgeons like Bloom, or cynical post-modernists like Bill Readings.

The reason for my sympathy has to do with my experience as a teacher at the New School for Social Research—an experience which I will say a little more about in a moment. But in order to explain the character, and doubtless the limits, of my experience, I should say something about my own eccentric background.

Before coming to the New School, I worked for a decade outside of the academy. For most of that time, I was an editor and writer for *Newsweek* magazine, covering two quite different beats, the world of books, and the world of popular music. As a result, I missed that wonderful decade in the history of the American university when many English teachers stopped teaching English— that is, stopped teaching novels and poems and plays—and started analyzing instead wild and wonderful things like the trans-gendering of pop culture. (I, meanwhile, had to struggle with an uptight executive editor in order to get the first transvestite ever on to the cover of *Newsweek*—this was the pop singer Boy George, in 1984; but that is another story.)

Because I had missed the rise in the humanities and social sciences of countless new fads and theoretical 'paradigms', I was bemused and astonished—and eventually depressed—by the new generation of students I met, first teaching part-time at Harvard and Brown in the late 1980s, and then teaching at the New School since the 1990s.

Let me be clear. These students were generally very smart. Most of them knew a great many things that concerned young intellectuals ought to know, things that I, at their age, knew absolutely nothing about. They knew, for example, about the history of the struggle for women's rights. They knew about the horrors visited by European colonizers on the indigenous populations of North America. And they almost all had come to hold very sophisticated views about the biases built into many, perhaps all, of our claims to know anything at all.

Still, committed as I was to some fairly traditional notions about the community of scholars and the value of familiarity with a small number of important facts and indisputably great books, I was struck—no, appalled—by the unabashed ignorance of too many of these very smart and often very jaded students.

Some anecdotal evidence: my first semester at the New School, I taught a course on Ancient and Modern Democracy, and also a course on Twentieth Century Social Thought. I discovered that most of the American students in these survey classes knew *noth-*

ing—absolutely nothing—about a surprising number of texts, events and facts, for example: the Funeral Oration of Pericles; the causes and consequences of the French Revolution; the decade in which World War I occurred. These, remember, were *graduate* students. They were explicitly interested in politics and philosophy. Yet even when my American students seemed sufficiently interested in philosophy to use properly the word 'Cartesian', if only as a casual term of abuse, chances were that they had never actually read Descartes, and furthermore felt absolutely no embarrassment about it. (I stress that I am talking about my *American* students, since my many students from Europe and Latin America and Asia are rarely so ignorant.)

Now it is true, of course, that, the Graduate Faculty being what it is, most of my American students did know a thing or two about Michel Foucault and the New Left and rock 'n' roll. Since I've written about all of these things, this was gratifying. Still, knowledge about such things was not enough—and it certainly couldn't compensate for the cheerful ignorance that in other areas seemed to prevail. (These observations, by the way, mean that I wish to stress anew what Carl Bereiter, in his paper, wishes to de-emphasize, namely the teaching, as a central part of the liberal arts curriculum, of "what others have already understood.")

As I came to realize while working on my essay for *Lingua Franca*, and while reading Allan Bloom as well as Bill Readings, I was instinctively holding on to a bizarrely old-fashioned conviction, about the value of a common cultural background in forging a truly *liberal* education, whatever the prevailing market demands for this or that kind of more specialized, or trendy, knowledge. In the humanities at least, and also I would argue in the social sciences, it is crucial to have a grasp of what has gone before, even if one hopes to hone a new mode of argumentation, or to pursue research in new areas. Gaining possession of some of the understandings of the world that have preceded our own allows a student to become a citizen in the republic of ideas, a realm larger than our own limited personal experience. Knowledge of this larger realm— of remote events, predecessor cultures, and conceptual possibilities, whichever ones we may choose to transmit—should ideally become instinctive, second-nature, like knowledge of a second language: providing a secure framework for a fluent conversation. By learning how to join in this conversation, students become, as Carl Bereiter nicely puts it, cosmopolitans—citizens of a world that transcends the contingencies and particularities of their ethnic and social backgrounds.   I believed—and I still believe—that one of the primary aims of higher education is to lead students to appreciate things they would otherwise have no reason to know about, or have difficulty understanding. If this is indeed a primary aim of a properly liberal education, then Foucault may be worth teaching, not because he is contemporary and fashionable, but because he is important as a thinker and because he is hard to understand. Popular music by contrast is a generally worthless area of study, since students can discover and explore it for themselves, and by themselves.

I can put my convictions in a more critical form as well. Like Ralph Waldo Emerson, one of our greatest native thinkers, I assume that, in our society, the virtue in greatest demand is conformity. It thus falls to liberal educators to combat this demand for conformity, by ignoring passing fads and the constant pressure of the marketplace. For Emerson, the American scholar must exemplify self-reliance. He or she will show others in practice how to think independently, how to live an examined life, how to obtain a due measure of wisdom and happiness.

Now something like this view, about the need, in a democracy especially, to cultivate non-conformity, will be familiar to anyone who has read not only Emerson, but also Tocqueville or John Stuart Mill. A version of it also appears in *The Closing of the American Mind*, where Allan Bloom puts it like this: "There is one simple rule for the university's activity: it need not concern itself with providing its students with experiences that are available in a democratic society."

Bloom's ambition, as I understand it, was, like Emerson's, frankly Socratic. Both men went against the grain of prevailing opinion. Both urged others to challenge the received wisdom. Both required of the American Scholar that he or she broaden dramatically the vision of his or her students. But unlike Socrates, both of these American Scholars, both of them profoundly idiosyncratic, paradoxically emphasized the importance of knowing about heroic models, of coming to appreciate exemplary predecessors in the adventure of thinking, like Socrates himself. Both wanted their ideal interlocutors to be eager to grapple critically with the work of what Emerson called "Representative Men"—that is, paragons of innovation and independent judgment, with the power to humble, to elevate, and eventually to transfigure one's sense of oneself, and also one's sense of one's own proper calling within the larger society.

Of course, it is unlikely that any university anywhere has ever fully realized this vision of the American Scholar's proper ambition. It is also worth recalling that Emerson, like Socrates, never taught in a university (his alma mater, Harvard, for a generation wouldn't let him lecture on its grounds). Still, however much one may disagree (as I do) with Emerson's occasional anti-intellectual quip, or Allan Bloom's extremely narrow conception of the 'representative men' who repay critical examination, their joint plea, for an arduous regimen of open-ended Socratic questioning, combined with a general knowledge of heroic precursors, makes a case that, I think, is still worth making.

Bill Readings, I thus decided, was both right and wrong. He was right, because the University really *is* in ruins. But he was wrong, because amid the ruins, something like the Socratic ambition remains both possible and essential—above all in a democratic society such as our own, where the cultivation of self-reliant judgment can act as a counterweight to what Tocqueville called "the tyranny of the majority."

This, at any case, was the basic point of the essay I ended up writing for *Lingua Franca.*

It is relatively easy, of course, to express a sharp point in a short essay. But as a famous Russian revolutionary once asked, what is to be done?

As I said at the outset, I am not an expert. Obviously, there are a host of structural problems that make reform difficult. For example, students, especially graduate students, are sinking ever deeper into debt. The government continues to slash funding for higher education. The curriculum in most high schools and colleges remains an incoherent jumble. The nation's K–12 system of education leaves countless students unprepared for advanced study.

I personally would like to see the institution of meaningful national standards for what students at every level are expected to know. I'd like to see colleges curtail the number of electives that are allowed. I'd like to see a resurrection of core courses aimed at providing a general education, in imitation of the kinds of curriculum still offered at Columbia and the University of Chicago. It is all well and good to talk, as Carl Bereiter does, about "knowledge production," especially as a device to teach scientific ways of problem-solving to younger students; but, especially in the humanities, there is also a need to transmit a shared fund of facts, and acquaint students with a handful of key texts, if only to create a common frame of cultural reference.

But of course, for the foreseeable future, American students will be graduating from high schools and colleges with no common fund of shared knowledge. It is these students who will continue to come to go on to graduate study.

Still, the situation is not completely hopeless.

As an example of what can be done on a very small scale, let me close by recounting my experience as director of the M.A. program in Liberal Studies at the Graduate Faculty.

I arrived at this program in 1992. After assessing the situation, I resolved to reinvent the free-form M.A. program I had inherited, transforming it into a more structured program, offering (among other things) a dose of liberal education at a graduate level. Acknowledging the reality that students have become consumers, just as Bill Readings says, I designed a mix of courses that still promised a lot of freedom, even touting the possibility of studying and writing about popular music in the context of putatively 'cutting-edge' kinds of post-modern theories.

But this was meant, frankly, as a bait-and-switch tactic. For despite the dire warnings of some colleagues that students wouldn't stand for it, I also instituted an old-fashioned core course required of every entering student. This core course was, in effect, a dose of remedial Western Civ. In this course, I forced my students to study Rousseau and Kant and Hegel, and the history of the French Revolution and the American Revolution and the Russian Revolution, and to read Abraham Lincoln alongside a slave narrative, and to read Darwin as well as Freud—and I forced them to do all of this, not simply in order to transmit a few fragments of a cultural tradition, but also in order to build a sense of intellectual community, a sense of being participants in a shared conversation.

Finally, I required my students to attend more closely to the art of writing. I did this by forcing everyone to attend a writing workshop. In this workshop, students are expected to generate multiple drafts of their M.A. thesis, and also to read the drafts generated by their peers, exchanging comments and suggestions for making the work better. The workshop format is meant to help students learn, together, to revise and rewrite for themselves, with a heightened awareness of needless jargon and the kind of academic pretentiousness that inhibits independent judgment.

Despite a variety of limitations, my little program has become a magnet for two kinds of students—those interested in receiving, however belatedly, a bit of an old-fashioned liberal education, and those keen to do interdisciplinary work, but unhappy with the more trendy alternatives, like the History of Consciousness Program at Santa Cruz, or the Rhetoric program at Berkeley. At the same time, my little program has developed a real sense of community among the students, who are distinguished within the New School by their high morale and their shared sense of idiosyncratic ambitiousness.

Proud as I am at what some of these students have accomplished, I must confess, in closing, a nagging doubt about the social and *economic* value of what they have learned. Perhaps (to use the language of Edwards and Ogilvie) they have learned to "experience beneficial forms of consumption" by slogging through treatises by great German philosophers. Some of them have in fact gotten jobs in the worlds of publishing and journalism. But most of what they have learned is, I'm afraid, *useless:* of scant productive value.

That is one of the dirty little secrets at the heart of our contemporary perplexities about 'liberal education'. Liberality, if one goes back to the Latin roots of the word, is a matter of *freedom*—not least freedom from economic necessity. It is relevant, surely, to ask educators to prepare students to live productive lives in our modern industrial societies: to that extent, Carl Bereiter's effort to link a fluency with abstract ideas with preparation to enter a 'knowledge society' intuitively makes good sense, if only for instrumental reasons.

Still, a properly *liberal* education, as Humboldt well understood, has another goal: not the training of knowledgeable workers, but the cultivation of well-rounded and thoughtfully independent individuals. And no matter the currents at play in our own increasingly complex society, and despite the unceasing demand, in a market society, to turn higher education into a mass-produced commodity with tangible economic benefits, the old (and in every society potentially disquieting) aim of Socratic critique—of a liberation, through enlightenment, of the spirit—is never impossible, since the Socratic ambition can be pursued in almost any setting. All it takes is a dedicated teacher, an eager student, and a readiness to work together. And as I concluded in my essay for *Lingua Franca*, "it shouldn't be impossible to have something like this model of teaching as one's goal, at least in the realm of higher education—even in Allan Bloom's all-too-worldly America or in Bill Readings's ghost-like University of Excellence." And even in our own 'knowledge society'.

6

Dialogue about Knowledge Building

Gordon Wells

I want to make it clear from the start that I am in broad agreement with Bereiter's vision of what liberal education might be in the twenty-first century. I, too, would like to "make knowledge building the principal activity in schooling," where this is understood as encompassing "both the grasping of what others have already understood and the sustained, collective effort to extend the boundaries of what is known" (Chapter 2 above, p. 25). In fact, for the last few years we have both, by different means, been exploring how to create communities of inquiry and knowledge building at various levels of education from particular classrooms, through whole schools, to the faculty of OISE/UT. At the same time, we have been engaged in an ongoing argument about the nature of knowledge and the status of knowledge objects in a knowledge building community.

To give an illustrative example of this running battle: Carl and I met for lunch a few weeks ago and, predictably, between mouthfuls of excellent food, we continued to argue over whether knowledge objects are 'really' material or immaterial. After an hour and a half of extremely interesting discussion—in which I thought I had succeeded in persuading Carl to modify his opinions, at least to a small degree—I said, as we prepared to leave, "Well, we have certainly done some useful knowledge building today." "Not really," he replied, "nothing has been written."

Whether I have captured his very words or not, the general point of his retort is extremely germane—as I hope to show—both for a general consideration of what we mean when we talk about knowledge and, more specifically, for a specification of the sorts of conditions that are required if classrooms are to become the sites for the kind of knowledge building communities that we both espouse. In most of this chapter, I intend to focus on the latter topic. However, I should first like to fire a few salvoes at the particular view of knowledge that is put forward in the target article for this volume (Chapter 2 above).

Knowing and the Objects of Knowing

The problems I have with Bereiter's theory of knowledge are largely the result of his having adopted Popper's (1972) 'three worlds' metaphor—although, in point of fact, I don't have too much difficulty with the distinction between Worlds 1 and 2. However I do have real trouble with the autonomous 'immaterial knowledge objects' of World 3.

Let us consider the way in which Popper himself presents the argument.

> If we speak of Platonism, or of quantum theory, then we speak of some objective import, of some objective logical content; that is, we speak of the third-world significance of the information or the message conveyed in what has been said, or written. (Popper 1972, p. 157)

My problem here is with the separation of form from meaning—of the message from the text in which it is realized. Popper seems to be subscribing to a 'conduit' conceptualization of linguistic communication (Reddy 1979), in which the 'message' is treated as an independent and pre-existing object that is merely 'conveyed' in the discourse. And it is the uncritical acceptance of this metaphor that makes it possible to draw the further implication that the message exists in its own right, and continues to exist, immaterially and autonomously, whether or not any particular individual engages with it.

Certainly, it may sometimes be convenient to speak as if ideas, theories, and concepts had an autonomous and immaterial existence—provided that such terms are recognized for what they are, that is to say, as synoptic constructs that function as shorthand expressions in particular genres of theoretical discourse. In general, however, this way of speaking can be seriously misleading. Serious not simply because it misrepresents the way in which knowledge is constructed and used, but serious also in its consequences for the way in which, in schools and other educational institutions, knowledge, by being reified, becomes a commodity to be transmitted to students and its possession subsequently assessed and quantified. As Bereiter himself notes with respect to his adoption of Popper's conception of knowledge objects: "Every way of dividing up reality has its problems, and so a pragmatic choice has to weigh gains against losses" (Bereiter 2002, p. 89). However, I would argue in response that to propose that knowledge exists in an immaterial World 3 is to be misled by our ways of speaking into a position that is neither plausible nor advantageous. We are not better off as a result. Let me spell out my objections in a little more detail.

Separating the 'message' from the form in which it is realized, as Popper does, ignores the process by which a theory or any other putative third-world object is developed. This process necessarily involves the creation of a representational artifact in a semiotic medium such as language. And, whether in speech or writing, in order to be made available to others, this artifact must be realized in a material form. But the choice of the medium and the way it is used also has a constitutive influence on the development of the theory. Language is not neutral. One has to use a particular language—English, Japanese, Urdu—and, with the choice of language, one inherits the affordances and constraints of the cultural worldview that is 'encoded' in that language (Halliday 1978). All languages abstract away from the particularities of experience; common nouns and verbs refer, not to unique, particular instances, but to categories of objects and processes, and these terms are combined in structures that apply to events treated as instances of event-types. But these categories do not entirely correspond from one language to another.

Theoretical writing typically makes use of a range of technical registers which construe experience from a synoptic perspective (Halliday 1988). In these registers, the event-types that, in everyday speech, are realized in active clauses of doing, feeling and saying, are nominalized as abstract nouns and noun phrases; these abstractions are then treated as 'things' that can themselves enter into processes and relationships in the construction of descriptive and explanatory texts. Finally, these sequentially-structured patterns of lexico-grammatical choices are abstracted still further and referred to as for example in Popper's theory.

However, the fact that we can use the metalinguistic term 'theory' as a way of referring to the current textual end product of this constructive process of synoptic abstraction does not mean that there is a corresponding immaterial object that then exists, independent of the linguistic formulation and argumentation through which it was constructed. Thus, although I can refer to my ideas about knowledge or my objections to the theory proposed by Bereiter, my ideas and objections, respectively, don't exist independently of some attempt to formulate them, as in presenting them now in this written text.

Certainly, we do habitually refer to theories and arguments, as well as to stories and literary and musical creations generally, as if they had an existence independent of any particular embodiment in a performance or engagement with a text of some kind. But this way of speaking is clearly implausible if it is taken literally. As I have argued in response to Bereiter's citing of Madame Butterfly as an example of such a third world object: "what is the status of such an object if all material representations of it are destroyed and all those who had engaged with it, in any mode, have gone the way of all flesh? Does Madame Butterfly continue to exist in World 3 when there is no longer any possibility of her being embodied by a human voice?" (Wells 1999). So when Popper argues that the unexpected new problems to which new theories give rise are "in no sense made by us; rather they are discovered by us; and in this sense they exist, undiscovered, before their discovery" (Popper 1972, pp.160–61), I find his claim to be at best hyperbolic, and at worst confusing.

One might try to play down the criticism of the use of such synoptic metaterms as 'theory' or 'story' as if they referred to real, although immaterial, objects by agreeing that this is merely a way of talking to which our language misleadingly disposes us. However, as Yngve (1996) has convincingly argued, a 'language' is itself merely a synoptic linguistic construct which refers to the set of patterned regularities that are constructed by linguists on the basis of observations of specific instances of languaging within a community whose members are mutually intelligible. In this sense, 'language' is itself a theory.

My point is that, while these linguistic constructs play an important role in mediating our thinking and communicating, by allowing us to refer to the outcomes of semiotic activity without specifying the particular material artifacts in which these outcomes are realized, these outcomes only play a role in human affairs when particular individuals engage with particular material textual objects on particular occasions. Furthermore, when they do so, it is not the texts that 'mean'; rather it is people who mean by deploying the linguistic resources of their culture in particular, occasioned utterances to achieve particular discursive effects (Edwards 1997). By the same token, as textual artifacts, theories do not explain; it is people who use theories as mediating artifacts to explain and to organize their actions in the material and social world.

It is in this context that we can most usefully consider the particular value of writing. Writing (or other modes of visuographic representation) greatly facilitate the activity of knowledge building. As Olson (1994) and many others have noted, the permanence of a written text means that, unlike a spoken utterance, it can be read, discussed and interrogated in places and times distant from the occasion of its actual production. For this reason, the recursive process of composing a written or other visuographic text is probably the mode in which we most effectively engage in theoretical knowing. Of course, as Bereiter emphasizes, to be of value, even to the writer, the composing, (re)reading and revising need to be undertaken within a community as part of a larger, jointly undertaken, activity in which there is an attempt at knowledge building with respect to a topic of common concern.

However, knowledge isn't *in* the text. Knowledge is what is (re)created and advanced in the course of the reader/writer's transactions *with* the text and in the oral discourse that frequently accompanies these transactions. The text is thus simultaneously an artifact that is produced in the course of knowledge building and a tool that both affords and constrains further knowledge building activity (Lotman 1988). But it must be emphasized that it can only function as a tool for those who are equipped to use it by virtue of their prior enculturation into the relevant knowledge building community through participation in its activities and through appropriation of the values, artifacts, and practices that are constitutive of those activities. And this can only happen through engaging with particular textual artifacts for particular purposes.

In sum, I believe that it is, on balance, unhelpful to talk about knowledge as existing autonomously as a set of immaterial third world objects. As I have tried to show, knowledge does not have an existence apart from the situated acts of knowing in which it is constructed, reconstructed, and used. Theories and explanations only exist in the particular occasioned use of the semiotic representations of various kinds in which they are realized (or the reconstruction of these representations from memory) by specific individuals who are enaged in some activity in which these semiotic artifacts play a central role in the knowing of those involved (Nuthall, in press). Certainly, knowledge artifacts exist, the products of previous attempts at knowledge building by all those who have contributed. But, as I have emphasized, these do not themselves constitute knowledge; they only play a role as tools that have a potential for facilitating problem solving and further knowledge building for those who, through participation in the activities of the relevant communities, have already learned—or are learning—how to use them through knowing with others.

For those who understand the 'in process' nature of knowledge, there is little harm in referring to theories and explanations *as if* they had an independent existence—as can be seen in the example Bereiter quotes of the student who wrote "Mendel worked on Karen's problem." However, I would contend that it is the frequent references to 'the knowledge out there' by those who believe that it *does* have an independent existence and that it *can* be transmitted to students through texts or teacher exposition that is one of the chief impediments to the creation, in classrooms, of the knowledge building communities to which both Bereiter and I are committed. Strategically, therefore, I believe there is more to be lost than gained by using Popper's three-world model to underpin the otherwise persuasive argument for 'transforming schools into work-shops for the production of knowledge' that Bereiter presents.

But, theoretical underpinnings apart, there still remains the question as to how such a transformation might be achieved. On this issue, Bereiter has rather little to say—though this is no criticism of his paper. However, as one sympathetic teacher to whom I showed his paper replied: "As a teacher, I'm very much left with the question: What does a knowledge building classroom look like?"

In the remainder of my response, I shall attempt to move towards an answer to this question, based on the work of the Developing Inquiring Communities in Education Project (DICEP), a collaborative action research group to which I belong.[1] Over the last ten years, we have been attempting to create knowledge building communities in elementary and intermediate grade classrooms; we have also been meeting together and communicating by email to reflect on what we are learning in the process. The following comments are my summary of the 'guiding orientations' we have established.

Guiding Orientations

Recently, a new high school was opened in Toronto named after Ursula Franklin, a distinguished Canadian scientist. The choice of name was not just a mark of respect, for Franklin is herself committed to a form of education that places a strong emphasis on knowledge building—as she made clear in introducing one of the speakers at a recent conference on the 'Ecology of Mind'. Knowledge, she asserted, is created and recreated "in the discourse between people doing things together" (Franklin 1996) and in this statement, she implicitly emphasized three critical features of the

---

1. The Developing Inquiring Communities in Education Project involves a collaborative action research group made up of school-based and university-based educators. Funded by a grant from the Spencer Foundation, whose support is gratefully acknowledged, the project has as its goal to promote an inquiry-oriented approach to curricular activities and to seek to understand and improve the role of discourse in the processes of learning and teaching. The project has produced a substantial number of publications, many of which can be found at our homepage, http://www.oise.on.ca/~ctd/DICEP/http://www.oise.on.ca/~ctd/DICEP/, and also in Wells 2001.

kind of knowledge building communities that the members of our group are trying to create:

- knowledge is an intrinsic part of 'doing things'
- knowledge is created between people
- knowledge is constructed in collaborative meaning-making through discourse.

I should like to elaborate on each of these points in turn.

KNOWLEDGE IS AN INTRINSIC PART OF 'DOING THINGS'

When our era is described by the business community as marking the advent of the knowledge society, clear recognition is given to the role that the collaborative construction of knowledge plays in solving practical problems across a wide range of activities critical for the continued existence and improvement of human society. In our educational system, by contrast, it is a 'banking' concept of knowledge (Freire 1970) that is most frequently emphasized—the acquisition of knowledge for display. In high-school and undergraduate courses, in particular, the curriculum is conceived largely as the transmission of theoretical knowledge that is decontextualized from activities in which that knowledge might play a productive role in doing something beyond simply 'learning' it; in these contexts, success is measured in terms, not of what new problems can be solved, but of how much knowledge has been acquired (that is, memorized) by individuals for reproduction under test conditions.[2]

In criticizing the curricular emphasis on theory, I do not wish to undervalue the important contribution that theoretical knowledge has made to human welfare (although not all advances in knowledge have had beneficial consequences). However, I do want to suggest that, as currently enacted in schools, this emphasis is both dis-

---

2. The serious consequences of this have become particularly apparent in rapidly expanding fields such as medical science; academically successful medical students are at a complete loss when they are faced with real patients whose presenting symptoms do not fit the text-book descriptions. It is for this reason that a number of medical schools have begun to experiment with 'case-based' approaches to learning.

torted and restricting. On the one hand, it treats knowledge as more important than knowing and loses sight of the fact that the purpose of coming to know is to be able to act more effectively and responsibly. On the other hand, it ignores the equally important modes of knowing that complement theoretical knowing in any major undertaking and on which theoretical knowing has, historically, been built.

As Wartofsky (1979) has argued, it is not simply substantive knowledge that changes over time. Over the course of human history, knowing itself has developed, as different modes of knowing have emerged as a result of the increasing range of types of activity in which people engage and of the types of artifacts that enter into those activities. Table 1 gives a schematic summary of the sequence of emergence of six modes of knowing, based on a number of recent reviews of the evidence (Deacon 1997; Donald 1991; Egan 1997).[3]

There are two important points to be made about this developmental sequence. First, each successive mode of knowing depended on the invention of a new form of semiotic artifact. More than two million years ago, our earliest ancestors found and then began to fashion the tools involved in transforming the material world for the purposes of survival; then, with *Homo erectus*, came mimesis as a means of co-ordinating group activity and passing on instrumental knowledge; the appearance of *Homo sapiens* saw the beginnings of oral language which, with its potential for representing not just objects and actions, but also the relationships into which they enter and the conditions under which these relationships are observed, gradually made possible the substantive mode of knowing that allowed joint planning and reflecting and the consideration of alternative, hypothetical actions and states of affairs. Combined with other semiotic modalities, oral language also gave rise to such macro-genres of aesthetic knowing as myth, ritual and drama, in which our ancestors first attempted to construct overarching expla-

---

3. As I point out in Wells 1999, metaknowing is certainly much older than its position in the table suggests. Although it was clearly involved, for example, in the ironic stance to be found in the plays of Sophocles and the dialogues of Socrates (Egan 1997), and probably even before the earliest extant written texts, the term itself only appears in writings in the latter half of the twentieth century.

TABLE 1.

Modes Of Knowing: Phylogenetic And Cultural Development

Time before Present	Mode of Knowing	Particpants	Donald (1991)	Wartofsky (1979)
2 million years	Instrumental	Individual in action	Episodic	Primary artifacts: material tools
1–1.5 million years	Procedural	Between individuals while engaged in action	Mimetic	Secondary artifacts: tools and practices; mimetic interaction
50,000 years	Substantive	Among members of a cultural group, reflecting on action and as a basis for planning further action	Linguistic	Secondary artifacts: representations of tools and practices; spoken interaction
50,000 years	Aesthetic	Among members of a cultural group, making sense of the human predicament	Mythic	Tertiary artifacts: artistic representations in myth, narrative, graphic, and musical modes
2,500 years	Theoretical	Among members of a specialist community seeking to explain the natural and human world	Theoretic	Tertiary artifacts: decontextualized representations, such as taxonomies, theories, models, etc.
?	Meta	Among members of a cultural group, also individuals, seeking to understand and control their own mental activity		Tertiary artifacts: representations of mental and semiotic processes

Adapted from Wells 1999

nations of human existence in the world as they experienced it (Donald 1991). Each new mode of knowing thus also significantly extended humans' ways of understanding and acting and their ability to solve the practical, social and ethical problems that arose in the course of doing things together in the progressively more complex ecosocial environment that they themselves were creating with the help of these successively more powerful artifacts.

As can be seen, the period of time represented in this table spans at least a million years, with the substantive and aesthetic modes of knowing going back perhaps as far as 50,000 years.[4] Against this background, theoretical knowing can be seen to be of very recent origin. It emerged only two or three thousand years ago, following the invention of writing (Olson 1994), and it only began to attain its current ascendancy at the time of the European Renaissance with the conjunction of three further inventions, the controlled experiment (Hacking 1990), the register of scientific writing (Halliday 1988), and the technology of printing (Ong 1982). Although this mode of knowing has certainly played a major role in the last two or three centuries in extending humans' ability to understand and exploit the material world, it has certainly not replaced the modes that preceded it. Furthermore, each new mode of knowing built on the achievements gained in the previous modes and continued to be supported by them. Indeed, in everyday life, the problems we encounter demand an orchestration of all the modes of knowing in which none can be seen as the most important. The different modes of knowing should not be seen as a hierarchy, therefore, but rather as together making up a tool-kit of artifact-mediated means of extending the range of human activity, from which the appropriate means is chosen according to the task in hand (Wertsch 1991).

The second significance of this phylogenetic development of modes of knowing is that, in large measure, it shapes the course of ontogenetic development in the present. As Vygotsky (1981) explains, individual intellectual development repeats phylogenetic development in the sense that it involves the progressive appropriation and internal reconstruction of the cultural artifacts and practices that mediate knowing in joint activity. Of course, this is not a simple recapitulation, as the cultural environment into which a

---

4. These figures are based on Donald 1991.

child of today is born is shaped by the accumulated effects of all the modes of knowing described above. They are therefore available to be appropriated and do not have to be invented anew in each generation (Scribner 1985). Nevertheless, there are strong grounds for treating the sequence itself as developmentally accurate, with theoretical knowing emerging only in the school years, along with mastery of the genres of written language and the other modes of representation by which it is mediated.[5]

However, the implication of this 'genetic' (developmental) account is not simply that an emphasis on theoretical knowing should await the adolescent years, as is proposed by those who appeal to Piagetian stages. In most settings outside the classroom, as I have already argued, knowing is both situated in relation to the specific activities it mediates and oriented towards changing that situation in ways that are of importance to the participants; such activities also call upon the integration of a variety of modes of knowing. These features should, in my view, also characterize knowing in the classroom.

Finding ways to put this principle into practice is a continuing concern of our research group and we find that workable solutions vary according to the age of the students, the topics to be studied, as well as to the characteristics of the individual participants— teachers as well as students. In general, though, we find that for each new topic area there should, wherever possible, be opportunities for gaining first-hand, practical experience of tackling problems in the relevant domain so that there will be a perceived need for the theoretical constructs that provide a principled basis for understanding those problems and making solutions to them. By the same token, since theoretical knowing should not be treated as an end in itself, there should also be opportunities to put the knowledge constructed to use in some situation of significance to the students so that, through bringing it to bear on some further problem, they may deepen their understanding.

---

5. Egan (1997) makes a similar recapitulationary argument for the sequence of 'kinds of understanding' that he proposes.

KNOWLEDGE IS CREATED BETWEEN PEOPLE

Outside classrooms, whether in the workplace or in the home community, the solving of problems and the creation of the knowledge involved in doing so is rarely an individual affair. Participants pool their existing knowledge—as well as their ignorance—and work together to come up with a solution that is typically in advance of what any individual could have achieved alone. Collaboration is the norm. In the 'knowledge-producing' organizations that Bereiter describes, the collaboration takes place between people who are already experts; however, what enables them to create new knowledge is that their expertise is in somewhat different specializations, and it is from the interplay between what each already knows that new ideas/solutions arise. In the home community, the diversity of kind and extent of expertise is often much greater and, because there may be no one who is particularly knowledgeable with respect to the particular problem to be solved, the solution that is jointly constructed may not constitute 'new' knowledge in the sense of not having been thought of before. Nevertheless, the principle is the same: by collaborating to find the best possible solution, the participants often generate knowledge that is new for those involved. At the same time, collaborative problem solving almost always involves learning for the individual participants involved as well as the creation of knowledge that is new for the group. As Lave and Wenger (1991) emphasize, learning is not a separate activity, but an integral aspect of doing things together in a community of practice that involves individuals with different types and degrees of expertise. Furthermore, although competition with other groups for prestige or profit may, in some cases, be a powerful motive for persuading the group to work together, it is the solving of the problem to the best of their joint abilities that is the immediate spur to their collaborative efforts.

Although not the principle on which coming to know is typically organized in the classroom, it can provide an equally effective mode of learning there as well, if the ethos of individual competition for high grades is abandoned in favour of an ethos of collaborative knowledge building. For this to happen, what is required is that the classroom be reconstituted as a *community* of inquiry, in which students are expected and encouraged to care enough about the topics of their inquiries to make collaboration with others in the construction of knowledge a natural and rewarding way to behave. That this can be achieved has been clearly demonstrated by a number of investigators working in curricular areas as diverse as math (Lampert, Rittenhouse, and Crumbaugh 1996; Cobb et al. 1992), science (Meyer and Woodruff 1997; Palincsar et al. 1998), social studies (Barnes and Todd 1977), and literature (Dias and Hayhoe 1988; McMahon et al. 1997), and with theoretical frameworks ranging from cognitive science (Brown and Campione 1994; Scardamalia, Bereiter, and Lamon 1994) to sociocultural activity theory (Hedegaard 1990; Roseberry, Warren, and Conant 1992).

However, as we have found in our own attempts to create communities of inquiry, collaborative knowledge building is not something that can be scheduled for certain lessons in the weekly timetable while the rest of the program continues in a more traditional mode. To be successful, it must become pervasive throughout the curriculum—a general stance with respect to the world of experience that might be characterized as a disposition to engage in systematic inquiry about the questions or topics in which one is interested and a willingness to join with others in working towards a shared understanding of them and of the principles that underlie them (Wells 2000).

With this emphasis on collaborative activities, it might seem that there is a lack of concern for individual mastery of the skills and information that are necessary for knowledge building. Yet this is very far from the case. In fact, the advances in understanding made by the group as a whole are dependent on the contributions of its individual members. If they do not make progress individually, they will have nothing of significance to add to the joint endeavor. However, by the same token, little will be gained if all students are expected to follow identical learning trajectories, by reading the same textbooks, listening to the same lectures, carrying out the same experiments and writing the same essays and reports. As with the out-of-school communities referred to above, some diversity of expertise and experience is essential if collaborative knowledge building is to be progressive (Bereiter 1994). Most importantly, however, from the perspective adopted here, individual and group progress are not seen to be in conflict; rather, as Vygotsky (1978) argued, they are mutually constitutive. To understand this, we have to appreciate the central role of discourse in knowledge building.

KNOWLEDGE IS CONSTRUCTED IN COLLABORATIVE
MEANING-MAKING THROUGH DISCOURSE

Constructivists have rightly drawn attention to the way in which each individual's understanding of an issue or topic is the result of an active transaction between new information and what the individual can bring to bear in interpreting it in terms of his or her past experience, culturally shaped beliefs, and personal interests and sense-making strategies. However, what this fails to explain is how, if each individual constructs an understanding that is idiosyncratic and unique, there can be progress in a group or community's understanding.

Here, Bereiter's distinction between 'learning' and 'knowledge building' is very much to the point. His two terms correspond, I suggest, to the inner and outer orientations of the discourse of collaborative knowledge building.

As I argued earlier, one of the dangers of treating theories and explanations as if they had an independent, immaterial existence is that this lends support to the view that ideas are merely expressed in words or some other semiotic medium rather than being brought into existence through them. However, as Vygotsky stated at the conclusion of his investigation of thought and utterance, "The relationship of thought to word is a vital process that involves the birth of the thought in the word" (Vygotsky 1934/1987, p. 284).[6] In similar vein, Halliday writes, "language is the essential condition of knowing, the process by which experience becomes knowledge" (Halliday 1993, p. 94, original emphasis).

What both Vygotsky and Halliday are proposing, I believe, is that utterance—or rather, the dialogue in which utterances respond to each other, as Bakhtin (1986) put it—is the site in which both knowledge building and learning occur. This is not the only site, of course, as I emphasized earlier in my account of the different modes of knowing. However, in almost every mode, language and other semiotic modalities play a crucial role in mediating knowing,

---

6. Although translated as 'word', Vygotsky's expression in Russian is now believed to be better rendered as 'utterance'. Furthermore, although his discussion was couched in terms of language, it is clear from his writings as a whole that an utterance can be realized not only in 'speech' but in any of the variety of semiotic modalities in which meanings are made.

whatever the object to which the activity is directed, and this is quintessentially true of theoretical knowing, in which representational texts of various kinds are most typically the objects on which attention is focused.

The term 'text' is usually used to denote something that has already been written; however there is considerable value in extending its denotation to include the products of meaning-making, whatever the modality in which they are produced. Maps, diagrams, numerical equations, and also spoken utterances can thus all be considered as types of text. Treating a text as an improvable object is one very powerful way of engaging in knowledge building (Scardamalia et al. 1994). However, for every text product there is necessarily a process of 'texting'—of bringing the text into existence or of proposing ways of improving one that already exists. It is in this interplay between the process and the product that learning and knowledge building are constitutive of each other.

One of the characteristics of utterance, whether spoken or written, is that it can be looked at as simultaneously process and product: as 'saying' and as 'what is said'. In uttering, the speaker's effort is directed to the saying—to producing meaning for others. To do this, s/he has to interpret the preceding contribution(s) in terms of the information it introduces as well as the speaker's stance to that information, compare that with her or his own current understanding of the issue under discussion, based on her/his experience and any other relevant information of which s/he is aware, and then formulate a contribution that will, in some relevant way, add to the common understanding achieved in the discourse so far, by extending, questioning or qualifying what someone else has said. It is frequently in this effort to make his or her understanding meaningful for others that the speaker has the feeling of reaching a fuller and clearer understanding for him or herself.

But in uttering, the speaker is also producing 'what is said', a material utterance to which s/he can respond in very much the same way as those to whom it is addressed: by interrogating the meaning of what is said, evaluating its coherence and relevance, and by beginning to formulate a further response. This is the second way in which speaking can enhance understanding. It was partly this function of uttering that Wertsch and Stone had in mind when they wrote that young language learners: "can say more than they realize and [that] it is through coming to understand what is meant by what is said that their cognitive skills develop" (Wertsch and Stone 1985, p. 167).

> In contributing to a knowledge-building dialogue, then, a speaker is simultaneously adding to the structure of meaning created jointly with others and advancing his or her own understanding through the constructive and creative effort involved in saying and in responding to what was said. (Wells 1999)

Another way of putting this is to say that learning is the 'internal' counterpart of participation in 'external' dialogue with others; not a consequence of being told, but the active construction of a personal understanding as an integral part of participating in knowledge building with others. This is what Vygotsky had in mind, I believe, when he wrote: "the individual develops into what he/she is through what he/she produces for others" (Vygotsky 1981, p. 162).[7]

Two further points need to be made in order to round out this account. The first is that collaborative knowledge building does not require that the participants be in face-to-face dialogue. Certainly, this is often a good way in which to get the dialogue going, particularly for those who are new to this community practice. However, the dialogue can often be more effectively carried on asynchronously, using any of the visuographic modes that is appropriate, since this allows for reflection as well as action. What is critical for the dialogue to contribute to advancing individual and collective understanding, though, is that all contributions be treated as tentative and improvable rather than final and unchallengeable, including the contributions made by the teacher or the writers of textbooks and works of reference. This emphasis on improvability, together with the need for contributions to be supported—or supportable—by relevant evidence, is what I take to be the central core

---

7. This is not to deny that there are other modes in which learning occurs. For example, there is clearly a place for instruction and guided practice in the component skills that mediate knowledge building, just as there is for being helped to master the physical skills required in sports. However, just as learning to play a backhand shot only takes on meaning and purpose in the context of playing tennis or squash, so the mastery of intellectual skills needs to be clearly recognized as not an end in itself but the means to substantive ends that are of significance to the learner.

of the 'progressive discourse' that Bereiter (1994) sees as the principle medium of knowledge building.

Following from this is the second point, namely that, having learned to engage in this inter-mental dialogue, one can carry on a comparable intra-mental dialogue with oneself. However, in order to internalize the use of dialogue as a medium for individual thinking and reasoning, there must be multiple opportunities to engage in it with others. Here, then, is a further justification for the importance of creating a community of inquiry in the classroom in which such collaborative knowledge building dialogue is an integral aspect of the way in which all curricular topics are approached.

Creating Knowledge Building Communities in Classrooms

Given the implied criticism of Bereiter's paper, that it does not provide specific guidance for teachers on how to create classroom communities of inquiry, the same objection may be raised concerning the previous section. However, this is not because of a lack of empirical work on which to draw. On the contrary, Bereiter's proposal and my guiding orientations represent a distillation of ongoing work in a variety of schools and classrooms in which knowledge building is a major goal for the teachers and students involved. See, for example, the work reported in Brown and Campione 1994; Cohen, McLaughlin, and Talbert 1993; Donoahue, Van Tassell, and Patterson 1996; Gallas 1995; Palincsar et al., in press; Pontecorvo and Girardet 1993; Roseberry et al. 1992; Scardamalia et al. 1994; Torbe and Medway 1981; Wells et al. 1994, as well as in publications by members of DICEP (Wells 2001). Significantly, moreover, a substantial number of these reports were written by, or in collaboration with, classroom teachers.

The reason for presenting the guiding orientations in such general terms was that they are just that: ways of thinking about the constitutive features of knowledge-building communities that individual teachers can engage with in planning how to proceed in their own classrooms. Proposals of a more prescriptive nature would be inappropriate for three reasons. First, knowledge building cannot be thought of in terms of implementing a pre-existing model. As the above reports show, there are probably as many ways of creating such communities as there are classrooms, and there is no reason to believe that there are 'best practices' that will be universally successful (Clarke et al. 1996). This is entirely to be expected from the social constructivist perspective adopted here. Although there may be commonalities across settings and across the activities in which participants engage, every classroom is unique, since it involves the coming together of diverse particular individuals in a particular setting with particular artifacts, all of which have their own histories, which, in turn, affect the way in which the activities are played out. Creating an ethos of knowledge building depends as much on making good use of 'teachable moments' as on following a prepared agenda, and such moments are emergent, arising from particular problems encountered and the human and material resources available for the making of solutions.

The second reason is intrinsic to the very nature of inquiry and knowledge building. To lead such a community effectively, the teacher cannot remain on the outside as an all-knowing authority, but must also be involved in inquiry him or herself. This ideally takes place on two levels: joining as co-investigator in the knowledge building around issues that arise from the students' inquiries; and making the practice of classroom inquiry itself the subject of inquiry. This latter involves adopting the stance of the teacher researcher who not only reflects on his or her practice (Schön 1987) but also systematically makes changes and collects and critically evaluates evidence about the consequences (Carr and Kemmis 1983). Here, it is teacher colleagues who constitute the co-participants in the community of inquiry, both teachers in the same school and kindred spirits in other institutions, both school and university. It is in such professional communities of inquiry that some of the most productive transformations of schooling are being carried out, often using a social constructivist framework to assist them.

Finally, as is clear from the teacher reports referred to above, creating a knowledge building community is not straightforward and there are many issues that still need to be resolved. As Seixas (1993) observes, to adopt a community of inquiry approach to the learning and teaching of any subject raises profound questions about the nature of knowledge and the extent to which it is possible for knowledge to be created in the classroom by students uninitiated into the practices and genres of the discipline when they are assisted by teachers who themselves are more accustomed to teaching the knowledge constructed by others than to participating in the professional community in which it is constructed. Seixas specifically addresses the case of historical knowledge, but the same arguments apply, *pari passu*, in other areas of the curriculum.

To give some idea of the problems that we have encountered and of the ways in which we are attempting to understand and overcome them, I should like to quote three extracts from reflections written by members of DICEP about changes that they have deliberately been making in their classrooms in an attempt to create an ethos of knowledge building. The first, written by a doctoral student part way through her collaboration with a grade 5 teacher, draws attention to the expectations that students bring to the classroom as a result of their previous experiences in school.

> Our lack of success [in encouraging 'progressive discourse'] made me conscious of the difficulty of changing patterns of classroom talk. Classroom rhythms, it seems, are determined over the years; expectations and practices for participating in classroom talk appear to be carried over from one year to another, as well as being influenced by participation patterns that the children bring to school with them that they have learned from early childhood in their families. . . . To change these normalized patterns of classroom talk required, we discovered, a great deal of persistence in trying out various strategies to see what might be effective. (Measures 1997, p. 18)

As the above quotation implies, students' expectations about appropriate ways to talk in the classroom owe a great deal to teachers' pervasive use of the 'recitation script' (Tharp and Gallimore 1988) as the principal means of instruction, and to their practice of reserving to themselves the right to ask questions, both as a means of controlling the class and in order to ensure that "incorrect information can be replaced with the right answers" (Newman, Griffin, and Cole 1989, p. 127). In order for the dialogue of knowledge building to flourish, therefore, there needs to be a major reorientation in teachers' conceptions of their role and of the genres of classroom talk that they encourage and model. This was the realization of two teachers who regularly join forces to teach grade 2 science.

> As classroom teachers, we felt a large responsibility for "covering the curriculum." However, what we came to recognize was that we had neglected the fact that we were not alone: that covering the curriculum also required students' active collaboration. The question we then began to ask ourselves was whether we trusted the students enough to guide us in fulfilling this responsibility. Over the preceding two years, we had observed many exciting and authentic learning situations develop when students had had an active role in the direction and course of study, but we had been reluctant to trust the implications of these observations. As a result of the present investigation, however, we recognized that a major shift had occurred in our understanding of our curricular responsibilities. As one of us wrote:
>
> We have come to identify that the most important thing we do in our science class is listen. We listen in order to ask questions. Because our focus has shifted to assisting students in their 'zones of proximal development', we are able to listen to the students and to each other. We did not know this was the shift we needed to take, nor did we anticipate it at the outset, but it was the most significant learning for us. . . . And, as with all learning, [it has] carried over into all other areas of our teaching.
>
> The change in us, as teachers, was reflected in our interactions with the children and in the changed climate of the classroom. Students' questions and knowledge were as valued in the learning process as those of the teachers. Consequently, the students were supported in their efforts to make sense of their world and were motivated to take risks to further their own understandings. Because of this act of being responsive, both to the students and to each other, the knowledge constructed over the course of the unit was much deeper and more meaningful than we had anticipated. (Galbraith, Van Tassell, and Wells 1997)

As all of us are aware, as we try to make the kinds of shift referred to in the preceding quotation, it is a long road with many blind alleys and few signposts to guide one. This is made very clear in the final quotation, written by a teacher who is committed to the 'idea' of knowledge building and who has the courage to make radical changes in her practice. Even after several years of teacher research, however, she still finds that more changes are required.

I had always thought inquiry to be an outgrowth of thematic teaching, in which there's a greater emphasis on students' questions and a more determined effort to answer the questions through a variety of means. Short (1996), however, says that the problem with thematic teaching is that it's still organized around activity. . . . As she puts it, "thematic units are models of how to teach content, not of how people actually inquire about something they want to understand." . . . Short claims that we teachers are in too much of a hurry to get to kids' questions and that our 'What We Know/What We Want To Know' charts result in kids posing questions that are meaningless to them because we haven't given them the time to 'wander and wonder' amongst text sets, or the time to observe and experiment in ways that allow them to create meaningful questions.

The above is pretty commonsensical if you already possess the theoretical framework, but it's very alien to most teachers, including those of us who used to think we were on the cutting edge with our integrated thematic programming! It's really difficult to create a brand new way of life in a school when not only the entire school culture, but all teaching resources are organized in a different form. Even when attempting to start fresh, I find myself pulled back into old, comfortable patterns. . . . (Hume, personal communication, 28th May 1997)

That these last comments were written by a teacher who has read many of the papers written about the CSILE project and has, for several years, been trying to foster an ethos of knowledge building in her classroom—and with considerable success—only serves to underline the magnitude of the difficulties that have to be overcome.

Knowledge Building in Society

A central tenet of sociocultural theory is that the identities we develop and our personal resources for acting and knowing are constructed through participation in communities of practice, first in the home environment, then in school and college, and on into the workplace and the formal and informal associations to which we belong. On the face of it, such a claim appears quite uncontroversial; it seems obvious that what we learn will depend upon the company we keep. However, it is not just the differential accessibility to us of information, or even of ideas, that depends upon which communities we belong to; more importantly, it is differences between them in the modes of knowing that are habitually used for different purposes that so significantly affects the development of community members. In Vygotskian terms, who we are and how we act depends less on what we know than on the dispositions we develop to use our resources for knowing effectively and appropriately. This is what we learn through participation in community activities with those that Lave and Wenger (1991) call the 'old-timers'.

Seen in this light, it becomes clear why educational change is so difficult to achieve. First, there are few old-timers who have developed the appropriate dispositions and, second, instead of forming and participating in communities in which the desired values and practices are regularly enacted, those who would bring about change too often tell others how to act differently while continuing themselves in their unregenerate ways.

This has been particularly true in the field of education, where mandates for change are handed down by 'experts' higher up the institutional pyramid who remain uninvolved in the arena in which the change is to take place. In teacher education, too, it is not unusual to find proponents, for example, of active learning in the classroom who behave as if this can be brought about simply by giving lectures on this subject to large classes of student teachers. Gallimore and Tharp make this point very forcefully when they write:

> Little actual teaching occurs in schools; this is characteristic of transactions in the entire educational apparatus. All the way down the educational ladder, teaching is peculiarly absent in transactions between children and teachers, teachers and administrators, students and professors. Each appears to believe that, somewhere below, someone is teaching someone. Each position attempts to create educational opportunities for those down the chain - good textbooks, good workshops, even good performance objectives - but no one attends to assisting the performance of those objectives. (Gallimore and Tharp 1990, p. 188, emphasis added)

'Assisting performance' involves the teacher (or administrator or professor) in engaging in the activity with the other participants, both doing it with them and providing help where necessary. Teaching, then—to paraphrase Vygotsky's account of working in the zone of proximal development—is to provide assistance in such a way that the learner will become able to carry out the new activity independently (Vygotsky 1978).

My teacher colleagues in DICEP have been experimenting with how to create communities of inquiry in their classrooms and with how to provide assistance in knowledge building. As they recognize, however, they are hampered by the fact that they have had very few opportunities to participate in knowledge building communities themselves. As students in school, this was not their experience; nor did knowledge building characterize their teacher preparation. Not having had this experience themselves, they naturally find it hard to model it for others. The same could be said, of course, for administrators and teacher educators; they too have little experience of learning through knowledge building with others—at least not in formal classroom settings.

If schools are to become workshops for the production of knowledge, then, the same change must simultaneously occur in teacher education and in the preparation of educational administrators. These settings, too, must become knowledge building communities. This is a tall order, but nothing less will achieve the desired result.

However, even that will not be sufficient. Schools and colleges of education are not self-contained communities; there are countervailing pressures on them from many other directions—parents, employers, politicians, as well as specialists in the various academic disciplines—to whom the idea of knowledge building as the real work to be done in schools will seem inappropriate, undesirable or just plain impossible. As Bereiter himself remarks: "something academics too readily forget: that a large part of the world has no experience of treating ideas as objects of inquiry and discussion."[8]

The size of the task that Bereiter sets for us is certainly daunting, therefore, so it is unlikely that it will be achieved early in the

---

8. Nor should the local and national political climate be ignored. Parental pressure to meet their agendas as well as the shifting demands of district and state educational policy-makers and administrators create significant constraints on what it is feasible to do in particular times and places. Building and sustaining a community in which progressive dialogic inquiry is practiced and valued can be more like steering a ship through rapids in a storm than driving a school bus along a well-mapped highway.

twenty-first century. Indeed, judging by the pace of change in the emergence of the different modes of knowing that I discussed earlier, we cannot expect that a change in the practices of knowing and learning that has such wide cultural ramifications can be brought about in a single generation—or even two. We can also expect that, as the project gathers momentum and more people join in the knowledge building dialogue, it will undergo substantial revision. But then, this is the purpose of knowledge building: to continue to work on an improvable object in collaboration with others. As the coiner of the term 'progressive discourse', Bereiter will surely be pleased if his paper has this effect.

References

Bakhtin, M.M. 1986. *Speech Genres and Other Late Essays*. Translated by Y. McGee. Austin: University of Texas Press.

Barnes, D., and F. Todd. 1977. *Communicating and Learning in Small Groups*. London: Routledge.

Bereiter, C. 1994. Implications of Postmodernism for Science, or, Science as Progressive Discourse. *Educational Psychologist* 29(1), 3–12.

———. 2002. *Education and Mind in the Knowledge Age*. Mahwah, NJ: Erlbaum.

Brown, A.L., and J.C. Campione. 1994. Guided Discovery in a Community of Learners. In K. McGilly, ed., *Integrating Cognitive Theory and Classroom Practice: Classroom Lessons* (Cambridge, MA: MIT Press/Bradford Books).

Carr, W. and S. Kemmis. 1983. *Becoming Critical: Knowing through Action Research*. Geelong, Vic.: Deakin University Press.

Clarke, M.A., A. Davis, L.K. Rhodes, and E.D. Baker. 1996. *Creating Coherence: High Achieving Classrooms for Minority Students*. Denver, CO: University of Colorado at Denver.

Cobb, P., T. Wood, E. Yackel, and B. McNeal. 1992. Characteristics of Classroom Mathematics Traditions: An Interactional Analysis. *American Educational Research Journal* 29(3), 573–604.

Cohen, D.K., M.W. McLaughlin, and J.E. Talbert, eds. 1993. *Teaching for Understanding: Challenges for Policy and Practice*. San Francisco: Jossey-Bass.

Deacon, T.W. 1997. *The Symbolic Species: The Co-evolution of Language and the Brain*. New York: Norton.

Dias, P.X., and M. Hayhoe. 1988. *Developing Response to Poetry*. Milton Keynes: Open University Press.

Donald, M. 1991. *Origins of the Modern Mind: Three Stages in the Evolution of Culture and Cognition.* Cambridge, MA: Harvard University Press.

Donoahue, Z., M.A. Van Tassell, and L. Patterson, L., eds. 1996. *Research in the Classroom: Talk, Text and Inquiry.* Newark, DE: International Reading Association.

Edwards, D. 1997. *Discourse and Cognition.* London: Sage.

Egan, K. 1997. *The Educated Mind.* Chicago: University of Chicago Press.

Franklin, U. 1996. Introduction to the Symposium, 'Towards an Ecology of Knowledge'. University of Toronto, 7th March 1976.

Freire, P. 1970. *Pedagogy of the Oppressed.* New York: Herder and Herder.

Galbraith, B., M.A. Van Tassell, and G. Wells. 1997. Learning and Teaching in the Zone of Proximal Development. (Original in Spanish.) Republished in English in Wells 1999.

Gallas, K. 1995. *Talking Their Way into Science: Hearing Children's Questions and Theories, Responding with Curricula.* New York: Teachers College Press.

Gallimore, R. and R. Tharp. 1990. Teaching Mind in Society: Teaching, Schooling, and Literate Discourse. In L.C. Moll, ed., *Vygotsky and Education: Instructional Implications and Applications of Sociohistorical Psychology* (New York: Cambridge University Press), pp. 175–205.

Hacking, I. 1990. *The Taming of Chance.* Cambridge: Cambridge University Press.

Halliday, M.A.K. 1978. *Language as Social Semiotic: The Social Interpretation of Language and Meaning.* London: Arnold.

———. 1988. On the Language of Physical Science. In M. Ghadessy, ed., *Registers of Written English: Situational Factors and Linguistic Features* (London: Frances Pinter), pp. 162–178.

———. 1993. Towards a Language-Based Theory of Learning. *Linguistics and Education* 5, 93–116.

Hedegaard, M. 1990. How Instruction Influences Children's Concepts of Evolution. *Mind, Culture, and Activity* 3, 11–24.

Lampert, M., P. Rittenhouse, and C. Crumbaugh. 1996. Agreeing to Disagree: Developing Sociable Mathematical Discourse. In D.R. Olson and N. Torrance, eds., *The Handbook of Education and Human Development* (Cambridge, MA: Blackwell), pp. 731–764.

Lave, J. and E. Wenger. 1991. *Situated Learning: Legitimate Peripheral Participation.* New York: Cambridge University Press.

Lotman, Y.M. 1988. Text within a Text. *Soviet Psychology* 26(3), 32–51.

McMahon, S.I., T.E. Raphael, with V.J. Goatley, and L.S. Pardo, eds. 1997. *The Book Club Connection: Literacy Learning and Classroom Talk.* New York: Teachers College Press.

Measures, E. 1997. A Grade 5 Teacher and a Researcher Negotiate a Shared Sense of Inquiry. OISE/University of Toronto, unpublished paper.

Meyer, K., and E. Woodruff. 1997. Consensually Driven Explanation in Science Teaching. *Science Education* 81, 175–194.

Newman, D., P. Griffin, and M. Cole. 1989. *The Construction Zone: Working for Cognitive Change in School.* Cambridge: Cambridge University Press.

Nuthall, G. In press. Understanding Student Learning and Thinking in the Classroom. In B.J. Biddle, T.L. Good, and I.F. Goodson, eds., *The International Handbook of Teachers and Teaching.* Dordrecht: Kluwer.

Olson, D.R. 1994. *The World on Paper.* Cambridge: Cambridge University Press.

Ong, W. 1982. *Orality and Literacy.* New York: Methuen.

Palincsar, A.S., S.J. Magnusson, N. Marano, D. Ford, and N. Brown. In press. Designing a Community of Practice: Principles and Practices of the GIsML Community. *Teaching and Teacher Education* 14 (1), 5–19.

Pontecorvo, C., and H. Girardet. 1993. Arguing and Reasoning in Understanding Historical Topics. *Cognition and Instruction* 11, 189–196.

Popper, K.R. 1972. *Objective Knowledge: An Evolutionary Approach.* Oxford: Clarendon.

Reddy, M. 1979. The Conduit Metaphor: A Case of Frame Conflict in Our Language about Language. In A. Ortony, ed., *Metaphor and Thought* (Cambridge: Cambridge University Press), pp. 284–324.

Roseberry, A., B. Warren, and F. Conant. 1992. Appropriating Scientific Discourse: Findings from Language Minority Classrooms. *Journal of the Learning Sciences* 2, 61–94.

Scardamalia, M., C. Bereiter, and M. Lamon. 1994. The CSILE Project: Trying to Bring the Classroom into World 3. In K. McGilley, ed., *Classroom Lessons: Integrating Cognitive Theory and Classroom Practice* (Cambridge, MA: MIT Press), pp. 201–228.

Schön, D. 1987. Educating the Reflective Practitioner. San Francisco: Jossey-Bass.

Scribner, S. 1985. Vygotsky's Uses of History. In J.V. Wertsch, ed., *Culture, Communication, and Cognition: Vygotskian Perspectives* (Cambridge: Cambridge University Press), pp. 119–145.

Seixas, P. 1993. The Community of Inquiry as a Basis for Knowledge and Learning: The Case of History. *American Educational Research Journal* 30, 305–324.

Short, K. 1996. *Learning Together through Inquiry: From Columbus to Integrated Curriculum.* York, ME: Stenhouse.

Tharp, R., and R. Gallimore. 1988. *Rousing Minds to Life.* New York: Cambridge University Press.

Torbe, M., and P. Medway. 1981. *The Climate for Learning*. (Reprinted by Boynton/Cook, Montclair, NJ). London: Ward Lock Educational.

Vygotsky, L.S. 1978. *Mind in Society: The Development of Higher Psychological Processes*. Cambridge, MA: Harvard University Press.

———. 1981. The Genesis of Higher Mental Functions. In J.V. Wertsch, ed., *The Concept of Activity in Soviet Psychology* (Armonk, NY: Sharpe), pp. 144–188.

———. 1987 [1934]. Thinking and Speech. In R.W. Rieber and A.S. Carton, eds., *The Collected Works of L.S. Vygotsky, Volume 1: Problems of General Psychology* (New York: Plenum).

Wartofsky, M. 1979. *Models, Representation, and Scientific Understanding*. Boston: Reidel.

Wells, G. 1999. *Dialogic Inquiry: Towards a Sociocultural Practice and Theory of Education*. Cambridge: Cambridge University Press.

———. 2000. Dialogic Inquiry in the Classroom: Building on the Legacy of Vygotsky. In C. Lee and P. Smagorinsky, eds., *Vygotskian Perspectives on Literacy Research* (New York: Cambridge University Press).

———, ed. 2001. *Action, Talk, and Text: Learning and Teaching through Inquiry*. New York: Teachers College Press.

Wells, G., L. Bernard, M.A. Gianotti, C. Keating, C. Konjevic, M. Kowal, A. Maher, C. Mayer, T. Moscoe, E. Orzechowska, A. Smieja, and L. Swartz. 1994. Changing Schools from Within: Creating Communities of Inquiry. Toronto: OISE Press/Portsmouth, NH: Heinemann.

Wertsch, J.V. 1991. *Voices of the Mind: A Sociocultural Approach to Mediated Action*. Cambridge, MA: Harvard University Press.

Wertsch, J.V., and C.A. Stone. 1985. The Concept of Internalization in Vygotsky's Account of the Genesis of Higher Mental Functions. In J.V. Wertsch, ed., *Culture, Communication, and Cognition: Vygotskian Perspectives* (New York: Cambridge University Press), pp. 162–179.

Yngve, V.H. 1996. *From Grammar to Science: New Foundations for General Linguistics*. Amsterdam/Philadelphia: John Benjamins.

7

Education, Knowledge, and the World of Objective Ideas: Some Philosophical Remarks

Erich H. Reck

The goal of Carl Bereiter's paper 'Education in a Knowledge Society', and more generally of the Conference on Liberal Education for which it was the centerpiece, is to reconceptualize, and thus to revive, the idea of a liberal education. I have been asked to comment on this paper, in particular on its more philosophical aspects. As I find the idea of a liberal education to be something that deserves our attention, I am happy to do so. And as I think Bereiter's target paper is provocative in the right kind of way—it brings up many ideas and suggestions that are well worth exploring further—my comments will stay relatively close to it, especially initially.

Bereiter starts his discussion by talking about some recent developments in what he calls the "futuristic business literature," on the one hand, and "cognitive learning research," on the other. I am not an expert on cognitive science or education, much less on futurism or economics, so I will only make a few general remarks about the corresponding aspects of his paper, leaving detailed criticism of them to more qualified commentators. However, Bereiter also uses ideas and terms from philosophy, in particular from the philosopher Karl Popper, such as the notion of 'World 3', the world of 'objective knowledge' or of 'objective ideas'. It is the use of these

Popperian ideas and terms, in conjunction with that of 'knowledge production' as found in the futuristic business literature, that allows Bereiter to articulate a new general vision for education. And it is this aspect of his paper to which I want to respond in detail, partly because it connects directly with my own philosophical interests, partly because it has important consequences for how to think about education.

The primary goal of my response will be to examine and to call into question the usefulness—for Bereiter's own purposes—of the Popperian notions mentioned. This will lead me into an exploration of some ambiguities, tensions, and potential problems created by using labels such as 'World 3' and 'objective knowledge'; similarly, or even more so, for 'knowledge production'. These aspects make Bereiter's proposal somewhat problematic, as I will argue. At the same time I am not unsympathetic to the underlying thrust of his new vision. In particular, I agree with his renewed emphasis on teaching "real content" in school, on opening up certain "traditions of inquiry" to students, and on making a kind of "cosmopolitanism" the aim of education. My second goal will, then, be to bring some of these ideas into clearer focus. In doing so I will explore how one can articulate them differently, modify them where necessary, and refine them in certain ways. Finally, I will raise some big questions along the way—basic philosophical questions about education, knowledge, and the world of objective ideas. These questions seem to me to be lurking in the background of Bereiter's proposal, and they need to be discussed more openly and fully if we want to make real progress about education.

Bereiter's New Proposal: Motivation and Core Idea

Let me start by reviewing briefly what Carl Bereiter's new proposal for education is.[1] In his paper he motivates it in terms of being a

---

1. My discussion of Bereiter's proposal will focus on his 'Liberal Education in a Knowledge Society' (this volume). All my quotations will come from the original version of this paper, the one that was at my disposal when preparing my comments for the conference and when turning them into this paper. For further elaboration of Bereiter's ideas compare Bereiter and Scardamalia 1996 and Bereiter 1997.

reaction to, and an improvement on, certain earlier models of education. What are these earlier models?

The initial foil for Bereiter is the model according to which education works basically as follows: the mind of a student is seen as a 'container', and this container, initially rather empty, needs to be filled with knowledge by the teacher. Now, this is an old model, and much subsequent research on cognitive learning processes has led to criticism of and opposition to it. Such criticism has, in turn, led to several alternative models, in particular models emphasizing 'child-centered learning activities' and 'self-initiated learning projects'. There has also been a new emphasis on the importance of 'classroom culture', including the encouragement of 'reciprocal teaching' amongst students, of creating 'communities of learners', and so forth. Clearly these more recent models are, in various respects, better than the old one. But a remaining problem with them, as pointed out by Bereiter, is that they tend to focus too much on 'process' and not enough on 'content'.

According to Bereiter, the excessive de-emphasizing of content in recent models of education has been reinforced from a different side: the futuristic business literature. In the view of many writers in this literature, as well as in that of some educators who already follow them in classroom practice, the goal of education should be to produce students who have developed certain 'general skills' and 'personal qualities'. Amongst these skills and qualities are prominently: imagination, the ability to collaborate with others, problem-solving skills, communicative skills, and the ability and desire to go on learning. Possession of these general skills and qualities is, from this perspective, what is needed to succeed in today's and tomorrow's business world.[2] The acquisition of more specific knowledge of, say, certain parts of modern physics or biology is perceived as much less important.

Current educators and education policy makers sometimes try to combine the two ideas or models just mentioned: that of a child-centered education and of creating a classroom culture of

---

2. Such skills and qualities are also what is needed to play one's part in a modern democratic and multicultural society. But the emphasis in the futuristic business literature is very much on economic considerations. I will return (critically) to this emphasis in later parts of my paper.

communal learning, on the one hand, and that of emphasizing the development of certain skills and personal qualities, on the other. The question becomes, then, whether such an eclectic, superficial combination of these ideas is really attractive, or simply good enough. Bereiter argues that it is not. What we need, according to him, is a "new vision" or a "radical new proposal," one that has more unity, more depth, and is thus more exciting. And he proceeds to offer us such a new vision. According to that vision, child-centered education, communal learning, and the skills and qualities mentioned are not rejected completely, but they are not the primary focus any more. Instead new weight is put on teaching 'real knowledge', as opposed to mere process, mere general skills, and mere personal qualities. Put slightly differently, students are again supposed to be confronted with 'real content' in the classroom, albeit in fresh and innovative ways. The core idea of Bereiter's vision is, thus, to reorganize classroom culture around the "pursuit of real knowledge."

Partly in order to clarify what is new about his proposal, partly to give it more rhetorical punch, Bereiter proceeds to introduce some special terminology. The fundamental idea for him is—first in words borrowed from the futuristic business literature—for school to become a "knowledge building organization"; or perhaps slightly better, the goal of school should be to draw students into a "shared knowledge-building enterprise." And to draw students into such an enterprise consists in—now using Popperian terminology—introducing them to 'World 3', the world of "objective knowledge" or of "objective ideas". The slogan becomes, then: let education be "enculturation into World 3"!

A catchy, engaging slogan, isn't it? Perhaps. I am not so sure, however, whether Bereiter's central metaphor of 'knowledge building', or 'knowledge production', is entirely happy and unproblematic. It certainly seems advisable to probe it further, in some detail, before assigning such a central role to it. Also, a lot more needs to be said now about the notions of 'objective knowledge', 'objective ideas', and 'World 3'. They too may turn out to be more problematic than assumed. But let me establish some common ground first, by explaining in which sense I basically agree with Bereiter's proposal, before turning to what I find problematic in it.

Basic Agreements and Initial Clarifications

Part of Bereiter's general assessment of the situation we are in is that knowledge will be an increasingly salient part of our world in the future. Here he follows the futuristic business literature, among others. But if so, then one should not only not exclude today's students from such a world of knowledge, but work actively on including them. Now, while I think one may debate whether the salience of knowledge is really so radically new,[3] it seems correct to me, in fact almost a truism, that knowledge will be of continuing importance in today's and tomorrow's world. It is probably also true, as Bereiter writes, that the more one knows (within certain limits, I would add), the greater the chance for learning something new.[4] But then, to teach students some real knowledge in school will indeed prepare them well for the future.

Beyond this basic agreement, I find the following three aspects of Bereiter's general position also attractive, and worth emphasizing further in the context of a discussion about education. First, he defends the view (clearly not a new view, to be sure) that we can find around us "a fund of accumulated knowledge that is passed on and of knowledge advancing through people's creative efforts." In this connection one may quibble with the degree to which, or the exact sense in which, our knowledge is cumulative.[5] But to deny that there is any fund of knowledge worth passing on seems clearly wrong. In fact, there is probably too much such knowledge, so that the problem becomes one of selection. (I will come back to this issue later.) Also, Bereiter's emphasis on human creativity, in the passage just quoted and elsewhere, deserves to be noted.

Second and relatedly, Bereiter directs our view towards 'communities' and 'traditions' of inquiry. The main goal of his new vision for education can then be re-described as follows: it is to

---

3. Cf. Edwards and Ogilvie 1998 (Chapter 3 of this volume).

4. I would argue, with Bereiter, that personal experience, common sense, various theories of understanding (such as ones involving the 'hermeneutic circle'), and some results from recent cognitive learning research all point in that direction.

5. Compare here Kuhn 1970, which argues against various simplistic views about the accumulation of knowledge in science, in particular as they can be found in many standard science textbooks. (I do not think it follows from Kuhn's work that there is no progress at all in science; compare, amongst others, his account of 'normal science' in this connection.)

make such communities and traditions genuinely open to students. This is indeed a very desirable goal, for various reasons.[6] One reason is the tremendous economical influence such communities and traditions have today, in particular the indispensable, or at least inescapable, role the sciences play in today's economic world. Another reason, not emphasized as much by Bereiter himself, is the role such communities and traditions can and often do play from a humanistic point of view, for example with respect to human intellectual flourishing. As human beings we seem to be inherently curious, that is, we have many questions about ourselves and about the world around us. And the communities and traditions mentioned are crucial sources for answers to such questions. Moreover, they provide important resources for overcoming various prejudices and misconceptions that tend to come up in our moral and political lives. In other words, such communities and traditions of inquiry tend to encourage a cosmopolitan, enlightened, and tolerant outlook in its participants. I agree with Bereiter that that is a good thing.

A third aspect of Bereiter's proposal that I find attractive, at least to some degree, is this: especially if considered as a counterweight to the earlier excessively child-centered and classroom-culture directed models of education, there is probably much good and practical sense in his urging us to see pieces of knowledge— 'ideas', 'concepts', and 'thoughts'—as in some sense 'objective'. Having said that, it needs to be made clearer now what is meant by these notions—in which sense knowledge is supposed to be objective. (Various different ways of understanding such a claim are possible, and not all of them are helpful and defensible in the present context, as will become clear later.)

It is, of course, exactly with respect to the idea of 'objective knowledge' that Bereiter appeals to Popper and his 'World 3'. Bereiter states: "(I)n order to carry on a serious discussion about knowledge in education we need distinguishing labels"; and he adds: "Popper has provided some, which can be quite useful as long as we are careful not to encumber them with excess meaning." I do

---

6. It is also an ambitious goal, to be sure, and it needs to be made clearer how to do so. Compare here Scardamalia, Bereiter, and Lamon 1994.

think that it can be very useful—for certain purposes, like to get a discussion started—to have catchy labels at one's disposal. But there are also dangers that come with relying on them. For one thing, certain labels, especially if borrowed from a philosopher, do not have to be "encumbered with excess meaning"—they already come with it. But if so, then one should at the very least be aware of that fact. Often it is even advisable to explicitly disassociate oneself from this excess meaning; otherwise people will be misled or simply put off by the use of the labels.[7] In addition, "serious discussions", about education or any other topic, should not remain at the level of just putting labels on things for long. Once one has made careful and productive use of certain labels initially, one should make sure to go beyond them, to move towards a more subtle language and towards more differentiated theses and arguments.

There is one particular way in which invoking notions such as 'objective knowledge', 'objective ideas', and so forth, may be seen as problematic that I want to address first, mostly so as to put it aside. Namely, relying on these notions may be taken to lead directly to debates about 'realism' and 'anti-realism' (in the philosophical sense). Especially metaphysically inclined thinkers are often drawn towards, and get stuck on, such debates. Let me say the following right away: While I don't want to deny that there are interesting philosophical questions one can raise in connection with these metaphysical issues, I don't think that we need to worry too much about them for present purposes, especially about general anti-realist objections.

Why not? Consider the sense in which Bereiter wants to treat knowledge as 'objective'. He stresses two aspects in this connection: first, he thinks it is useful to see knowledge as 'something that people acquire and that becomes part of them'; second, he thinks it is useful to see knowledge as 'something to work with and that takes on a life of its own'. I have already agreed above that it may be useful in our context—especially as a corrective to certain earlier views about education—to see knowledge in that way. Beyond that, it

---

7. Note here that Karl Popper's philosophy is today very much out of fashion amongst large parts of the philosophical community (especially in North America, but also elsewhere). Consequently, the mere appeal to him, or the use of terminology closely associated with him, will put some people off.

seems to me that both a 'realist' and an 'anti-realist' (some kind of instrumentalist or social constructivist, say) should be able to accommodate both of these aspects, at least if they are sensible about it. In other words, the kind of 'objectification' of knowledge that Bereiter needs seems relatively harmless, at least metaphysically speaking.[8]

This is not to say that I see such 'objectification' as completely unproblematic. But the problems I want to focus on in this paper are conceptual and practical, rather than metaphysical. Let me now turn to some of these problems, in particular ones that have their source in the terminology used by Bereiter. I will start with a discussion of his phrase 'knowledge-producing organizations' and some of its implications. After that I will turn to 'objective knowledge' and 'World 3'. In connection with the latter I will add a few metaphysical clarifications, coupled with some historical asides.

Different Kinds of 'Knowledge-Producing Organizations'

According to Bereiter, education should not just be a matter of 'taking in' knowledge, in particular knowledge handed down by authority (as suggested, for instance, by the mind-as-container model). Nor should it simply be a matter of developing certain skills and personal qualities, or merely a matter of learning to learn. Rather, education should be a matter of 'building' or 'producing knowledge'; in Bereiter's own words: "What I shall propose is that the schools be reconstituted along the lines of other organizations whose function is to produce knowledge."

This way of putting the point immediately leads to the following question: what kinds of 'knowledge-producing organizations' are we supposed to think of as models here? If we follow Bereiter's paper carefully, we can see that he basically appeals to two kinds of

---

8. At some point a real case would, of course, have to be made for such a claim, in particular in a more philosophical setting. I will come back to it later in this paper, but only briefly. At this point, it might best be taken as an orienting remark, that is, as an indication of the kinds of issues I want to focus on in this paper: conceptual and practical issues, rather than metaphysical ones. For a discussion of some of the metaphysical issues involved, compare Reck 1997.

knowledge producing organizations. They are: first, the research and development departments of big commercial companies; second, university research centers, especially science laboratories. Let us reflect a bit more on the similarities and differences between these two kinds of organizations.

Modern high-tech businesses such as Microsoft or Apple probably exemplify best the first kind of knowledge-producing organization mentioned. Examples suggested by Bereiter also include: Nike's research and design department, some market research centers, and opinion research groups. What is crucial about them, for Bereiter's purposes, is that in such organizations "problems are solved and new knowledge is generated within the working group"; and these organizations strive to "make everyone a contributor" in these activities. In addition, what is striking—to me at least—is that these are all organizations in which knowledge is produced for economic or business purposes, in other words, for external customers or for profit. As such, they can be seen as paradigm cases for a pragmatic or instrumental view of knowledge, a view according to which knowledge has its value because of its practical, especially its economic, use.[9] But this is not the only possible view about the value of knowledge. Instead, one can value knowledge, or at least certain kinds of knowledge, either as an end in itself or insofar as it contributes to human intellectual flourishing. Both of these would reflect a more Aristotelian or humanistic view of knowledge, rather than a pragmatic, instrumental one.

How appealing and appropriate is it to regard the first kind of 'knowledge-producing organization' mentioned by Bereiter, and thus a pragmatic or instrumental view of knowledge, as the model for school? Well, first of all it is no mystery why this would be appealing for writers in the futuristic business literature, since this whole literature is driven by economic considerations. Also, there

---

9. Notice here also the economic language often used by Bereiter in this whole connection: Knowledge is a "commodity," or a "third factor of production, along with capital and labor." Actually, this language sounds rather old-fashioned to me: it suggests various kinds of nineteenth-century economics, especially Marx's theories. Adopting such language opens Bereiter's proposal up to various recent criticisms directed against corresponding Marxist views. But that is a topic for another paper, and for a commentator more competent than I in this large area.

seems to be a more general trend, or fad, today to let economic and management considerations dominate everything else, including education.[10] More basically, it is not hard to see why some students, and even more some parents, may find it attractive to think about school and 'knowledge production' along these lines, namely as something that will profit them economically. However, should we, as people trying to reconceptualize the idea of a liberal education, follow that trend? In other words, is it really so appropriate to try to turn students into 'knowledge producers'? To be fair, Bereiter clearly doesn't have a Dickensian vision of child exploitation in mind when he talks about 'knowledge production' in school. His goal is more benign: he wants to give the students "the experience of producing knowledge of real value to someone". Still, what is the "real value" supposed to consist in here—merely and purely economic value?

The question I have just raised is whether it is desirable to see students in school as 'workers' along the lines of our first model of 'knowledge-producing organizations'. Putting it this way also leads to some related questions which I will only formulate, but not discuss further, namely: Which age group do or should we have in mind here? College students? High-school students? All the way down to first grade? Perhaps the closer the students get to the end of high school, the more the model considered so far—that of producing knowledge with economic value—is useful and attractive, at least for some people. But should exactly the same model be used for all age groups? Also, should the school world of first-graders, say, not be kept a bit more playful and innocent, as well as primarily directed towards their general learning and intellectual development?

Let me now turn to the second kind of knowledge-producing organizations appealed to by Bereiter. Its main example is the research university, and perhaps most clearly the research laboratory, say a physics or biology lab. If we take this second kind of organization as the model for school, we get a somewhat different picture. Students are now supposed to see themselves as working on

---

10. Compare *The Economist* 1997b for a discussion of this trend in connection with the research university—again from an economic point of view.

real scientific problems, including very 'pure' scientific problems, just like the scientists in such labs. Bereiter quotes a phrase one of his students used in class in this connection: "Mendel worked on Karen's problem". He also mentions the names of Aristotle and Newton. The latter were thinkers who, according to him, wanted "to construct an understanding of the whole world", that is, who worked on very big, encompassing scientific and philosophical theories.

Along such lines, a question about the appropriate age level arises again; very briefly: how old are the students supposed to be who are to behave like Aristotle, Newton, and Mendel, and are supposed to be involved in the kind of "authentic knowledge construction" Bereiter has in mind? To be fair again, he emphasizes that one should see the originality of the research involved as "relative to the context." In other words, one shouldn't expect a first-grader to write a scientific dissertation. Nevertheless, wouldn't it be useful to think and say more about various gradations in this connection, to make the model more age-sensitive?[11]

My main point in this section does not concern age, though. It has to do with the following contrast. Along the lines of this second kind of model—the research university, Aristotle, Newton, and Mendel—the driving force for knowledge production is not, or at least not just, pragmatic or economic. Instead, what plays a bigger role, especially for someone like Aristotle, is our human interest in pure intellectual inquiry, including the search for knowledge to satisfy our human curiosity (apart from, or in addition to, satisfying more basic needs). To push this thought even further, what is crucial, in the end, is the philosophical motivation of wanting to understand our place in the universe, including what it means to be fully human. Exactly that motivation was, of course, at the very center of an older, more humanistic vision of a liberal education. It is interesting to observe, then, how some aspects of Bereiter's proposal relate to this older vision.

When considering this general issue one may feel a strong tension between two opposed visions for education that both seem to play a role in Bereiter's overall vision: one very pragmatic/

---

11. Because of its emphasis on developmental aspects, the work of Jean Piaget (on the genesis of children's conception of number, space, causality, and so forth) comes to mind here; cf., for example, Piaget 1965.

economic, the other more humanist/Aristotelian.[12] This was my initial reaction to it. On further thought, however, it is not clear whether the opposition is more ideal than real. Perhaps there is a continuum of cases, rather than just two opposite poles, and perhaps most examples of human inquiry, including most scientific research, are located somewhere in the middle—they are never completely pure, always to some degree also economically, or at least pragmatically, oriented. Just think of most contemporary microbiology labs in this connection. Conversely, perhaps research in some of today's high-tech businesses can also, at least sometimes, satisfy one's intellectual curiosity. In other words, perhaps 'purely theoretical' and 'purely practical' knowledge are not so isolated from each other as one may think initially.[13]

But even if this is the case, we have arrived at an important question. What should the ultimate goal of education be: simply to satisfy certain economic needs (perhaps as revealed to us by the futuristic business literature), or something beyond that (for example, to contribute to human intellectual flourishing along Aristotelian lines)?[14] Without answering this question myself, my main point so far may be put this way: the choice of one kind of knowledge-producing organization over another as the main model for education will, to some degree at least, reflect an answer to this question.[15] Bereiter himself does, of course, not explicitly make such a choice: he does not single out one of his models as the

---

12. Perhaps this tension is also connected with the difference between a 'knowledge economy' and a (more general) 'knowledge society', as these terms were used by some of the participants at the conference.

13. In addition, this would not be the first time a more practical or business-oriented vision for education was seen as being in line with a more scientific or even a humanistic education. Consider, for instance, the way in which vocational training in late nineteenth-century Germany, influenced by Humboldt's vision for education, emphasized both the acquisition of very practically oriented skills and the cultivation of a broader humanistic or philosophical *Bildung*. Compare here the presentations by André Carus, Blouke Carus, and James Miller at the conference.

14. My source for Aristotle's views on human flourishing is Aristotle 1992.

15. The answer to this question will also have various more practical and pedagogical ramifications. Consider the following example: The different kinds of knowledge-producing organizations mentioned do their 'producing' to achieve somewhat different ends. But these different ends bring with them different criteria for what counts as being good, or as becoming better, at the kinds of work involved. Thus, being able to satisfy some external, fixed need in a reasonably self-contained form and in a restricted amount of time may be crucial in one case; being able to

primary one. Insofar as that is the case, he remains uncommitted and open as to the ultimate goal of education. At the same time, his repeated appeal to the futuristic business literature and its demands does, it seems to me, reveal some implicit bias towards the pragmatic/economic side. Moreover, the very use of 'knowledge production' as the guiding metaphor is not quite neutral either.

Bereiter's other guiding metaphor, closely related to that of 'knowledge production', is that of 'World 3'. Let me turn to this notion now. We will see that its use, too, is not exactly neutral and unproblematic, in several respects.

World 3: Popper versus Frege, Bolzano, and Plato

'World 3', as understood by Popper and Bereiter, stands opposed to 'World 1', the physical world of tables and chairs, and to 'World 2', the mental world, or worlds, of sensations, memories, and mental images. Put more positively, World 3 is the world of 'objective ideas' (or of 'intelligibilia', as Popper puts it at one point). A good example, mentioned both by Popper and Bereiter, for an inhabitant of this world of objective ideas is a piece of mathematics: Pythagoras's Theorem (about triangles).[16]

However, it is not just theorems that inhabit World 3, again both for Popper and Bereiter. Also included are, for example, "explanations of theorems, intuitive proofs, examples of applications, formulated problems." At one point Popper gives the following general list of what is in World 3: "discussible propositions or declarative knowledge—theories, conjectures, problem formulations, historical accounts, interpretations, proofs, criticisms, and the like". Bereiter himself provides this more qualitative characterization: "The boundaries of World 3 are approximately the boundaries of what can be profitably argued about in general terms."

---

raise new questions, even to make the inquiry really open-ended may be crucial in the other case. Now, which of those kinds of criteria are more appropriate for students in school? (This way of looking at the issue was suggested to me by a question Sheilagh Ogilvie raised at the conference, in the discussion after Carl Bereiter's presentation.)

16. For Popper's general views in this connection see in particular Popper 1968. Similar ideas are brought up in passing in Popper and Eccles 1977.

Later I will come back to the interesting fact that included in Popper's list are things like "historical accounts" and "interpretations", that is, the typical results of inquiry in the humanities, the arts, and the social sciences, not just the more usual examples from mathematics and the natural sciences, such as Pythagoras's Theorem. But first I want to go on a brief historical detour. I want to compare Popper's and Bereiter's notion of World 3 with some other, similar notions from the history of philosophy.

Many contemporary philosophers will associate the notion of a separate world of 'objective ideas', or of 'objective thoughts', 'objective meanings', and so forth, with Gottlob Frege's work, some also with Edmund Husserl's work. Both of these thinkers wrote about such notions late in the nineteenth and early in the twentieth century. Earlier, during the middle of the nineteenth century, Bernard Bolzano, the Bohemian philosopher and mathematician, put forth the closely related notion of a 'proposition in itself'. Since Bolzano clearly influenced Husserl, perhaps also indirectly Frege, he can be seen as the modern father of the notion of 'objective idea'. However, one can go back even further: The Stoic philosophers, in Hellenistic Greece, used a notion of 'lecta' that is similar in some ways to that of 'objective meanings'. Finally, it is Plato who is best known for having developed a theory of objective 'ideas' or 'forms' which points in a similar, if not exactly the same, direction.[17]

Being well aware of these earlier thinkers and their views,[18] Karl Popper wants to differentiate his own notions of 'objective knowledge' and 'World 3' from theirs in a certain way. Namely, he insists that the content of World 3, as he understands it, is wholly 'a human construction'. In contrast, for Plato, for Bolzano, and for Frege, say, 'forms', 'propositions-in-themselves', and 'objective thoughts' are supposed to pre-exist human understanding, and more generally all human production or construction. Now, Bereiter is explicit in following Popper on this point; he even insists on the following: Not only have the contents of World 3 been constructed by us, they are also "undergoing continual renovation."

---

17. For Frege's views see Frege 1884 and Frege 1918; for Husserl's see Husserl 1913; for Bolzano's see Bolzano 1837 or Bolzano 1978; for the Stoics' views see Long and Sedley 1988, esp. pp. 196–202; and for Plato's see Plato 1974.

18. See Popper 1968, especially footnotes 1, 4, 5, 6, and 12.

This claim is important to him because of his emphasis on human creativity; remember that he wants students to be 'knowledge producers'.

Many people today, if they consider such issues seriously at all, will find the notion of 'objective ideas' as things existing in some special, separate 'world' or 'realm', apart from the physical universe and our minds, highly problematic. In fact, it is rather popular these days to be 'anti-platonist' in this sense. This is especially so if the alternative is to follow Plato, Bolzano, or Frege in taking that realm to be in some strong sense independent from what we humans think and do. I, on the other hand, am not completely unsympathetic to that alternative. More precisely, I think there is, at the very least, a way to understand it that saves it from being absurd, perhaps even a way that makes it defensible.[19]

While I don't intend to go much into the corresponding metaphysical subtleties, as indicated before, I do want to offer a few basic clarifications. To begin with, Popper's and Bereiter's 'constructed', thus more 'dependent', inhabitants of World 3 are in a certain respect actually more problematic than Plato's 'forms', Bolzano's 'propositions-in-themselves', or Frege's 'objective thoughts'; or so one may argue. Moreover, considering this argument briefly will lead us to certain ambiguities and tensions in Bereiter's notion of 'objective knowledge' that have not only metaphysical, but also practical implications.

First, though, a more general clarification: remember that according to both Popper and Bereiter the inhabitants of World 3 are things we can "argue about in general terms." I do agree on this aspect. In fact, I think it is crucial to recognize that there is a direct connection between what is in World 3 and the notion of 'argument'. Put slightly differently (in more Fregean terms), there is something correct about connecting 'objective thoughts' to the notions of 'judgment', 'inference', and 'reasoning'. The connection consists in the fact that 'objective ideas' or 'objective thoughts' are

---

19. That is to say, I believe there is a way to conceive of 'objective ideas' and similar entities that makes their existence and independence at least understandable, partly also defensible, even if some other questions about them remain. Compare here again Reck 1997, which contains a discussion of such views in the case of certain other 'abstract objects' such as numbers and sets.

distinguished, or gain their identity, by how they are related infer-entially to other such ideas or thoughts. That is to say, they are dis-tinguished by what implies them and by what follows from them.[20]

But now, clearly inferring and reasoning are things we as human thinkers do, aren't they? And if that's the case, does it not follow that such objective ideas are 'created' by us after all? Not necessarily. In fact, assuming so leads to some immediate prob-lems. Take the Pythagorean Theorem as an example. Let us grant, for the sake of the argument, that this theorem was created by us humans, in particular by the historical figure Pythagoras, a Greek philosopher and mathematician of the fifth century B.C. This leads to a number of questions. When exactly was it created, that is, when did it come into existence: was it when Pythagoras wrote it down explicitly for the first time; or when he talked about it ini-tially; or perhaps when he started to think about it, in some vague form? None of these answers seems quite satisfactory. In addition, suppose some sage in China, say, came up with the same theorem some time later (or earlier). Would that mean that he or she created the same theorem again, perhaps a second copy of it; does it even make sense of think of 'a second copy' in this connection? Similarly, suppose a student today 'produces' it for the first time. Do we then get more and more copies of the theorem, all created at different points in time? Finally and most importantly, if the theorem came into existence at one of those points (pick any one), does that mean it wasn't true before? That sounds funny, too.

While these (Fregean and Husserlian) challenges may not be completely clear and conclusive in themselves, together they do, or should, make us feel uncomfortable. They put the claim that the Pythagorean Theorem was 'created'—by a particular person, at a particular time—in a strange light. What that indicates, I would argue further, is the following: it may be better to give up the claim that such theorems or ideas are 'created' at all, on pain of having to answer all those questions. This is not to say that they have, in some strange sense, existed 'eternally'. Rather, we should think of such ideas and theorems as a-temporal. In other words, any attempt to locate 'objective ideas' or 'objective thoughts' themselves

---

20. This 'inferentialist' idea is worked out in great detail in Brandom 1994.

in space and time, including any attempt to describe them as 'created' by us, is just inappropriate.[21]

It is important to add the following immediately: this does not mean that we cannot talk about certain closely-related things or events as being locatable in space and time. For example, it makes perfect sense to say that Pythagoras, or someone else, was the one who formulated that theorem for the first time explicitly at a certain date and location.[22] Likewise, it makes sense to say that a student today proves it for the first time at a certain point, or applies it at another, or formulates it in another language at again another point in space and time. It also makes sense to say that the theorem became part of the state of knowledge in a community during a certain period, or that one person transmitted the knowledge of it to another person at a certain date and place.[23]

What I have just suggested is to treat 'objective ideas', on the one hand, and human knowledge (both individual and communal), formulations, applications, and so forth of such ideas, on the other hand, separately. This leads to a related point: namely, that the phrase 'objective knowledge', as used both by Bereiter and by Popper, involves an unfortunate ambiguity. To understand this ambiguity better we need to separate the notion of 'states of knowing' more clearly from that of 'content of knowledge'.

------

21. It is interesting to compare Pythagoras's Theorem with a poem, say a Shakespeare sonnet or Whitman's *Song of Myself*. Insofar as the latter are more 'subjective', it makes sense to talk about a point in space and time when they came into existence; also that they were created at that point. Note here that it is much harder, if not impossible, to identify a poem with respect to its inferential relations to other ideas; its identity is tied to other, less abstract features. Consequently, it makes sense to say that two people discovered the same theorem , while this would be strange to say in the case of a poem.

22. For most purposes we don't need to make a distinction between, say, the Pythagorean Theorem itself (seen as a 'proposition-in-itself' or as an 'objective thought') and specific and explicit formulations of it (conceived of either as tokens or types). But in more philosophical contexts as here—when discussing their objectivity and similar questions—this distinction becomes crucial (as Frege and Husserl pointed out).

23. Similarly, it makes sense to say that a particular formulation of the Pythagorean Theorem is, or at some point becomes, part of some computer program, or that it is now contained in some electronic database. Compare here the CSILE/Knowledge Forum programs and databases presented by Marlene Scardamalia at the conference.

States of Knowing versus the Content of Knowledge

It is 'objective ideas' and 'objective thoughts' that live in World 3. For them it does not make sense to be located in space and time, as I have just argued (following Frege and Husserl). States of knowing, on the other hand, should clearly not be located in World 3, since for them it does make sense to be located in space and time. Actually, the latter is also what Bereiter states in his paper, at least at certain points. Thus he puts individual students' knowledge of, say, the Pythagorean Theorem (such knowledge now thought of as a mental state) in World 2. At one point he even adds: "Without doing violence to Popper's concept, we can expand World 2 to include situated knowledge as well—knowledge that is implicit in the practices of communities and not assignable to individual minds."

Let us reflect on the latter suggestion critically. To begin with, is it really coherent to think that 'situated knowledge', in this sense, is part of World 2? Well, it depends on what exactly one means by "being implicit in the practice of a community." Take, for example, an ancient copy of Euclid's *Elements*, a concrete text in which the Pythagorean Theorem was formulated and transmitted by the Greeks. This text is, or was, clearly in World 1. What about the 'practice' of the corresponding community in which this World 1 object played a role? Well, doesn't a lot of that practice—for example, the text being stored in a library, it being read and copied, and so forth—again take place in World 1? More generally, isn't this a point where the separation between World 1 and World 2 loses its sharpness and usefulness? But then, wasn't Bereiter's adoption of Popper's notions motivated exactly by their usefulness?

My main point in this section is slightly different, though. It concerns the following question: should either individual or collective knowing be located in *World 3?* I hope it is plausible by now that they should not. Instead, they should either be located in World 1 or in World 2. The problem is that sometimes, although not always, Bereiter does put 'knowledge' into World 3. He seems to be led into this ambiguity, or tension, by the term 'knowledge', especially in phrases such as 'objective knowledge' and 'knowledge production'. Underlying this tension is the fact that the term 'knowledge' can be used in a number of different senses. These senses include: a. individual states of knowing (to be located in World 2!?); b. the knowledge embodied in the practices of a community (Worlds 1 or 2?); and c. knowledge 'objects', that is, the contents of either a. or b. (World 3?!). It helps to be more aware of the differences between them, I think.

It should be noted that Bereiter is not just following Popper in his use of the term 'knowledge'; he is also influenced by the futuristic business literature. And in that literature the meaning of the term 'knowledge' is extremely vague and slippery, it seems to me. That is to say, in it the term is used in a very crude and slogan-like way, as when people talk about 'knowledge management', 'knowledge banks', and the like.[24] Probably that usage approximates most closely to my sense c. above: knowledge as 'content'. In contrast, most philosophers and psychologists talk about 'knowledge' in the senses a. or b. above, that is, as 'state of knowing' either of the individual or of some community. Now, I do not mean to legislate in favor of one particular usage of 'knowledge' over against others. I simply want to urge that it helps to avoid confusions if one is clear, or at least clearer, about the usage of one's key terms.

It does not necessarily follow that Bereiter's basic vision for education is made inconsistent or incoherent by such ambiguities. For example, one can still say that it is important for students to become familiar with the world of 'objective ideas', such as the Pythagorean Theorem, in the sense that it is important for them to get to know what that theorem amounts to: what it implies, how to prove it, how to apply it, and so forth. Furthermore, in doing so the students may even be said to 'produce' something new, namely: explicit formulations of the theorem, applications to new situations, an awareness of connections to other theorems and other problems, and so forth. Finally, such 'production' may very well be crucial for acquiring 'real knowledge' for the students, since an excellent way to get to know something may be by being 'creative' about it in the right kind of way. In other words, the process of coming to understand the Pythagorean Theorem, especially in a thorough and lasting way, may be very much like the corresponding processes of creation or invention.

---

24. Compare, for instance, *The Economist* 1997a.

The latter is, of course, a psychological question, to be decided by empirical observations and studies. My more basic point here is that, as a matter of conceptual clarity, it is better not to claim that it is the Pythagorean Theorem itself that is being created, but rather new states of knowing of the theorem, new explicit formulations of it, new applications, and so forth. Perhaps it is even best to drop the phrase 'objective knowledge' altogether in this connection, since it brings with it so many ambiguities and problems.

Truths, Conceptual Possibilities, and Traditions of Inquiry

Let me turn to another general worry about World 3, one again related to an ambiguity in the various usages of 'knowledge', but now a different ambiguity. Consider the following question: is what is in World 3—and what should thus be known by students—only truths; or is it all kinds of ideas and thoughts, including some false ones? This issue has, once more, a metaphysical side, connected with the question of how to think about truth and falsity. But I am, as before, more concerned about its conceptual and practical consequences.

Some brief historical comparisons may again be helpful at this point. First, it is clear that for Bolzano, Frege, and Husserl, say, it is not just truths, but also all kinds of falsehoods that count as 'propositions-in-themselves', 'objective thoughts', or 'objective meanings'. Take the negation of the Pythagorean Theorem or, even better, the negation of Euclid's Fifth Postulate. Such a negation, like the negation of any truth, can be studied in terms of how to prove it, what follows from it, how to apply it, and so forth. And it is that kind of study that is crucial for Bolzano, Frege, and Husserl. Second, Popper agrees with these earlier thinkers on this particular issue; he, too, puts both Euclid's Fifth Postulate and its negation into World 3.[25] Finally, observe that Bereiter follows Popper in putting all kinds of 'conjectures' in World 3 as well.

---

25. It is also good to remember another side of Popper's epistemology here, namely his 'fallibilism'. According to it, all human knowledge consists of 'conjectures', of claims which, although perhaps seemingly true now, may always turn out to be false on further examination. Thus we can never be sure that what we currently think is true is really true.

So all these thinkers agree that it is not just 'truths' one can find in World 3, but also many 'falsehoods'. Actually, perhaps we even need to go beyond the whole truth-falsehood dichotomy. Remember that both Popper and Bereiter include 'problem formulations' and 'questions' in World 3, and such problems and questions are not strictly speaking true or false. Now, if one wants to do that I suggest a bit of new terminology (related to Popper's use of 'intelligibilia'). Namely, instead of talking about '(pieces of) knowledge' it might be better to talk about 'conceptual possibilities' as what World 3 contains. It is, then, such conceptual possibilities that we want students to become familiar with in school.[26]

Why would the introduction of such new terminology be helpful? We have already seen various problems with the phrase 'knowledge' above. A further consideration is this: some people will probably object to Bereiter's new vision for education because they are suspicious that with his notion of 'objective knowledge' he is trying to force on them a particular 'canon' of what is 'objectively true'. To do so would, of course, be in conflict with something he says explicitly in his paper: he states that he wants to "leave open such questions of what constitutes established knowledge and what needs to be mastered and in what way." In other words, he wants to remain non-committal about what exactly should be taught in school. Then again, perhaps such a brief disclaimer by him is not enough, especially since his general perspective seems not completely neutral in this respect after all. Arguably, certain biases, for example, in favor of scientific knowledge, seem to be built into it in a more covert way. (I will support this claim further in the next section.) Whether this is true or not, it is again the notion of 'knowledge' that gets in the way here: 'knowledge' seems to imply 'truth', and then one is led to wonder who decides here what is to count as true.[27]

---

26. As I think about them, 'conceptual possibilities' are not isolated; they can only be understood in their interconnection. Thus we also immediately need to consider various 'conceptual connections', etc.

27. Since the work of Plato many philosophers have found an equation of 'knowledge' with 'justified true belief' attractive (in spite of some remaining problems, such as the so-called Gettier counter-examples). And even someone who does not accept this exact equation may still think that 'knowledge' does, in some way, imply 'truth'. This raises the question of whether such an implication is accepted by Bereiter.

As a way to sidestep this whole problem, or at least to make Bereiter's proposal look less suspicious, let me suggest another bit of new terminology: why not talk about 'inquiry' as what education should (teach to) do, as opposed to 'knowledge production'? Note that adopting that terminology would also tie in nicely with the "communities and traditions of inquiry" to which Bereiter himself wants to introduce students.

Cultural Objects and the Boundaries of World 3

There is another question about World 3, or about its boundaries, that may lead to resistance to Bereiter's vision. To be able to formulate it, let us remind ourselves, once more, what World 3 is supposed to contain: "discussible propositions or declarative knowledge—theories, conjectures, problem formulations, historical accounts, interpretations, proofs, criticisms, and the like." At one point in his paper Bereiter remarks that beyond this world there exists "the larger world that includes other cultural objects such as: poems, sonatas, folk tales, food recipes, rituals, and monuments." He adds that with respect to this "larger world of cultural objects" there may exist significant differences for different people, for example, for "a liberally educated Indonesian or Italian." In contrast (and in spite of many recent claims to the contrary), Bereiter insists that "there are no culture-specific sciences, mathematics, literary or historical theories."

So somewhere beyond World 3 there exist these other "cultural objects." But where exactly do they live, if not in World 3, as we may ask now? Take a poem or a sonata: should it be located in World 1; or rather in World 2? Neither seems quite satisfactory, since such objects are almost as 'abstract' as a mathematical theorem.[28] Where else could we locate them? The answer is not clear. What this reveals, once more, is that Popper's and Bereiter's 'World 3' picture has significant limitations. Now, suppose we simply add a World 4 to their schema, and we put poems, sonatas, and so on, in that world. This proposal leads immediately to another question: can we really draw clear boundaries between this new World 4 and World 3? More importantly, even if we can do so conceptually, do

---

28. But compare note 21 here.

we want to uphold such clear boundaries for present purposes? (Similar questions can be raised if we put "cultural objects" into World 1 and/or World 2.)

Remember here that 'interpretations' and 'criticisms' are supposed to inhabit World 3. What is it that they are about? Well, presumably such things as poems and sonatas, also folk tales, rituals, and monuments, perhaps even food and recipes, so exactly the things listed as further 'cultural objects'. In other words, there is clearly a close connection between World 3 and our new World 4. (Similarly, historical accounts, say, are about historical events, and these are located in Worlds 1 and 2. Thus there is also a close connection between Worlds 1 and 2 and World 4.) But, as Bereiter and Popper would have to argue at this point, there is still a strict distinction one can make, isn't there? After all, what is located in World 3 are things that "can be profitably argued about in general terms", for example, general questions, hypotheses, and theories about, say, a poem or a ritual. The poem or ritual itself, while providing the 'raw material' for them, should still be located in another world, shouldn't it?

I am not sure whether such a strict conceptual separation can be defended in the end. But let us suppose we can do so. What are the implications of accepting it for education? More specifically, what does upholding such a separation reveal about Bereiter's vision for education? One way to understand his vision is this: its core is to emphasize, or re-emphasize, 'theory'; in Bereiter's own words, it is to emphasize "science and scholarship", especially in the natural sciences, but presumably also in the social sciences and the humanities. That is exactly what the emphasis on World 3—on "discussible propositions and declarative knowledge," or on "what can be profitably argued about in general terms"—amounts to, as becomes clear now.[29]

In contrast, according to more traditional conceptions what a liberal education amounts to is not just, and perhaps not primarily, an introduction to 'theory' in this sense. Rather, it consists of an introduction to exactly, at least also, the larger world of culture

---

29. Bereiter is explicit about this point when he writes: "What I am proposing is that World 3 needs to become a larger part, if liberal education is to rise to the challenges of the knowledge age." Note again the nod towards the futuristic business literature and economic needs in this passage.

mentioned above: to works of art such as paintings, theater productions, music, and dance performances. Bereiter himself admits that this larger world is "very valuable" and "gives richness to life." Nevertheless, by separating it from World 3 he clearly relegates it to secondary status in his vision for education. To bring out the contrast more sharply and concretely, note that the more we emphasize 'science and scholarship' in education, the less time, energy, and money remain for getting students involved in the production, performance, and enjoyment of 'cultural objects'. Is that what we want from a liberal education?

A related question arises if we consider the case of, say, creative writing. Namely, shouldn't the teaching of such writing be an integral part of a liberal education, even if it is not exactly, in itself, an example of 'science and scholarship'? In fact, this points to the following further and deeper question: can 'science and scholarship' themselves actually flourish if we cut off the larger cultural world of creative writing, plays, concerts, rituals, mythology, and so forth, so much from them? For one thing, the humanities and the social sciences depend on observing various parts of the 'larger cultural world' to have something to theorize about (think especially of sociology, anthropology, or art history). For another, all scientists benefit from good writing skills at some level.

To be fair again, I assume that Bereiter does not want to argue for the complete exclusion of creative writing, or of the performance of theater, music, and dance, from a liberal education.[30] Rather, his emphasis on World 3—on 'science and scholarship', thus on theoretical inquiry and theoretical explanation—should again be seen as a corrective: as re-emphasizing a side of education that has not been emphasized enough recently. And as such it probably has something to recommend itself, especially in today's and tomorrow's worlds. Still a question remains here: how far do we need, and want, to go in that direction?

---

30. In conversation Bereiter told me about attempts within his own research group to get students more actively and 'productively' involved in creative writing. These attempts include working with Lewis Carroll's *Alice in Wonderland* in the context of using CSILE/Knowledge Forum computer programs in the classroom. It would be helpful to hear more about such examples, I think.

Let me close this section by briefly formulating three related questions, or challenges, as food for further thought: a. Is Bereiter's emphasis on theory not again, at least partly, an effect of being too impressed by the futuristic business literature, with its strong and somewhat superficial stress on business needs?[31] b. Is this emphasis perhaps also a reaction, indeed an over-reaction, to postmodern claims about the importance and unbridgeability of cultural differences, or to corresponding challenges to 'the canon'? Finally, c. are we not in danger of throwing out the baby—large parts of the humanities—with the bathwater here, namely by sep- arating too sharply "what can be profitably argued about in gen- eral terms" from what's more particular and culturally specific? This third question also leads over to my next and final general point.

Enculturation, Cosmopolitanism, and the General Goals of Education

Education, we have been told by Bereiter, should be "encultura- tion into World 3"; and World 3 is the world of general ideas and thoughts, not that of particular cultural differences. This vision of education is presented to us as a corrective to earlier approaches. In particular, it is presented as a corrective to models "so intent on preserving indigenous culture or ethnic pride that it relegates World 3 to the status of a foreign culture"; also to edu- cational programs "so child-centered or so intent on learning objectives that there is no participation in any larger intellectual world." According to Bereiter, education should, instead, take us beyond our specific cultures and beyond our particular situations in life. It should, in other words, introduce us to a cosmopolitan life.

I agree wholeheartedly with Bereiter that being enculturated into World 3, in this cosmopolitan sense, can be very enriching and liberating. (I wouldn't want to have missed it in my own life!) However, a number of questions can be raised now about how

---

31. Note here that a good familiarity with at least some 'cultural objects' seems essential for certain businesses. Think of, say, architecture or the design of computer programs for 'edutainment' and so forth.

exactly to think about 'enculturation'.[32] Most basically, when a student gets enculturated into World 3 what is supposed to happen to her broader cultural background, or to her more particular identity and situation in life: is she supposed to give those up completely, just leave them behind; or is she supposed to carry them along, perhaps to connect them in some way with what is in World 3? More generally, how are we supposed to think about the relation between the two spheres, World 3, on the one hand, and one's particular identity and situation in life, on the other?

As we just saw, certain statements Bereiter makes seem to imply that World 3 is rather separate, and should be kept separate, from more particular aspects of one's life; remember his exclusion of 'cultural objects' from World 3.[33] Now, this could mean that for him enculturation amounts to entering a wholly new world, rather unconnected to one's old world. Then again, other things Bereiter writes seem to point in the opposite direction. Remember, again, his remark about Mendel being relevant to a student's "current knowledge problems"; compare also his repeated emphasis on knowledge that is "important to the intellectual world that the students live in." In such remarks we have, presumably, to see the "current knowledge problems" of students as growing out of, thus as somehow closely connected with, their particular lives and cultures; similarly for "the intellectual world that the students lives in." What we have, then, is another tension in Bereiter's views that deserves further attention.[34]

---

32. There is a huge literature in anthropology on 'enculturation'. As I am only marginally familiar with that literature, what follows are just some general philosophical reflections on the topic.

33. Insofar as Bereiter excludes large parts of what's usually considered 'culture' from World 3, there is actually a considerable irony in his use of the term 'enculturation'. I expect that this irony—and, as some will argue, an underlying insensitivity to or devaluation of larger cultural issues—will not be lost on people coming from the humanities, arts, and social sciences.

34. That there is such a tension in Bereiter's views can also be seen from a slightly different angle. Remember that what's in World 3 is "what can be profitably argued about in general terms." To this Bereiter adds the following clarification in a footnote: "The qualifier, 'in general terms', is needed because most of what people argue about, of course, in everyday life are particular cases, and these are not World 3 objects." On the surface, this footnote suggests again a clear separation between World 3 and what is more particular about everyday life. However, the very way in

The issue we are dealing with here has again potentially important practical and pedagogical consequences. If students' particular lives, on the one hand, and World 3, on the other, are taken to be as separate as Bereiter sometimes makes it seem, one wonders how it will be possible at all to get the students interested in World 3. If, on the other hand, the two spheres are seen as not so separate, as Bereiter himself suggests at other points, it makes sense to exploit that fact further, i.e., to try to draw students into World 3 by means of connecting the two sides very explicitly. The latter does not necessarily mean that every idea, explanation, or theory in World 3 has to be connected directly to a pre-given question in the student's life. But a few such connections may serve as bridges between the two sides.

The latter kind of consideration leads to the following suggestion. Perhaps we should think of education, in particular of Bereiter's 'enculturation', as a 'weaving together' of World 3, on the one hand, and the students' different, culturally specific, particularly situated lives and cultures, on the other hand. Note, among others, that such a weaving together is potentially enriching for both sides. It can add new cosmopolitan dimensions to the students' particular lives, thus providing them with new tools to solve some old problems they already have. And it can enlarge World 3, or at least our knowledge and appreciation of World 3, by leading to new applications for certain ideas, explanations, and theories; perhaps also by leading to surprising new twists and extensions of these ideas, explanations, and theories.

In addition, this way of thinking about education seems to fit together well with some other, general aspects of Bereiter's own proposal, for example, with his emphasis on the dynamic character of knowledge and learning. Remember in this connection his suggestion—quite plausible and attractive in its own right, I think—

---

which it is formulated also leads to questions about whether such a separation makes sense. In particular can and should we really see the 'general arguments' and the 'particular cases' as so distinct? Note here the following: Even in 'science and scholarship' we are sometimes dealing with particular cases, particular questions, and particular arguments, aren't we? Conversely, can't we have general arguments about particular cases in everyday life as well? In the end my suggestion would be this: it is probably best to think of a whole spectrum—from the particular to the general, with many cases in between—both in everyday life and in science and scholarship.

that the process of acquiring real knowledge may be profitably modeled on the process of invention or discovery in science. Where could there be more occasions for such processes to take place than in connecting World 3 with various new situations, new cultural settings, and so on? In other words, what could better stimulate the students' creativity, their 'production' of new ideas, new applications, new interpretations, and new theories?

However, it is easy to go too far in this direction as well, or to be too one-sided and simple-minded with respect to such a weaving together of cultures.[35] One immediate danger is this: If we always try to connect World 3 with the students' more concrete worlds and lives, we may never get very far into World 3—we may spend all our time on building the bridges, and very little on crossing them.[36] An implicit recognition of this kind of danger is, I take it, what motivates Bereiter's emphasis on World 3 in the first place. It is similar to what he sees as having gone wrong in many schools recently: only concrete skills and personal qualities are being taught in them, and no, or very little, general, abstract knowledge.

To provide a more balanced point of view overall, I now want to turn around and add three considerations in favor of Bereiter's emphasis on World 3. First, it is arguable that for some things in World 3—think of certain parts of abstract mathematics or of quantum physics, but not only these—the best way to teach them is not by trying to connect them, immediately and directly, to what is already familiar to students from their everyday lives; actually, for some of them it may even be harmful to try to do so. Why? Well, compare learning about such things with learning a new language. There is good evidence, it seems to me, that one learns a new lan-

---

35. In what follows I am heavily indebted to comments by André Carus on an earlier draft of this paper.

36. As André Carus pointed out to me in correspondence, this is what happened with the Deweyan 'progressive education' program in the U.S. early in this century. According to it theory and practice were supposed to be 'woven together' in real-life settings: everything academic was to be integrated into real-life tasks. Attractive as this may sound at first, it degenerated (especially in the 1940s and 1950s) into a kind of schooling in which very little general and abstract knowledge was being taught any more (even: where boys only worked on various concrete construction tasks and girls on cooking and sewing), thus disadvantaging the students who went through it severely. (Since I grew up in the German educational system of the 1960s and 1970s, where the problem was the opposite, perhaps I still underestimate this danger.)

guage best by direct and prolonged immersion, as opposed to always connecting it with one's native language, that is, translating back into it. But some things in World 3, like abstract mathematics and quantum physics, may be very much like a new language, and learning about them may be similar, too.[37]

A second, different consideration is this: certain things in World 3 may have their value largely independently from being usable for solving concrete, everyday problems; or at least their value may go substantially beyond solving such problems. Think of astronomy here, also of various parts of history, anthropology, and philosophy. It is possible, indeed quite plausible, that the main value of such disciplines lies in instructing us—in a general, deep way, but without immediate practical 'pay off'—about the world we live in, about our place in it, and ultimately about ourselves. Perhaps part of their value also lies in simply giving us new things to think about, beyond our practical everyday problems. If this is the case, then to introduce and motivate these studies by always connecting them to everyday problems will again not be really appropriate.

Third and most importantly, we should ask ourselves the following basic question: What is, or should be, the main goal of an education, in particular of a liberal education? Suppose, first, that this goal is to make people able to deal better with their everyday problems. In that case we should always keep those problems in the foreground, including when introducing students to World 3. But is that all there is to it? Shouldn't we also take into account certain more ambitious goal or goals? Consider the following three related goals in this connection: 1. to enrich the students' lives beyond what they already know, especially by broadening their intellectual horizons; 2. to urge them to overcome prejudices and narrow, parochial categories and assumptions, not the least so as to make them more tolerant and responsible citizens; and 3. to

---

37. Of course to learn a new language by direct immersion is not easy (at least if attempted as an adult, not a child), and it takes time; likewise for getting to know the corresponding World 3 objects. Then again, ease and speed shouldn't be the main goals here anyway, real and lasting learning should. An aside: I think it would be interesting to explore further the similarity between learning about certain World 3 objects and learning a new language. (I will come back to this issue briefly later in the paper, but only briefly.)

make it possible for them to overcome the limitations of their particular situations and cultures, thus also to make social mobility possible?[38]

If we adopt any of these further goals—and I think we should, at least to some degree—then it will be too restrictive, and largely ineffective, always to start from familiar everyday problems in education. Adopting any of these goals will also have other implications. In particular, pursuing them will bring with it real changes for those being educated, including a certain (at least initial) alienation from their original situations in life and from their particular cultures. In other words, education will now mean to leave home— in more than a physical sense—for the students. And perhaps they will never feel quite at home again afterwards (at least in the original sense).[39] The language analogy used above may again be helpful here. Learning a new language often does change one's attitude towards, and one's feeling for, one's native language.

Of course, someone who learns a new language will usually not lose the ability to communicate in the old language; he or she may even get better at it. Ideally a person who learns a new language will become bi- or multi-lingual. And that will open up all kinds of doors for that person, economically, socially, and otherwise; similarly, and perhaps more so, for other kinds of knowledge. Now, this is precisely one sense in which getting enculturated into World 3 does have tremendous value, both instrumentally and intrinsically. And this aspect is something that makes Bereiter's proposal fundamentally attractive, I think. Then again, we shouldn't forget that many things (and people) we encounter in our particular lives or in specific cultures have considerable value as well.

Since it is so easy to be one-sided in this connection, let me close this discussion with a plea for balance. I agree with Bereiter that it would be bad, for the reasons discussed, to "relegate World 3 to the status of a foreign culture." But it would be equally bad to

---

38. For further considerations of these goals, or of the roles they have played in our changing visions about education in Western history, cf. André Carus's and James Miller's contributions at the conference, or their corresponding papers in this volume.

39. Compare here Serres 1997. In it the author argues, along similar lines, that to become really educated means to depart from home so as to encounter 'otherness'; or, in even more colorful language, to become a "harlequin, a crossbreed, a hybrid of our origins." He, like myself, sees this as positive.

see World 3 as being somehow intrinsically and diametrically opposed to 'indigenous culture', and then just to reject the latter.[40] Similarly, while "an educational program so child-centered or so intent on learning objectives that there is no participation in any larger intellectual world" would clearly be detrimental, it would also be detrimental to under-emphasize the importance of skills and personal qualities in a child.[41] In the end the aim should be to reconcile both sides so as to get the best of both worlds, shouldn't it? Then again, to achieve this goal is easier said than done, especially given the usual scarcity of resources in education.

Summary and Conclusion

In retrospect, what I have done in this paper is the following. Initially I focused our attention on the core of Bereiter's new vision for education, especially its renewed emphasis on teaching real content in school. I agreed with several basic aspects of this vision, including its cosmopolitan side and its aim to open up various traditions of inquiry to students. Then I brought up a number of questions, problems, and criticism concerning this proposal, or rather concerning Bereiter's particular way of presenting it. First, I looked at his suggestion to think of school as a 'knowledge-producing organization'. I did so in order to raise the question of what our

---

40. Instead one can, for instance, take various culturally specific things (such as pieces of literature, works of art, historical events, examples of rituals) and try to discuss them 'in general terms'. Of course, two immediate problems arise: a. the question which specific things to select, and why; b. the challenge not to be too general in discussing them, thus missing what is interesting about their particularity. Yet these are problems one can deal with in a balanced way, it seems to me; or at least one should try.

41. As to the latter issue, it is important to recognize that theorizing, explaining, and interpreting, the activities valued especially by Bereiter, do depend in crucial ways on various prior skills and personal qualities (for example, could we really do without the theorizer's writing skills, or without her communicative skills, intellectual curiosity, and so forth?). In other words, high-level 'science and scholarship' can only flourish against the backdrop of various lower-level skills, abilities, and competencies. Furthermore, the latter are fundamentally rooted in particular lives and specific cultures. In this connection, it may be helpful to use some terminology introduced by Gordon Wells: 'General intellectual understanding', understanding at the 'theoretic' and 'meta-theoretic' levels, is always built on top of (or perhaps better, is enmeshed or entangled with) other modes of understanding, such as 'aesthetic' and 'substantive understanding'; even all the way down to very basic skills. See Wells 1998 for a further discussion of such issues.

primary model should be here: profit-oriented businesses or pure scientific research? The answer to this question has important practical implications. It is also tied up with the bigger question of whether we should see the value of an education as purely instrumental or as something more.

Next, I tried to clarify how we could and should think about the 'objective knowledge' to be produced in school according to Bereiter. While it seems to me to be possible, for certain purposes, to talk about 'objective ideas', perhaps even to see them as existing in some 'World 3', I suggested that it is better to think of such ideas as the content of knowledge, and to separate them conceptually from corresponding states of knowing. After making that separation, I argued that it is not clear where to locate 'objective knowledge' in Popper's '3 Worlds' schema. This is, then, one problem with that schema, or with the corresponding notions of 'objective knowledge, 'knowledge production', and so forth. I also argued that it is not just truths that are of interest to us, as the use of the notion of 'objective knowledge' may be taken to imply, but more general 'conceptual possibilities'. Moreover, perhaps we should replace talk about 'producing knowledge' with talk about entering into certain 'traditions of inquiry', especially given all the ambiguities and problems connected with the former notion.

I then explored the boundaries of World 3 relative to the "larger world of cultural objects." I argued that it is problematic to see these boundaries as absolute, or indeed to take them to be clear in the first place, both for conceptual and practical reasons. And insofar as Popper's Three Worlds schema suggests such clear boundaries, this is another problem with it. Finally, I raised the question of how exactly to think about education if we conceptualize it, with Bereiter, as "enculturation into World 3." Here I discussed two things pointing in opposite directions: On the one hand, there are reasons to think that such enculturation should amount to a 'weaving together' of World 3 and the more particular worlds and lives, or homes, of students. On the other hand, there are also reasons to think that this will be too restrictive overall, and that to become educated and cosmopolitan really means to 'leave home', including becoming alienated to some degree. What we need, in the end, is a balance between these two sides.

What is my overall evaluation of Carl Bereiter's new proposal? I do consider it a valuable contribution to an old and open-ended discussion about education. More particularly, I see it as a helpful corrective to the deficiencies of some other recent models. I also think that its underlying thrust is quite attractive in its own right, at least in certain respects. At the same time, the particular way the proposal has been presented so far is problematic. In order to bring to light some of the corresponding problems my strategy has been to criticize it 'from within'.[42] In response one can now try to work out various refinements, and it would be worth doing so. Beyond that and most importantly, there is also a need to address more directly and to discuss more fully some of the general questions raised along the way by me, especially those about the ultimate goal, or goals, of education. Without good answers to those questions our thinking about education will not be as clear as it needs to be for making real progress at this point.[43]

––––––––––

42. A more external criticism of Bereiter's proposal could proceed as follows (as suggested to me by André Carus). His appeal to Popper's notion of World 3 gives the impression that there is a completely culture-neutral realm of objects that education should open up to students. (Compare here, in particular, Bereiter's statement that "there are no culture-specific sciences, mathematics and literary or historical theories.") But, so goes the criticism now, that is wrong: it's a myth. Really Pythagoras's Theorem, say, is very much part of some particular cultures, that of the Greeks and that of the Modern West; even more so for 'literary or historical theories'. Furthermore, Bereiter would do much better to admit that much. What he should do, really, is to defend the view that the particular cultural achievements he values have some kind of universal validity and universal appeal (since they are liberating, empowering, and enriching in various ways).

My partial defense of the notion of objective idea in the text shows why I am somewhat hesitant about the starting point of this line of thought (I would like to distinguish objective ideas themselves more sharply from our knowledge of them.). On the other hand, I do agree with this general, more external criticism in the following sense: our human interests in things in World 3, our descriptions, discussions, and knowledge of them, and the traditions of inquiry in which they have been studied are very much part of certain specific cultures. Furthermore, insofar as Bereiter's aim is precisely to produce such interests, descriptions, discussions, and knowledge, and to open up such traditions of inquiry to students, a large part of what he is dealing with is, in fact, not culture-neutral. Finally, it would be better to admit as much and then to argue, in a careful manner, for the broader appeal of certain ideas.

But such considerations are really the topic for another paper (cf. here, again, André Carus's contribution to this volume). In the present chapter I chose to respond to Bereiter's proposal more from within, in the hope that this would be the most constructive contribution I could make at this point.

43. I would like to thank André Carus and Open Court for inviting me to their conference on Liberal Education, the participants of the conference for very stimulating presentations and discussions, and André Carus, Stuart Glennan, and Sally A. Ness for helpful comments on earlier drafts of this paper.

References

Aristotle. 1992. *The Nicomachean Ethics*. Oxford: Oxford University Press.

Bereiter, Carl. 1998. Liberal Education in a Knowledge Society. Chapter 2 of this volume.

——. 1997. Situated Cognition and How to Overcome It. In D. Kirshner and J.A. Whitson, eds., *Situated Cognition: Social, Semiotic, and Psychological Perspectives* (Hillsdale NJ: Erlbaum), pp. 281–300.

Bereiter, C. and M. Scardamalia. 1996. Rethinking Learning. In D.R. Olson and N. Torrance, eds., *Handbook of Education and Human Development* (Oxford: Blackwell), pp. 485–513.

Bolzano, Bernard. 1837. *Wissenschaftslehre: Versuch einer ausführlichen und größtenteils neuen Darstellung der Logik*, 4 vols. Sulzbach.

——. 1978. *Grundlegung der Logik: Ausgewählte Paragraphen aus der Wissenschaftslehre*, Band I und II, F. Kambartel, ed. Hamburg: Meiner Verlag.

Brandom, Robert. 1994. *Making It Explicit: Reasoning, Representing, and Discursive Commitment*. Cambridge: Harvard University Press.

The Economist. 1997a. Mr. Knowledge. 31st May, p. 63.

——1997b. Inside the Knowledge Factory. 4th October, pp. 3–22.

Edwards, J.S.S. and S.C. Ogilvie. 1998. Educational Objectives in Advanced Countries: Some Economic Considerations. Chapter 3 of this volume.

Frege, Gottlob. 1884. *Die Grundlagen der Arithmetik*. Republished as a bilingual edition, English translation: J.L. Austin, ed., *Foundations of Arithmetic* (Evanston: Northwestern University Press, 1968).

——. 1918. Der Gedanke. Republished in *Kleine Schriften* (Hildesheim: Olms Verlag, 1990). English translation: 'Thought', in M. Beaney, ed., *The Frege Reader* (Oxford: Blackwell, 1997).

Husserl, Edmund. 1913. *Logische Untersuchungen*. 2 vols. Republished as E. Ströker, ed., *Gesammelte Schriften 2 und 3* (Hamburg: Meiner Verlag, 1992).

Kuhn, Thomas S. 1970. *The Structure of Scientific Revolutions*. Chicago: University of Chicago Press.

Long, A.A. and D.N. Sedley, eds. 1988. *The Hellenistic Philosophers. Volume 1*. Cambridge: Cambridge University Press.

Piaget, Jean. 1965. *The Child's Conception of Number*. New York: Norton.

Plato. 1974. *Republic*. Indianapolis: Hackett.

Popper, Karl R. 1968. On the Theory of the Objective Mind. Reprinted in *Objective Knowledge: An Evolutionary Approach* (Oxford: Clarendon, 1972).

Popper, K.R. and J.C. Eccles. 1977. *The Self and Its Brain*. Berlin: Springer.

Reck, Erich H. 1997. Frege's Influence on Wittgenstein: Reversing Metaphysics via the Context Principle. In W.W. Tait, ed., *Early Analytic*

Philosophy: Frege, Russell, Wittgenstein (Chicago: Open Court, 1997), pp. 123–185.

Scardamalia, M., C. Bereiter, and M. Lamon. 1994. The CSILE Project: Trying to Bring the Classsroom into World 3. In K. McGilley, ed., *Classroom Lessons: Integrating Cognitive Theory and Classroom Practice* (Cambridge, MA: MIT Press), pp. 201–228.

Serres, Michel. 1997. *The Troubadour of Knowledge*. Ann Arbor: University of Michigan Press.

Wells, Gordon. 1998. Dialogue about Knowledge. Chapter 6 of this volume.

8
Moral Expertise
A.W. Carus

What is the point of liberal education? Why should anyone invest in it? An economist, looking only at self-interest and social consequences, might give two sorts of reasons: first, to increase one's market value—one's value to society, roughly speaking. From this point of view, liberal education (in any of its traditional senses) may not be as good an investment as, say, specialized training in dentistry or accounting. But an economist can also give a second kind of reason for investing in liberal education, which sees the payoffs to such an investment not primarily in terms of one's value to *society* but rather in terms of one's value to *one's self*. This viewpoint looks at human beings as instruments of *consumption* rather than as instruments of production. Though every human being is both producer and consumer, the human capital literature (and thus much of the literature on the payoffs to education) has focussed almost exclusively on investments people make in their *productive* capacities (Becker 1975). However, Edwards and Ogilvie (Chapter 3 above) have developed a suggestion by Gary Becker (1996) that general education can be understood more as an investment in people's skills and capacities as consumers. So liberal education, it is suggested, more than dentistry or accounting, improves the *quality* of the choices people make—about partners, jobs, cultural and political alternatives as well as the more usual objects of consumption in the market.

Such 'investment in consumption' has not been systematically studied by social scientists.[1] It seems reasonable to suppose, however, that one way general education improves the quality of choices is by encouraging certain mental skills (such as the exercise of the imagination) that make it easier to appreciate and envisage the future consequences of present choices, and thus to give the future more weight, in comparison to present gratification, than it would be given without such education. In this view, people may be able, by investing in general education, to bring their current preferences into closer conformity with their true long-term preferences (the preferences they *want* to have), their 'meta-preferences', their preferences about the kind of person they would ultimately like to be.[2]

Though expressed in economic terms, this view is consistent with traditional arguments for liberal education. Since antiquity, one central aim of liberal education has been the development of 'character', the making of a better person, and especially the development of the ability to make one's present choices conform with one's long-term view of the kind of person one wants to be (Kupperman 1991, pp. 173–78). Though this view is no longer popular, it seems obvious that some people *are* better than others at making their present choices consistent with their overall view of the kind of person they want to be. And this ability would seem essential not just as a component of human capital, a person's social usefulness, but above all for the person's *own* well-being.[3]

---

1. Though it is obviously of significance in consumer behavior (see Stigler and Becker 1977), it is not discussed in mainstream textbooks of consumer behavior (e.g. Deaton and Muellbauer 1980). Nonetheless, there is a great deal of interest in the subject; see e.g. de Vries (1993), who assigns such investment in new consumption bundles an important role in motivating the revolution in work habits during the late seventeenth century that underlay the subsequent industrial revolution in England and northwest Europe.

2. Harry Frankfurt, who made this distinction standard in the moral-philosophy literature, restricts his scope for simplicity to 'first-order' and 'second-order' preferences, though he recognizes that in principle a more extensive hierarchy is implied (Frankfurt 1971).

3. It has not, however, received much sustained attention in the literature of moral theory, and of philosophical reflection on concepts of 'welfare' and 'well-

This paper is an attempt to give this idea empirical content. Taking my cue from cognitive science, I will suggest that this ability of fitting current choices to long-term preferences, can usefully be regarded as an *expertise*, and perhaps studied empirically just as cognitive scientists study expertise in chess or basketball. Behind this suggestion, of course, is the possibility that it may be teachable—that the main goal of various historical programs of liberal education may be realizable. But those traditional programs are not only, at present, extremely unfashionable; they also, as we will see, greatly underestimated the difficulty of their task.

I. Moral Expertise

Let us provisionally call the ability to make current choices consistent with long-term meta-preferences 'consistency-across-time expertise' (making one's preferences consistent across time). Some people evidently have more consistency-across-time expertise than others. It would seem to vary as much among people as, say, chess ability or basketball ability. Perhaps it shares at least some characteristics of those simpler kinds of expertise. Empirical knowledge about human expertise has increased dramatically in recent years, and although this research has focussed mostly on domains where superior skill is quickly recognizable from standardized behaviors (like chess and basketball), one of the most remarkable findings is that widely different domains of expertise share certain fundamental characteristics. These are the subject of Bereiter and Scardamalia 1993,[4] whose findings I summarize, for present purposes, in four theses:

---

being'. James Griffin, for instance, in one of the most sustained recent meditations on these concepts (Griffin 1986, 1991), though often using examples about the 'kind of life' a person leads, never considers specifically the question of cross-temporal consistency as an essential component of well-being.

4. Bereiter and Scardamalia's summary of the expertise literature takes a point of view, of course, as any such summary of a nascent field must. Their view is in many respects consistent with other, less complete discussions (such as Sternberg 1997, Hoffman, Feltovich, and Ford 1997); it differs from them mainly in its emphasis on the *open-ended* nature of human expertise. Given that much of the available literature comes from the artificial intelligence community, its bias in favor of more static and narrow-gauge expertise is perhaps not surprising, any more than its relative lack of interest in the exceptional forms of higher-level human expertise that Bereiter's and Scardamalia's account focusses on.

1. Human expertise can largely be explained, in all the forms in which it has been empirically studied, as a collection of certain kinds of domain-specific *knowledge*—not just knowledge in the formal sense ('knowledge that'), but also practical knowledge ('knowledge how'), and many other kinds of informal knowledge (or 'knowledgability'), including impressionistic knowledge and self-regulatory knowledge, of the particular social practice in which expertise is sought or attained.

2. This domain-specific knowledge is built piece by piece through a dynamic *process* of continuous improvement; it is not a static *state* of arrival at achieved mastery, but a never-ending, self-conscious process of improvement. Bereiter and Scardamalia adduce empirical evidence for a principled distinction between genuine experts (in this dynamic sense) and skilled non-experts, whose development is arrested at a target state.

3. This process is driven by the *voluntary direction of mental effort* toward continuous improvement. As routine or lower-level components of processing in the domain of expertise are automated, the resulting spare capacity is reinvested in the pursuit of new subgoals within the domain itself. As processing becomes easier and more fluent, the genuine expert (in Bereiter and Scardamalia's sense) addresses new challenges and, rather than resting on her laurels, makes things *more difficult* for herself.

4. The continuous reinvestment of mental effort in the domain itself reshapes and reorganizes the knowledge constituting the expertise, continually changing and expanding the expert's view of the domain (the social practice in question, e.g. chess or basketball). The skilled non-expert maintains the same view of the domain over long periods, while the genuine expert is always moving on to a larger view of which her previous views form a particular subset or special case.

Can such a characterization be applied to 'consistency-across-time expertise'? It is, after all, a much more general ability than chess or basketball. Bereiter and Scardamalia have applied their framework to the case of written composition, a similarly broad and ill-defined domain (Bereiter and Scardamalia 1987b). But writing ability, like other kinds of expertise studied empirically, applies to an identifiable activity that one can isolate and consciously focus mental effort on. Expert writers, like expert programmers or musicians, commit huge investments of time and energy on the activity, continuing for long periods even when the payoff is low and the prospects bleak. What could be the equivalent in the case of consistency-across-time expertise? Isn't this rather something that, by its very nature, one does *jointly* with other things? Isn't it impossible to isolate and *focus* on (as one can, for instance, on re-writing a passage or editing for brevity)?

One can't imagine 'practicing' consistency-across-time expertise, as one practices the piano; it is clearly not the sort of thing one could break down into component skills to work on one at a time, as a basketball coach does with his team. But this is only because the components of consistency-across-time expertise *are* the things one does in one's life. The expertise is one of choosing the right things to become expert in—deciding how best to employ the particular resource endowment one finds one's self with, deciding where to direct one's *attention*. Not once for all at the beginning (or in adolescence), but every day of one's life, in the allocation of one's time and effort.

Isn't 'consistency-across-time expertise', then, just a fancy name for *morality*?[5] Isn't it, in fact, the subject of a great deal of art, literature, and everyday pop sociology? Yes, but only in one view of the matter. There is also an opposed view—currently dominant among thinking people—that wholly rejects the idea of morality as an expertise.

II. Cosmopolitan vs. Romantic Moral Traditions

In most historical traditions of literate moral thought, the expertise view was dominant. This includes nearly all moral traditions of antiquity: Judaism, Platonism, stoicism, epicureanism, ancient skepticism or Pyrrhonism, Christianity, Buddhism, Confucianism, and many more. In each of these traditions, a person is viewed as progressing, or potentially progressing, from an original state (of sin, ignorance, worldliness, dogmatism, or entanglement in appearances) to a state of 'enlightenment' or grace or redemption—

---

5. Here taken in a rather broad sense to include a substantially larger superset of the narrower definition sometimes given, e.g. by Bernard Williams (1985). This broad view of 'morality' is represented by, among others, Socrates, Aristotle, and R.M. Hare (1952).

the *exit* from sin, ignorance, dogmatism, appearances, and the like. What such traditions share is a negative attitude to the 'original state'; this state is to be overcome, and they all offer a program of techniques to achieve that critical task. Let us call this subset of the world's moral traditions 'cosmopolitan'.

Most thinking people today find it hard to take the ancient cosmopolitan moral traditions at face value; they are the classic ideologies of social control in traditional societies. They codify the values of a small elite which, though it often failed to live by them itself, used them as a standard by which the mass of illiterate peasants were judged unworthy. As ordinary people began to gain greater control over their lives, in the past two centuries, and there was less need for deference, the ancient moral traditions in which authority wrapped itself were increasingly challenged by ideologies of *liberation*. The moral traditions associated with these can perhaps be called 'romantic'; they come in many versions. What all these versions share, though, is their rejection of the basic premise of the cosmopolitan traditions, that morality is a matter of expertise, and of overcoming one's 'original state'. On the contrary, say the romantic traditions, morality must be *based on one's origins*, social and/or biological. In contrast to the cosmopolitan traditions, they *affirm the value* of the 'original state'; nothing else can confer authenticity and conviction on life choices and make them integral to one's identity or character. The socialization of origin is not to be despised, or overcome by an expertise in life-management, but to be prized and preserved. It is what gives one an *identity* distinct from that *imposed* on one as a subordinate or subaltern.

Historically, the most influential romantic ideologies come in two broad varieties: those of *individual* liberation and those of *group* liberation; the latter have their roots in the glorification of 'national' or 'folk' culture by figures like Herder or Tolstoy; authenticity is conferred by one's social or cultural ('ethnic') origins. Nationalist and anti-colonial movements throughout the nineteenth and twentieth centuries have drawn on such ideas, as have identity politics in the U.S. and other modern democracies. Romantic ideologies of *individual* liberation, on the other hand, see the locus of authenticity not in cultural origins, but in personal assertion. The most familiar example is American individualism; though most Americans nominally adhere to one or other descendent of the ancient cosmopolitan moral traditions (Christianity, Judaism), they don't in practice much rely on those traditions to guide their choices—least of all the basic life-choices here under discussion. They follow heart, conscience, gut. Above all, they rebel: they shatter the paradigm, break the mold, color outside the lines. 'Originality' is highly valued. Serious rebellion is of course as difficult and frowned on as anywhere, but Americans see themselves as wild and untamed. The individual defines himself in a single-handed struggle with 'raw nature' (his resource endowment), like Ahab with his whale, Huck with his river, the old man and his sea. It makes no sense, in this fluid and uncharted struggle, to accept any sort of rule book or set of techniques in which one could conceivably become *expert*. Belief in *one's self*, not reliance on any outside framework, is the way to shape one's life. Frameworks of all kinds are to be rebelled against, broken out of, escaped from, as in that archetypally American story *One Flew over the Cuckoo's Nest*.

Morality, say both romantic traditions, cannot be a matter of expertise because it is a matter of *conscience*—of feeling or inner intention. One makes basic life-decisions (how to allocate one's time and resources, what to become expert at), in this view, just as one makes all decisions: one is guided by one's conscience. One does, or ought to do, what *feels right*, not what, according to the rule framework of some moral tradition, *is* right. Where the 'cosmopolitan' traditions relies on objectivity (an external framework), the romantic views rely on subjectivity (internal inspiration; feelings of loyalty or identification).

But each kind of moral tradition, the cosmopolitan and the romantic, comes in many versions, so there is no sharp dichotomy between them but a continuum. Between Plato at the extreme cosmopolitan end ('expertise counts for everything') and Herder or Tolstoy at the extreme romantic end ('expertise is contemptible'), there is a broad spectrum of possible views, almost any given point on which has been occupied by some tradition or thinker at some time. Rousseau might be considered a kind of midpoint on this spectrum; cosmopolitan in many ways, he also idealizes simplicity, nature, and the unspoilt 'simple soul'. One could make a parlor game of locating various writers on this spectrum; Goethe, for instance, is clearly to the left (the cosmopolitan end) of Rousseau,

Novalis to the right; English writers are (with some interesting exceptions) generally to the left of German writers; and so on.

Nonetheless, there are clusters of reasonably stable attributes that distinguish *both* romantic 'liberation' traditions, as a group, from the cosmopolitan ones they rebel against. The romantic views, whether of group or of individual liberation, tend to trust 'native' impulses, especially those of children or the *Volk* (if it is uneducated). To interfere with such 'natural' flourishing is to *stunt* the healthy thriving of a child's spontaneous inner resources.[6] To induct a child into an expertise is to *distort* this natural growth, and to impose something *artificial*, to imprison the child in a straight-jacket of lifeless concepts that separate her from the wellsprings of natural (or folk-socialized) vitality. The overriding priority is to ensure that one retains inner access to one's natural, authentic, uncorrupted self, and isn't alienated into a way of thinking or talking that is false to one's (individual, biological, or social) roots.

Cosmopolitan traditions and thinkers, by contrast, share an ideal of moral *objectivity*: a standard or metric by which one can gauge the individual's *distance* from her untutored, original self. For cosmopolitans, the most important thing is to outgrow or transcend the self one started from, to *step back* from it and see it in a larger context. (Berofsky 1995) The ideal of maturity is co-extensive with the growth of a more objective point of view, a transcendence of one's parochial self, an escape from the prison of one's origins. A typical example is this well-known literary image, from *Middlemarch*:

> An eminent philosopher among my friends, who can dignify even your ugly furniture by lifting it into the serene light of science, has shown me this pregnant little fact. Your pier-glass or extensive surface of polished steel made to be rubbed by a housemaid, will be minutely and multitudinously scratched in all directions; but place now against it a lighted candle as a centre of illumination, and lo! the scratches will seem to arrange themselves in a fine series of concentric circles round that little sun. It is demonstrable that the scratches are going everywhere impartially, and it is only your candle which produces the flat-

---

6. As applied to schooling, the roots and influence of this attitude have been described by Hirsch (1996).in manuscript.

tering illusion of a concentric arrangement, its light falling with an
exclusive optical selection. (Eliot 1872, p. 297)

The particular application, in that passage, is to the egregiously
self-centered Rosamond Vincy, but the entire novel (like many nineteenth-century English novels) is about the variously successful
efforts of the characters to achieve a more objective view of themselves and the events affecting them. Cosmopolitan moral traditions, wherever they are on the spectrum, all seem to agree on the
desirability of that aim.

George Eliot's version of cosmopolitanism differs, of course,
from that of the ancient, mostly religious, traditions discussed so
far. The ancient traditions envisage the state of moral objectivity as
an end state or final state, achievable at a reasonably well-defined
terminus of personal and mental development. In many cases, this
terminus or end state requires the adoption of specified beliefs,
depicted as necessary to attain the sought-for state of objectivity
(exit from sin, appearances, or whatever). These beliefs have a special place in each of the ancient cosmopolitan traditions; they are
defined clearly, often in explicit creeds or catechisms (though of
course differently in each tradition), and their content serves as the
standard of moral objectivity. They are, in short, the ultimate foundation for all knowledge and all morality.

The modern age brings a new kind of *non-terminal* cosmopolitan moral tradition, exemplified by figures like Hume and Diderot,
whose philosophical critiques undermined the idea of a fixed terminus in previous moral traditions like Christianity. But for the
Encyclopédistes (as, later, for many others, including George Eliot),
dispensing with a terminus did not undermine the ideal of objectivity. In place of a fixed terminus, they put the idea of permanent
striving; they thought that although we can never *attain* a "view
from nowhere" (Nagel 1986), we can continually broaden our perspective, continue to step further and further back. This
Enlightenment attitude became for a while an integral part of the
bourgeois ethos in western Europe; the national (and even to an
extent European) traditions of art, philosophy, science, reflection
were a substitute for the certainties previously held out by the religious moral traditions (Mandelbaum 1971; Collini 1991; Skidelsky
1983, Chapter 2). They served as a basis and framework for a kind

of expertise in the conduct of life, to guide 'experiments in living' (Mill 1859; Donner 1991), from one's everyday interactions and time allocation to one's choice of mate and profession.[7] This Enlightenment aspect of the nineteenth-century European 'bourgeois ethos' finds canonical expression in the thought of Locke, Shaftesbury, and Diderot, the plays of Lessing, the novels of Jane Austen and Charlotte Brontë.

This Enlightenment view dovetails nicely with the cognitive-science view of expertise summarized above (from Bereiter and Scardamalia). Moral expertise, in the view I have attributed to Hume, Diderot, and George Eliot, is not an attained state, but a constant process of search and reconceptualizing one's life, and seeing it in progressively larger and larger contexts. The ideal of maturity in this non-terminal view is not one of arrival or mastery but of an equilibrium between acquiescence in uncertainty, on the one hand, and resolve to continue the search, on the other. It is a process of continuous improvement, both for one's self and for humanity at large, a process of restless, never-ending work on one's self and one's view of things.

The romantic (and American individualist) view of moral choice, by contrast, does not accord with the cognitive-science view of expertise at all. It views the taking of life decisions not as an expertise, in the cognitive-science sense, but as a matter of individual conscience. Such life decisions cannot be made or improved by reference to an established social practice such as a moral tradition; they grow organically from one's native culture or one's wild individuality. They are a matter of one's roots and of who one is, or a matter of direct interaction with nature, including one's own nature, one's own strengths and weaknesses.

These conceptions of moral choice, the cosmopolitan and the romantic, are at some level obviously incompatible. A great deal can be, and has been, said on both sides, and it can't be our task to address such a deep and long-running conflict of values here. The purpose of this paper is, rather, to work out a few elementary empir-

---

7. The American bourgeoisie differed, in this respect; its ideology was more traditional (ancient cosmopolitan moral traditions remained widespread, even among the elite), and there was no corpus of national folk or elite culture on which to base such an alternative cosmopolitan tradition.

ical consequences of the cosmopolitan view, *bracketing* the more fundamental alternative between cosmopolitan and romantic.

This requires some preliminary clarifications. First, we step back (in the next section) to see expertise in context as a particular kind of interface between social practices and individual subjectivity; we find that what we have called 'expertise' (in Bereiter and Scardamlia's sense) pertains mainly to *ill-defined* social practices, and 'moral' expertise to domains (which we have called 'moral traditions') that are very ill-defined even within this spectrum. They are not constituted by relatively clear rules (like the domains of chess or basketball). Still, they are organized around written-down texts whose interpretation, and whose relation to everyday life, is a central preoccupation within the social practice itself (whether it is a religion or some other sort of moral tradition). This raises the question how the 'objective' knowledge codified in such canons of texts and their interpretation relate to action, i.e. to the living of life and the making of choices. We address this issue (in section IV) with the help of Bereiter and Scardamalia, once again, and employ their concept of a *mental life* ("a conscious life of mental activity superimposed on the life of action in concrete contexts") as the locus of the assimilation by an individual of an ill-defined social practice; here is where the rubber hits the road. This attempt at a sketch of what 'moral expertise' concretely involves puts us in a position, then, to assess the historical program of Humboldtean liberal education (in section V), the problems faced by institutions who seek to realize some version of this program, especially universities (in section VI), and, finally, Bereiter's own proposal (in section VII).

III. Expertise as an Interface between Subjectivity and Social Practice

Expertise is a species of the larger genus 'assimilation of a social practice by an individual'. In this it resembles many other cognitive/biological phenomena, like language acquisition (in infancy) or learning to read (as a young child); like expertise, they represent the acquisition, by an individual, of something that exists outside the individual, something codified into a set of social practices. They each represent an interface between individual subjectivity and a practice or institution beyond or outside the individual—the internalization of something external. Language acquisition (in infancy) is perhaps the simplest and most widespread of these interfaces. Learning to read is somewhat less simple, and as we know from the existence of illiteracy, it is not always successful. Expertise is even less common; by definition it is an *exceptional* degree of assimilation by an individual of a social practice.

The interface between individual consciousness and social practice has inspired centuries of speculation, and has, until very recently, proven almost impervious to empirical inquiry. The speculation came from many angles—epistemological, psychological, sociological, historical, biological, anthropological, and, of course, metaphysical—and focussed on many different aspects of this interface.[8] Interestingly, though, almost none of this speculation about the interface between individual consciousness and social practices focusses on the *exceptional* degree of internalization we are calling expertise. Emphasis was always on the rudimentary, or, in sociology and history, the typical; it was expected, reasonably, that to understand the rudimentary and unexceptional would make it easier to understand the exceptional. The result is that although we now know quite a lot about language acquisition (Pinker 1994), and have been finding out about literacy (Adams 1990), even cultures of literacy (Olson 1994; Goody 1977; Fox 2000), the amount known about expertise is comparatively limited.

But certain structural facts about any such interface are obvious. In the case of language and literacy acquisition, the social practice to be assimilated or internalized is widely agreed on, and

---

8. Philosophers have concentrated mainly on the simplest kinds of interface, like those involved in language acquisition. Psychologists, linguists, computer scientists, evolutionary biologists, and neurologists have done the same, though with the attempt to impose empirical constraints on their inquiries. Sociologists and anthropologists have focussed on the character and content of social practices as they are internalized by individuals, but not on the internalization process itself. Historians, likewise, have studied the social transmission of ideas and practices, but not their acquisition by individuals. Psychoanalysts since the early twentieth century have speculated about the mechanisms by which the ego (self) and the superego (internalized social practices) interact, but the empirical basis of these accounts is now generally regarded as inadequate. Metaphysicians like Hegel were even more daring in their speculations, and are generally accorded even less credibility.

sometimes even explicitly set out in canons of correctness (as for spelling and grammar). To some extent this is also true for expertise, as in the traditional case of learning a well-defined craft by apprenticeship. But in less well-defined cases, the very nature of expertise makes it impossible for agreement on the canons of the social practice in question to be as complete as in the better-defined ones. There is a range of social practices, from simpler and more well-defined to more complex and ill-defined; at the one end are practices like chess or basketball, where the criteria of success are clear and universally agreed on, while at the other end are practices like gardening or written composition, where there is agreement among experts about clear failures, but little agreement on canons of success. More generally, then, interfaces between individual consciousness and social practices range from extremely well-defined (learning one's first language) to extremely ill-defined (written composition), along a more or less continuous scale:

well-defined	A	B	ill-defined
language acquisition	learning to read	chess	written composition

Learning to read would fall somewhere in between these extremes, at a point like A; the simplest and best-defined forms of expertise would fall to the right of it, say at B; it is an arbitrary decision where (between A and B) one defines simpler kinds of interface to end and expertise proper to begin. The important point here is that *moral* expertise is, almost by definition, at the extreme end-point of the scale on the right (well off the page); as discussed above, it is even less well-defined than written composition—and it is hard to imagine an expertise with an even larger, less well-defined scope than moral expertise.

The social practice that moral expertise represents an exceptional assimilation of is, as discussed above, a (cosmopolitan) 'moral tradition'. Such a tradition is not simply a conglomeration of ideas and doctrines, with associated behavioral prescriptions for overcoming the socialization of origin; it is a 'social practice', a way of talking, a way of seeing things, a *language*. But it is not a natural language, like those we learn in infancy and speak with each other for everyday communication; it is a consciously shaped language, embedded in a culture of *literacy*. And just as the invention of writing made us self-conscious about language (giving us the concepts of 'word' or 'sentence', for instance; Olson 1994), so a moral tradition, as a human institution, is anchored in, and made self-conscious by, a group of texts. The ancient moral traditions discussed above (section II) were embedded in well-organized religious institutions. These operated in a framework of explicit rules, which one could find *written down* in the relevant places: creeds, catechisms, regulations for religious orders, canon law, and so on; behind these lay scripture and the writings of the church fathers. Though in certain ways quite rigid, these rules could not be as clear and unambiguous as the rules of, say, chess or basketball, and the social practice they constituted was accordingly less well-defined.

But of course the religious institutions were much more than these explicit, written-down rules. They were groups of human beings who lived and worked according to certain habits and unspoken agreements, inherited from past generations—habits that most participants were not consciously aware of because they took them completely for granted. Such systems and networks of agreements and ways of acting were passed on from one generation of participants to the next by informal assimilation or enculturation by apprenticeship. This applied also to the subcultures of literacy within these religious traditions. (Irvine 1994; McKitterick 1989; 1990) What was explicitly taught was the written-down rules; how these were to be understood, how seriously they were to be taken, how they related to each other—this was learned by watching the senior members of the institution, imitating them, and being corrected by them.

The cosmopolitan moral tradition of the Enlightenment had even less well-defined institutions. European bourgeois culture did have its canonical texts; certain things written down were central to the social practice. But the institutions for maintaining and transmitting the language were less integrated, more plural. The scientific institutions were perhaps the closest, in their structure and mode of apprenticeship, to the ancient moral traditions; and science had an important place in the general culture. But the various sciences were not doctrinally integrated like the written-down aspects of religious cultures; nor was there an institution whose job it was to attempt and promulgate such integration. The problems raised by this will be the subject of section VI below. For now, the point is just that for European bourgeois culture, the social practice around the texts (and other cultural artifacts, like paintings and operas) was even less well-defined than it had been in the ancient and medieval moral traditions. And the education of post-Enlightenment Europeans (and Americans) has generally not been aimed at the inculcation or passing down of this ill-defined general culture. It has been much more specialized. Even as this process set in, though, an awareness grew that specialized training was not adequate to the demands of a whole life; to be equipped for the world at large, and not just some small part of it, one needed some sort of orientation in the general culture. The most comprehensive and articulate program to address this need was that of Humboldtean liberal education.

Before we can discuss this program, however, we must look more concretely at the nature of the interface between a social practice and the individual mind assimilating it. To make choices that will enable a person to live a life maximally resembling the one she would ideally desire to live, *information* is required about a range of alternatives to choose from (the broader the range, presumably, the freer the choice), and this information must be *available* to the person having to choose on the basis of it. It must *mean* something to that person. (It is no good 'knowing' about some option if it cannot be imagined in sufficiently vivid detail that one can compare it to the other options one is entertaining.)

But this requires a mental apparatus that can reduce a broad range of heterogeneous information about possible choices to a single language or conceptual system—a mental apparatus that can make this jumble of information mutually 'commensurable', to give it some minimal kind of coherence in the mind of the person using it as a basis for making choices. Such a mental apparatus is indispensable if one is to live a life conforming as closely as possible to one's ultimate meta-preferences—if one is to achieve a kind of 'moral expertise'. People do, to varying degrees, acquire some such mental apparatus. But as we will see in the next section, the coherence or commensurability it provides is parasitic on a social practice, and is only as good as the social practice on which it feeds.

IV. Knowledge and Coherence

How does the acquisition of moral expertise differ from the acquisition of expertise in better-defined domains? What is involved in acquiring expertise in a very ill-defined domain that goes beyond what we observe expertise to require in a domain like chess or basketball?

One of the earliest major discoveries in recent empirical investigations of learning to read, in the 1970s, was that skilled readers employ 'metacognitive' skills to *monitor* their reading (to check, for instance, whether they have understood a sentence or passage); these monitoring skills, it was found, less skilled readers lack (Brown, Bransford, Ferrara, and Campione 1983). Though the nature and workings of metacognition are still to some degree a matter of speculation, the existence and importance of such processes is hardly in doubt (Metcalfe and Shimamura 1994). It is a matter of speculative extrapolation, of course, to extend this insight to assimilation processes further to the right on the scale—to entertain the hypothesis, in other words, that higher and higher degrees of metacognition are involved in such processes. But this conjecture is not uncommon, even among empirically very scrupulous cognitive scientists (like Kintsch 1997, pp. 15–19). It has rarely been worked out in any detail, though. One of the few exceptions is an earlier article by Bereiter and Scardamalia (1983), in which they explore the genesis in children of what they call 'intentional cognition', i.e. the voluntary direction of mental effort in a cumulative and progressive way, so that children can take control of their own learning process. The idea of intentionally applying mental effort back into a process to improve it cumulatively is of course exactly the idea we saw described in their expertise book (as summarized in the four points in section I above). In the 1983 paper, though, they are concerned not with expertise in particular domains, but with an overall expertise in building a coherent mental picture of the world—precisely the kind of mental lingua franca discussed in the last section as required for the making of decisions among *prima facie* incommensurable choices. The knowledge in which this more general expertise in coherence-building consists, say Bereiter and Scardamalia, is not knowledge of a particular domain, but metaknowledge, knowledge about knowledge, knowledge of connections. As they put it, the discussion of intentional cognition raises "the larger question of how we develop a mental life—a conscious life of mental activity superimposed on the life of action in concrete contexts" (Bereiter and Scardamalia 1983, p. 254).[9]

Learning and action in concrete contexts have preoccupied cognitive science in the past decade or so; the important role, in such concrete learning, of *informal* knowledge in the mastery of formal knowledge has become very evident (Case and Okamoto 1996; Lave and Wenger 1991; diSessa 2000). It has become apparent how learning a formal body of knowledge like physics or mathematics is surprisingly similar to learning a language or learning one's way around a neighborhood; both kinds of learning have been compared to learning by traditional craft apprenticeship. Much of what one acquires when one begins to find one's way around even an abstract subject is, to use the current term, *situated* knowledge (Brown, Collins, and Duguid 1989; Greeno 1993; Kirshner and Whitson 1997).

The internalization of formal knowledge requires, in other words, that one literally develop a personal relationship with it, and forge links between one's subjective experience and the impersonal knowledge structure as one does with the physical configuration of a neighborhood one is getting to know. This process Bereiter, in the paper under discussion in this volume, has called "acculturation into World 3." From the viewpoint of the acculturee, this means developing links and connections between one's personal experience and perspective, on the one hand, and the culture surrounding the formal knowledge, on the other. It means the construction of a coherent mental world embracing *both*—subjective experience and formal knowledge—and *placing* that personal knowledge within the formal structure, thus both giving *coherence* to personal knowledge and concrete *applicability* to the abstract knowledge. This is the development of what Bereiter and Scardamalia, in the passage quoted above, called a *mental life*, "a conscious life of mental activity superimposed on the life of action in concrete contexts."[10]

---

9. The paper by Bereiter and Scardamalia referred to here and in the following paragraphs was never published in its original English, though it circulated widely in manuscript. It appears as an appendix to this volume, pp. 245–277. Page references are to the present volume.

10. In subsequent papers, Bereiter (1985; 1990) has discussed in more detail the kind of mental unit or 'contextual module' of which a 'mental life' in this sense would be a large-scale example, and how such a unit might interact with other

Learning in concrete contexts is of course exactly the kind of 'apprenticeship' that has been so popular in cognitive science recently (Greeno 1993; Lave 1997). But as Bereiter and Scardamalia pointed out even back in 1983, transfer from concrete contexts to larger ones, or across contexts, has proved problematic. Learning about scientific method, for instance, does not generally enable students to apply it, or even to recognize when an application might be appropriate (Bereiter and Scardamalia 1983, p. 255). "Still", they say,

> as educated moderns we would like to think that we have a great deal of knowledge that we can apply in varied contexts—scientific knowledge, mathematical knowledge, social knowledge, and even just a kind of common sense that seems to provide us with guides to reasonable action in most situations. How do we acquire such generalizable knowledge? . . . We want to argue that our attainment of generalizable knowledge is not a simple matter at all but that it depends on a great deal of mental effort expended in a context created by that effort itself. (*Ibid.*)

In ordinary concrete contexts, the goal of voluntary mental effort is mostly defined by the context, i.e. by something outside one's self. But the same sort of effort can be expended *without* a concrete goal; it can be focussed on itself, i.e. on the mental effort required to deal with a particular concrete context or with several. Then it gives rise to a more generalized, cross-contextual sort of knowledge. Also, contexts overlap, so there can be several relevant contexts at any given moment. So to organize their lives, people develop a larger context, accompanying and embracing specific contexts of action and learning, but going beyond them. "It seems that, in order to give coherence to their lives, people need a super-context that embraces all the other contexts in which they function" (*Ibid.*).

A cosmopolitan moral tradition of the kind described above provides a framework for such a super-context. It offers a ready-made coherence in which the individual can partake by assimi-

---

modules and account for many of the well-known phenomena and difficulties of learning. It is greatly to be regretted that neither Bereiter himself nor anyone else has built on the very promising foundation sketched there.

lating and personalizing the knowledge embedded in the moral tradition, developing a mental (only partly conscious) complex of formal and informal knowledge that Bereiter and Scardamalia call a "mental life." By forging links of coherence, local and of wider scope, the mental life establishes an overall commensurability among a large number of actual and possible concrete contexts. With time and thought, and prolonged investment over years, allocative decisions based on a framework of increasing internal coherence become at least partly a matter of conscious, intentional choice rather than instinctive habituated responses based on one's socialization of origin.

The construction of a mental life, Bereiter and Scardamalia emphasize, is a constant and life-long investment. "Work is required to extract . . . knowledge from activity in concrete contexts, work is required to develop it into a self-consistent whole, and work is required to bring it into use in other concrete contexts" (*Ibid.*, p. 257). Moreover such work, just as in the development of any sort of expertise, leads to a process of automaticity of lower-level functions, and re-investment of thereby freed-up mental capacity in the activity itself, which makes one better at it:

> As is true of any other context, work within the context leads to your coming to know the context intimately and becoming skillful and clever at operating within it. Coming to know the context means acquiring metacognitive knowledge. You come to understand your own thought processes, to recognize when you are comprehending something and when you are not. Becoming skillful in the context means developing strategies for analyzing, planning, solving problems, etc. strategies that are tied to abstract characteristics rather than to concrete cues. Thus, for instance, you become able to recognize and solve proportionality problems in all kinds of concrete contexts. Ability of this kind . . . is distinguished not by the mental operations involved but by the fact that these operations can be performed without support from a concrete context. That is, the thinking that goes on within the mental life context is not fundamentally different from that which goes on in other contexts, it is simply applied to different objects and tasks. (*Ibid.*, p. 258)

A mental life, then, is the development, within the support framework of a canon, of cross-contextual commensurability. Experiences in different contexts can thereby, with time and effort, be related to each other. *General* (or abstract) knowledge can thus be brought to bear on particular concrete contexts.

This same way of learning to apply general knowledge to particular contexts also extends to moral self-development (the development of consistency-across-time expertise). Bringing general knowledge to bear on a particular context is a necessary condition for being able to see one's *self* in a larger context (for what we called the moral 'objectivity' sought by cosmopolitan frameworks). The context of acting (in the first person) and the context of viewing the same action from outside are two different contexts. Bringing these two into focus with each other—making them coherent, commensurate with each other—has often been regarded in cosmopolitan moral traditions (by George Eliot, Kant, and many others) as a criterion of moral maturity. And this is not just a matter of bringing *two* contexts into focus, but one's own first-person perspective on a large number of contexts with one or more third-person perspectives on one's self in each of those same contexts separately, each involving different people, different concepts, different specialized languages.

To establish *subjective coherence* (and thus comparability) among the enormous number of contexts encountered in even a fairly restricted life requires a *framework*—a mental life organized around an 'objectively' coherent set of symbolic artifacts, texts, things written down.[11] A subjective coherence (or 'mental life') of such wide or general applicability depends on the wider and more general applicability of the structure of symbolic artifacts it forms

---

11. The romantic view is bracketed in this paper, as stated above. Still, it seems worth pointing out that it makes some staggering assumptions with respect to this task of establishing coherence across contexts. The American individualist version of romanticism suggests that one could not only undergo the Herculean labor of *assimilating* these different cultures and languages and making them commensurable, but that one could actually, beyond this, *invent one's own framework* for this commensurability. This seems an absurdly inflated view of individual capabilities. Obviously each person invents her own language within her native language, her own idiolect—but to invent the language itself, from scratch? More traditional romanticism makes the equally heroic assumption that one could dispense with a historically *constructed*, 'artificially' developed framework for this purpose and use instead a naïve 'folk' culture uncontaminated by cosmopolitan influences. Such a culture could, of course, serve as the basis for a mental life, but a restricted one; its efficacy or applicability would be limited to the narrow contexts in which it was developed.

around or assimilates and uses as a framework. Subjective coherence is parasitic on external (and in that sense 'objective')—symbolic, linguistic—frameworks for coherence.[12]

Without a mental life to effect this subjective comparability, then, one can consume only in a single context, on only one level or one time-scale, and one's choices are not part of a larger pattern, they don't contribute to the ongoing project of living the life one ideally wants to be living. Only by virtue of a mental life can the choices available at a given moment be made commensurable (comparable) so that the decision among them is an intentional decision, consistent with what one 'really' (at the level of longest-term meta-preferences) wants. Indeed, only by virtue of a mental life is there even a connection between decisions across time, i.e. between current ones and those in the future. Unless one has established some sort of commensurability among possible choices, unless there is a mental life that spans the contexts in which the choices reside, no genuine, intentional decision is being made.

We have seen (in the previous section) how moral expertise consists in the assimilation, to a high degree, of an extremely ill-defined social practice, and now (in this section) how such assimilation might concretely work, at least in schematic outline. This gives us a vantage point, at last, from which to review the historical proposals for the systematic *teaching* of moral expertise—the historical proposals, that is, to develop character through 'liberal education'.

V. Liberal Education

An expertise of any sort is inherently defined with respect to an existing social practice—one is expert *at something*. Moral expertise has also been defined here with respect to a social practice, only that it is a much broader and more encompassing social practice (a

---

12. This is a deep issue of wide ramifications that cannot begin to be discussed here. It does have an empirical dimension, and has been studied by cognitive scientists in connection with the operation of human memory, for instance, which appears to depend heavily on its coding in language (Kintsch 1974). But at a deeper level this is the very problem Wittgenstein addressed in his argument against the possibility of a purely subjective or 'private' language (Wittgenstein 1953).

moral tradition) than the narrower kinds of expertise generally studied by cognitive science. Such a tradition is foundational and integrative; it is not just a set of precepts and axioms, but a super-context or 'canon' within which most of life's decisions can reasonably be situated. And it is, above all, a *culture* of lived practices surrounding that canon. The mental life of an individual, as we saw in the last section, is parasitic on such a culture; though it can of course develop its own idiolect, it *consists* essentially in the assimilation of an existing structure, no less than learning one's native language or learning to read.

In fact, a certain popular image of morality regards it as akin to the assimilation of the *most* well-defined social practices, like learning one's native language. It is conceived as consisting in the assimilation and following of a fairly short list of unambiguous rules or precepts. The 'expertise' in this popular image is essentially that of Bereiter and Scardamalia's 'skilled non-expert', the person for whom expertise is not a continual process of improvement, but an achieved state—the person whose development is arrested at a target level. In the realm of guiding action (values, morality), as in other realms, this 'skilled non-expertise' requires little knowledge and no mental life. It does not require that one weigh the maxims or commandments in question against each other and decide which is preferable under which circumstances; the meta-preferences are assumed to be fixed and shared. The widespread popular genre of self-improvement manuals falls largely into this category, as do programs of 'time management' for business people, 'study skills' for students, and many other eleven-step programs for success. The rules or maxims, in this popular view, are all at the same level; they do not come with meta-rules informing the user which is to have priority over which others in case of conflicts in their application.

Moral expertise, in contrast, involves a *hierarchy* of meta-preferences. The simplest kind of hierarchy is a fixed one, like St. Ignatius Loyola's instructions for deciding what to do with one's life (Loyola 1548, pp. 164–65). One should, he says, consider this question at four successive levels: 1. the choice should proceed solely from the love of God, and not from any personal inclination (that is, from long-term meta-preferences rather than current preferences); 2. one should think of the arguments one would address, for or against a choice, to the most perfect human being one can imagine; 3. one should think of one's self at the point of death, and decide what one would then have wished that one had chosen now; 4. one should think of one's self before the Last Judgment, and decide what one would then have wished one had chosen now. These are progressively larger and (within the framework of Loyola's knowledge canon) more 'objective' viewpoints from which to make a decision; they invoke progressively larger considerations of which the person making the decision is a smaller and smaller part. Movement up these levels presupposes, in the decision maker, not only the knowledge that gives these levels a more or less definite meaning, but, above all, a mental life that can work out the consequences of each of these successive viewpoints for the choice in question.

Loyola's canon was a fixed or *terminal* one; the goal hierarchy was fixed. Though his canon was dominant in his time and place, it was not the only one used, even in the European past, for the development of a mental life. In western elite education, two others of special importance are often called the 'sciences' and 'humanities' or, after their supposed founders, the Platonic and Isocratean traditions (Kimball 1986). They have been rivals from the start. Each has, at various times, overlapped with or been grafted onto the Christian canon, but they have also retained their separate identities, increasingly so since about 1500.

The Platonic tradition was long an austere and quasi-mystical one. It was not quite as inflexible as Loyola's, but equally unworldly, given over to the pursuit of truth and wisdom. Since 1500 it has transformed itself into a somewhat less austere, though equally single-minded (and still rather forbidding) scientific culture whose unexpected practical uses in the last century or two have given it enormous and much resented prestige.

Its Isocratean rival began as something much more level-headed, worldly, and vocational: as rhetorical training for lawyers, courtiers, and politicians. Isocrates and other Athenian orators added an ethical dimension, particular reinforced and emphasized later by Quintilian and the early modern humanists, not only of self-marketing but also of self-improvement in a moral and spiritual sense (Irvine 1994; McKitterick 1989; 1990). The use of language, in this view, had a moral dimension; a person could not be a genuinely good speaker or writer, it was taught, without also being a good person. Until very recently (a century or two ago) this tradition and its descendent, the literary studies, have easily dominated educational thought, and formed the backbone of most ancient and early modern European programs for education in the 'liberal arts', or 'liberal education'.

In contradistinction to this traditional view of liberal education, a later and more modern view, associated particularly with Wilhelm von Humboldt and his reforms of Prussian secondary education in the early nineteenth century, seeks to *combine* the Platonic and Isocratean canons. This is the sense in which 'liberal education' has mostly been used since then, especially in the American context.[13] The idea has generally been that, in addition to the special vocational knowledge required, the student should receive a broad background in more general, widely applicable (or at least widely shared) knowledge, and should be socialized into the particular World 3 canon formed by the elite culture of the country in question. The U.S. has lacked such an established and accepted elite culture, so a smattering of various European bourgeois elite cultures was substituted. (This has now, of course, been expanded to include even more superficial smatterings of even more diverse cultures.)

There is a very basic practical problem with the Humboldtean program of liberal education, however: no social practice exists into which it could be the enculturation. This is not a local failure of some particular educational system. There just *is no* practice, or associated canon, that embraces both the Platonic and the Isocratean canons. There are of course liberally educated people, in the Humboldtean sense—individuals who have been socialized into both canons, and have found personal ways of relating them to each

---

13. As exemplified, for instance, by the famous Harvard 'red book' (Harvard Committee 1945) and in many discussions since then. An institutional realization or embodiment of such principles is the International Baccalaureate (Peterson 1972, 1987). However, the older view also survives; Jacques Barzun's 'house of intellect' (Barzun 1959) is solely humanistic, and more recently Roger Scruton, rejecting C.P. Snow's "suggestion that there are now two (high) cultures" says that ". . . there can be no more a scientific culture than there can be a scientific religion; culture, like religion, answers the question which science leaves unanswered: the question what to feel" (Scruton 1998, p. 16).

other. But there is no *canon*, no self-consistent system of values and knowledge, embracing both the Platonic and Isocratean traditions, that one could look up somewhere, or that forms a basis of some group's *culture* or way of life, into which new members could be socialized (around which they could develop a mental life).

This may appear to be a quibble, a far-fetched and perhaps fastidious theoretical objection to an obvious practical reality. But the gap between the 'two cultures', as they have been known since C.P. Snow's famous lecture (Snow 1959) is neither recent nor superficial. To cite an example of the fundamentally different value systems of these two canons we need go no further than the classic novel already cited. In *Middlemarch* the implied moral hierarchy reaches from Rosamond, at the bottom, through Casaubon, Bulstrode, Lydgate, Fred Vincy, Celia Brooke, Mary Garth, to, at last, the two central characters, Will and Dorothea. One could quibble with the details of this ordering (and certainly George Eliot did not have a one-dimensional scale in mind). But in general terms these characters stand for stages of moral development or 'objectivity' in much the same way as Loyola's stages or levels of deciding about one's life. No character in *Middlemarch* approximates even the first of Loyola's stages; Eliot's and Loyola's value systems do not even intersect.[14]

But Eliot's value system does intersect, if somewhat obliquely, with the scientific/Platonic canon. Note the position occupied in the *Middlemarch* hierarchy of values by the man of science, Lydgate. It is above that of the banker (Bulstrode) and the pedant (Casaubon), but that isn't saying much—and it is below Fred Vincy, the spoiled, feckless young man who, after a series of irresponsibilities, redeems himself in the end. Lydgate is, in fact, the really tragic character in the book, the one who, unlike Fred, fails to redeem himself, though he clearly has the potential to do so.

---

14. Though Eliot herself compares Dorothea's yearning for spiritual heroism with that of St. Teresa of Avila. The substance of this analogy is, in fact, the drive or yearning to get beyond the complacently ordinary existence prescribed by the socialization of origin, to strive for perfection, and never to be satisfied—precisely the drive identified above as characteristic of cosmopolitan moral traditions. But the specific values pursued by this yearning are very different in Eliot and Loyola, and as we saw above, Loyola's moral tradition is terminal, while Eliot's is non-terminal, open-ended.

It is perhaps no accident that the man of science occupies this position. For Eliot, Lydgate's mixture of worldly and cognitive ambition leaves him a stranger to his own emotions, and vulnerable to a low-quality schemer like Rosamond Vincy. At the critical moment when personal feelings suddenly erupt and cloud his vision, his Promethean scientific ambition, one-sidedly overdeveloped, leaves him with no guidance. He lacks both the character and the familiarity with his feelings to stand back from them and act in accordance with what his intellect would have been perfectly capable of telling him had he but had the courage (or humanistic education) to use it on himself rather than just on medicine. He is the prototype of many subsequent worldly types in literature whose one-sided, purely intellectual development has left them ignorant of their inner lives, leaving them defenceless in the face of emotions and clueless in relating to other humans. On this literary scale of values, exaggerating the importance of intellectual goals (truth, knowledge, insight) is as likely to distract one from one's personal values as an excessive attachment to money or any other sort of worldly pursuit.

This literary commonplace is simply not reconcilable with the emphasis in the scientific/Platonic canon on truth at all costs. Here nothing counts but a better theory; a scientist can be as wicked as he likes in his personal life; only his contribution to knowledge is of interest. The radical skepticism embedded in the scientific culture[15] notoriously recognizes no obligation to value systems constraining this pursuit of knowledge. From the literary/humanistic/Isocratean viewpoint, this attitude is dangerous for exactly the reasons Eliot and her successors illustrate in their characters.

How, then, can one be acculturated, as Humboltean liberal education prescribes, into both these canons? The problem is not so much that they conflict as that they *don't even* conflict. One could easily imagine real-life situations where the two value systems lead to different choices, but the more serious problem is that the scientific and humanistic canons dictate completely different *interests*, different mental and emotional stances, different and incom-

---

15. Described in some detail by Campbell (1986), who takes ample account of views such as those put forward by Barnes, Bloor, Latour, Woolgar, Knorr-Cetina and others.

patible attitudes toward what is worth taking seriously and what is not. They direct the *attention* in different directions, so that often a choice between them isn't even readily articulable or available. Though Snow did not begin to explore the properly sociological or anthropological dimensions of the problem he raised, he was right to call these *cultures*.[16] Most educated people, it seems (this has not been studied empirically, as far as I am aware), have developed their mental lives around some form of one or the other of these cultures of knowledge-organization. In most, this is probably not wholly conscious, is so much taken for granted that they are not even aware that such a culture lies at the basis of the way they make the world coherent to themselves. Personal inclination or an exceptional teacher led them to drift toward the assimilation of a disciplinary canon on one side or the other of this divide (physical science, for instance, or ancient philology) as the mental framework of explicit doctrines *and* informal attitudes within which they approach the whole of life, and articulate their major options and life decisions to themselves. They tend then, as a rule, to work in settings that makes best use of this socialization, and spend their time with people with whom they share a language, and with whom they share the values built into it.

There are, of course, individuals who have somehow been socialized partly or fully into more than one canon, and perhaps even into ones that lie on different sides of this divide. But since there is no *group* of people out there who speak a language that bridges those two canons or who live within a *practice* that spans both ways of articulating the world, the two canons tend, in such people, to remain separate and unintegrated. Such people are in the position of a typical immigrant to the U.S. from a nationalistic country like Ireland or Serbia,[17] who have two entirely distinct lives, their old life and the new one. In the new life, it is clear to

---

16. Though he was not right to say there were only two; even in the 1950s, the situation was much more complicated. While it may still make sense to see a single pole of opposition pervading all disciplines, with some at one extreme, some at the other, and some (social sciences like history and sociology) as split, this is not always how it is seen by the actual participants; see below, section VI, where the oversimplified view taken in the present section is complicated.

17. This was written in 1997.

them that people of different skin colors, beliefs, nationalities, and personal habits can and do live together in the same society. They may disapprove, but they certainly understand and accept the result, which is greater wealth and freedom for everyone. However, they also maintain mental ties to the old life, in which the Irish or Serbian nationalism inculcated in youth, and brought over the ocean with them, lives on. It would hardly occur to them that the principles they live with every day in their new context should apply in the old homeland, and they often go on advocating, even giving money to, nationalist causes that preach intolerance, violence, and ethnic cleansing in the homeland. More educated members of such immigrant communities are in a difficult position; their loyalties are divided. Although they can readily identify, in their hearts, with the national aspirations of the homeland, they also recognize, reluctantly perhaps, that some degree of pluralism is the only long-term solution even on the sacred soil of their fathers. This divided loyalty makes them eternally uncomfortable; they can never feel at ease among their compatriots because they cannot identify whole-heartedly with nationalism, but they can never be whole-hearted liberals, either.

That is also what it is like to be genuinely, deeply acculturated into *both* some form of the Isocratean/literary culture *and* some form of the Platonic/scientific one. Normally they are kept separate (as in the case of the less educated immigrants). Those who do attempt some genuine integration (like the more educated immigrants) between these very different registers of human articulation feel uncomfortable in communities of either culture; they have divided loyalties, they are permanent exiles. They do not feel at home in the world as do those whose socialization is unequivocally within a single culture. The latter may *know about* other cultures, may have undergone 'liberal education' and been exposed to examples of novels, say (if their primary focus is science), and even enjoy reading them, but this represents little more than amusement or entertainment; it is not something serious, not the basis of their mental life. It is not what they articulate their life-decisions in terms of.

This form of enculturation into a knowledge canon ('enculturation into World 3', Bereiter calls it) has become the rule; rarely is an 'educated person' today 'liberally' educated. To be 'educated' now is, rather, to have been encultured into *one* particular discipline.[18] Though still the official goal of American undergraduate education, Humboldtean liberal education *does not occur* in the real world (which is not surprising since, as we saw, there is no practice into which it could be an enculturation). Here, in fact, is the crux of the unhappy realization that has inspired so much hand-wringing over the past century or two: Humboldtean liberal education isn't happening, but the one-sided, single-discipline mental lives that people develop without it are too narrow. Such narrow, one-sided mental lives are inadequate to the range of choices modern people face; they are incapable of spanning and integrating—and so of genuinely *choosing* among—anything like the full range of decisions or options incumbent upon them (and about which informed, rational choice is possible). A narrow, single-discipline mental life leaves people facing decisions about which the frameworks they were socialized into have little to say. Inevitably, a non-rational or non-voluntary (Lydgate-like) default enters to fill the void. The frameworks or canons around which their mental lives were developed are unsuited as frameworks for a complete mental life. The ancient cosmopolitan frameworks were rejected for very good reasons, but one can also understand the nostalgia for them, since their modern replacements are too narrow; they lead to stunted, half-baked mental lives. This nostalgia, this awareness that the Enlightenment has left us without a canon-bridging social practice to be socialized into as the basis for a full or complete mental life, was first identified by Hegel and the romantics as 'the modern condition' (and one of 'alienation').

The Humboldtean response to the modern condition was based on a program to *overcome* it, by founding a new kind of canon-bridging secular culture based on the philosophy of Kant (especially the *Critique of Judgment*) and the world-views of Goethe and Schiller (both much influenced by Kant). This 'German classical' culture *did*, in fact, have a strong integrative role in secondary and higher German education over the nineteenth century, and even

---

18. As Max Weber (1918, p. 491) already saw clearly. 'Intellectual integrity', for him, was *all* a university education can convey, apart from specialized training. That he did not, however, mean this as a rejection of a broader 'mental life' in Bereiter's and Scardamalia's sense is plainly evident in his 'Wissenschaft als Beruf' (1919).

into the twentieth. Eventually it fell prey, though, to the same forces that had undermined the ancient cosmopolitan traditions; it could not accommodate (had never been able fully to accommodate) the more radical elements in the Enlightenment that were triumphantly vindicated by Darwin and the progress of mathematical science; German classicism came to seem like just another version of the Isocratean canon, despite increasingly heroic attempts by writers as diverse as Nietzsche, Simmel, Cassirer, Wittgenstein, and Musil to bridge the gap.

At the level of *content*—leaving aside cultures or ways of life— such reconciliations are entirely feasible; though the content of the Isocratean and the Platonic canons are in *tension* (as illustrated by the example of *Middlemarch*), there are no grounds for supposing that they are inherently or objectively irreconcilable. German classicism is not the only example of a culture or social practice that embraced both; most other European bourgeois cultures of the nineteenth century had their own version.[19] There is nothing in the *propositional content* of the two canons (as opposed to the culture of the respective social practices surrounding them) that requires them to be in conflict with each other. It has sometimes been proposed, in fact (Rorty 1998, p. 33), that there is natural division of labor between them: the sciences are about how things work, and the humanities are about how we want things to be (in economic terms, science provides the constraints, the humanities the optimands). On the surface this sounds entirely reasonable. The problem, again, is that there is no social practice embodying such a rapprochement; apart from the vestigial remains of European bourgeois culture in France and Germany, no substantial group of people has been acculturated into any such two-aspect single culture or discourse.

This is also the central weakness of Bereiter's proposal, in Chapter 2 of this book, to make liberal education the enculturation of students into World 3. World 3 is not organized around a single

---

19. In some of these cases (even German classicism) the present European bourgeoisie continues, not very self-confidently, to maintain an ever-fainter version of the previous integrative canon, in the face of onslaughts from pop culture and Americanization. Only in the U.S. are the consequences of the modern condition fully apparent.

canon; it contains a number of different, partly incompatible, and mutually hostile or indifferent ones. Which are we to choose as the basis for Bereiter's proposed enculturation? Into which *culture* is the student to be *en*cultured? This is not the same question as the more elementary one: which subjects should be taught? But it echoes that simpler question at a meta-level; it asks: which set of criteria should we choose to decide which subjects should be taught? Bereiter does not mean to deny the modern condition, and return to an ancient or terminal cosmopolitan tradition like that of Loyola. Nor does he think, like Humboldt, that he can *overcome* the modern condition. So he owes us an answer to the question 'which culture is to provide the criteria?' He never actually tells us, but it is evident from Bereiter and Scardamalia's educational *practice* (described in Scardamalia's paper in this volume, Chapter 4) that they opt for the Platonic/scientific canon as the basis for the development of a student's mental life. In the final section, this policy will receive qualified support, especially as a practical solution to the immediate problems of North American mass education.

But from a broader, more utopian point of view, and for those who aspire to a mental life whose scope is not one-sidedly abridged, who are willing to pay the price of divided loyalties and permanent exile to see things steadily and, as far as possible, whole—for such people, the practical solution is not enough. They do not want to rest complacently within a single canon, with predetermined limits of scope and use, to structure their mental life. Though Bereiter's practical solution is socially progressive, in that it proposes a realistic way to give any child, from any background, a mental life (this would be completely unprecedented in any human society), it is unsatisfactory from the viewpoint of moral *expertise*, if expertise is taken in Bereiter's and Scardamalia's sense as a process of continuous improvement, without limit.

VI. Utopia

Humboldtean liberal education is not, outside of continental Europe (and there only vestigially), the canon of an existing social practice. Its implementation is necessarily, therefore, an attempt to enculturate students into a culture that does not exist.

What does exist is a proliferation of disciplinary cultures. Up to here I have grouped these, somewhat artificially, under the historical banners of the Platonic/scientific and the Isocratean/literary cultures or canons; this gross oversimplification has not, up to this point, distorted the argument too badly. But it is time to look now at the consequences of the fact that the Enlightenment was not a single moral tradition, but rather a loose alliance of many different new kinds of intellectual and practical activity. Some had roots in antiquity, indeed some had roots in the ancient Platonic and Isocratean traditions—physics and mathematics in the former, humanistic scholarship in the latter. But there were many new ones. Biology and medicine, though picking up where Aristotle and Galen had left off, were soon almost unrecognizeable. Chemistry was almost entirely new. Exploration, new measurement technologies, and mapmaking skills made Europeans aware of a wider world, geographically and culturally. Scholarship of the Bible and of sacred texts in other traditions (Arabic, Hebrew, Sanskrit, even Chinese) combined with a new literature of travel and ethnography to produce the beginnings of historical philology, anthropology, and comparative human science. Legal scholarship, enriched by the same streams, led by the eighteenth century to a more rigorous and document-conscious discipline of history.

These new bodies of knowledge, the origins of our modern disciplines, were not all developed within a single over-arching program, either of a Platonic or of an Isocratean kind. And they were not mutually compatible. Each developed its own characteristic methods and approaches, which required a long apprenticeship to assimilate. Each developed its own language, its own heroes, traditions, taboos. It is *this* proliferation, beyond the coarser division into Platonic and Isocratean categories, that constitutes and gives real force to the modern condition. Nor did it stop there; the proliferation of disciplines has continued in the past two centuries, and continues now at an accelerating pace. The constant call for 'interdisciplinary' work does not undermine disciplines; it creates new ones (Damrosch 1995). The modern condition continues to grow more acute.

But what is *wrong* with it? This question is asked, for instance, by epistemological anarchists like Feyerabend and by radical pragmatists like Rorty. What is wrong with this plurality of canons?

Why can't we just live with them in a pluralistic free-for-all? The market for ideas will decide, in the end, which ones survive and which die out. Why should pluralism of canons be any worse than pluralism of species, or of cultures, or of languages? It is up to each individual to reach her own choice among the throng of options competing for her attention. It is the role of undergraduate education in the modern "multiversity" (Kerr 1963) to dangle as many of these options as possible in front of students' inquiring eyes, so that they can decide which is right for them; the romantic American individualism described in section II above has thus become institutionalized.

Individual students will obviously find their own solutions in any case; there is no returning to the compulsory enculturation in a cosmopolitan moral tradition of the days before romantic liberation ideologies. But the question for individual students, the question they cannot escape, is the Socratic one this paper began with— what strategy to adopt so as to enable them to live the life they ultimately, at the level of their highest aspirations, want to live. Pluralism is not an answer to that question; it merely restates it. Or, taken in another sense, pluralism might be seen as a restatement, rather, of American individualism; it might be taken as the assertion that *there is not* or *cannot be* such a thing as an expertise in the optimization of lifetime consumption (i.e. moral expertise), so that what one chooses as the basis for one's mental life (insofar as one needs such a framework at all, and doesn't just invent it for one's self from whole cloth) is a matter of personal conscience and belief in one's self, not something one could possibly do within a preexisting social practice or framework of rationality, in which one could acquire anything like expertise.

But from the utopian viewpoint we are adopting in this section, pluralism—complacency toward the modern condition—has a much deeper and more disastrous weakness: it concedes ultimate sovereignty to the disciplines. This may sound paradoxical, since pluralism *denies* sovereignty to any *given* discipline; it refuses to those disciplinary canons that once claimed to be *the* central organizing ones (theology, philosophy, physics, history, sociology, anthropology) any form of supremacy or organizing power over other disciplines. But by doing so it leaves each discipline in complete control of *its own* canon, and makes the disciplinary canons the ultimate, uncriticizable options available. In particular it excludes the possibility that an individual *could*, by genuinely internalizing two widely distant canons (becoming the permanent exile with divided loyalties) develop a broader view, a more inclusive mental life, than is possible using either canon by itself.

But why should disciplinary canons be so privileged? They are historically contingent, and have changed substantially in content and doctrines since they originated. Why should they now be immune from criticism? In fact, they aren't; disciplines criticize each other all the time. A consistent pluralism would have to argue that this criticism (the source of so much cognitive process) is somehow not just unwelcome, but pointless or impossible.

The romantic individualist rhetoric in which this liberation doctrine of complete pluralism (complacency toward the modern condition) presents itself, then, is really quite misleading. It does not *liberate* the individual from structures of (disciplinary) authority, but on the contrary *imprisons* the individual in precisely those structures. Not only is humankind as a whole locked into the possibilities inherent within the present disciplinary matrices available in institutions of higher education, but there is no escape route from disciplinary authority for the critical individual who desires a mental life broader than that offered by any single modern discipline, who voluntarily wants to be socialized into mutually hostile or indifferent disciplines. There is no room, in other words, for the free-floating critical intellectual.

But this means there is no room for moral expertise, of the kind striven for by Humboldtean and other utopian programs for liberal education. Rorty and other pluralists would probably agree that students should be equipped to live the life they ultimately, at the level of their highest aspirations, want to live, though they would point out that these aspirations differ. And they would probably agree that for some given aspiration or goal, some things are more important to learn than others. What they really resist—and rightly!—is, I suspect, the idea that some *particular* goal should be accepted as 'true' or 'correct' for all students, and especially the idea that this goal should be the maximization of the student's *productive* potential, her human capital. Unfortunately, this is almost the only consideration it is now respectable to discuss, so much so that many students have internalized it and think they are at university solely for that reason (apart from the direct consumption to be had in frat parties, courtship, and football).

But pluralism only plays into the hands of this deplorable prejudice, since it encourages the idea that there is no rational way to adjudicate the co-existence of disciplines within the larger institution of the university. The result of this is that universities are managed, more and more, not by academics, or people with academic vision, but by generic 'managers' (of just the kind that business believed in for the half-century or so between the rise of Alfred Sloan and the fall of John Scully); at best, academically-oriented administrators follow the recommendations of consulting firms. What such managers or consultants take as their starting point is the 'demand' for the university's 'product'. If students are of the belief that their studies have only the purpose of increasing their personal market value, then it is clear where such 'management' will ultimately steer the university.

If the reflective part of the university community—the intellectuals themselves—are ever to take back the initiative from the 'managers', it has to be by making a genuine attempt to develop a basis of communication among the ever-proliferating disciplines. And disciplinary pluralism of the Feyerabend or Rorty kind is simply the assertion that no such communication is possible or desirable; it is therefore, *in practical terms* ('objectively', as Marxists used to say), a certain recipe for the long-term ascendancy of worldly and commercial considerations in the running of universities. This ascendancy is already far advanced, of course. Still, it seems premature to throw in the towel altogether, and this is what disciplinary pluralism effectively advocates. Within the apparently civilized procedures and hallowed traditions of the university, the negotiation among canons is carried out at an appallingly crass and superficial level. Deep issues of genuine conceptual and philosophical importance are involved in the claims and counter-claims of both the ancient and the newly synthesized canons, but these debates are rarely joined at the conceptual level. The Foucauldian diagnosis of ideas as expressions of power relations is nowhere more thoroughly and cynically confirmed than in universities. Whatever intellectual integrity exists *within* each of the canons involved, altogether different standards apply in the Hobbesian war of all against all *among* the canons. And it is the sober, uninvolved financial people, with their aura of being above the battle, who every day use this dissension to their advantage.

This is not to say there is no solution; from a utopian point of view, one can easily imagine ways to bring about platforms for intercommunication among canons, so as to bring some rationality into the negotiation among them.[20] The problem, as before, is that there is no *existing* social practice in which participants in such negotiations have all been socialized to communicate. The basic question facing any imagined solution, then, is how to *bring such a social practice into existence*. This takes us far beyond the scope of this paper. It should be mentioned, though, that the problem here has a close analogy in another problem recently faced by cognitive science, one to which Bereiter alludes in his paper. This is the problem that metacognitive comprehension strategies could not, it was found, be taught in isolation from actual content, or, indeed, in isolation from a *culture* of inquiry in the classroom. Much effort has been devoted since then to the *creation* of a such a culture in the classroom—with considerable success in some cases (Brown and Campione 1990; Scardamalia et al. 1992; Scardamalia, Bereiter, and Lamon 1994). The present problem is essentially the same one at a higher level. Once the boundaries of inquiry are extended beyond a relatively narrow range, and there is interaction with people or sources of information outside the classroom, then it is the larger culture that must be relied on as the version of World 3 for the students to be enculturated into, to serve as the basis for a mental life. But the only framework available for this purpose, the only existing social practice that qualifies, in any given case, is that of a particular discipline.

For practical purposes, such a framework will serve, and provide children with the basis of a mental life. It can make the classroom a provincial extension of a disciplinary canon. What it cannot do is serve as the basis for anything that goes beyond the point where a particular canon gives clear guidance. It cannot serve as the basis for enculturation into anything like Humboldtean liberal education. For that to be possible, one would have to bring into

---

20. Some practical proposals, for instance, specifically in the context of the modern American research university, are argued for with admirable clarity by David Damrosch (1995).

existence a culture not just in a particular classroom, but in the society at large.

This may sound even more utopian than the preceding part of this section. But there may be ways of starting a movement toward such a (sub)culture. One way of approaching this might be to found a school (as a model school, in the hope that the model would spread) in which 'knowledge building' in Bereiter's sense is the central activity, but in which the school community as a whole is organized around the task of deciding what is most important for students to know (the task would be constrained by the need to get good grades on a standard examination, such as the International Baccalaureate). A good deal of the students' inquiry would focus on this question itself, and one could even imagine that students could take some form of responsibility for deciding the answer, for the next generation of students, all the way down to the elementary level. One interesting feature of the International Baccalaureate, a reflection of its founder's preoccupations, is the (somewhat forbiddingly named) 'Theory of Knowledge' component (Peterson 1974; 1987). The approach suggested here would turn this feature from a peripheral afterthought (which is what in practice it often becomes) into the central focus of school life, since it would have a very concrete application that could hardly be lost from view.

There is no harm in dreaming such utopian dreams, or even in doing something about them. Utopian reflections can give direction to real-world reformers, and provide an overall agenda around which specific reforms can be organized. It can make real-world reform movements more coherent. But Bereiter's paper was not addressed to this utopian level of reflection; it was intended as a contribution to the debate about what should go on in classrooms everywhere, right now. I conclude, therefore, by addressing his proposal on its own terms.

VII. Science as a Basis for Moral Expertise?

Bereiter proposes a program of cultural upgrading or "cultural bootstrapping" (as he and Scardamalia describe it in an earlier paper: Bereiter and Scardamalia 1987a) to enable all children to acquire mental lives. He calls it 'enculturation into World 3', but as we saw, he does not specify which particular culture, which disciplinary canon, he means. Still, it is clear from his paper itself as well as from the history of his and Marlene Scardamalia's project *Knowledge Forum* that the canon in question is, broadly speaking, the Platonic/scientific one.

There is considerable evidence that the Scardamalia-Bereiter program has something like the desired effect. The measures used to test student achievement do not, of course, say anything directly about the acquisition of a mental life, but it is clear that much deeper involvement in conceptual questions is encouraged by *Knowledge Forum*, and participants are much more concerned with interconnections (that is, with coherence), than is the case in conventional classrooms, even challenging ones (Scardamalia 1992; 1994). The idea is to get students actively engaged in the production of knowledge, just as they would be in an applied research lab or in a university, only somewhat further from the actual frontier. They gain an understanding of inquiry and of knowledge production by themselves becoming genuine members of a knowledge-producing community that extends beyond their own classroom to include people actually working on problems nearer the frontier. This also gives them an appreciation for the artifactual, improvable (and thus objective) nature of knowledge, and to see how it enters into the human and social world we have built around us.

These features of Bereiter's proposal underscore its embeddedness in the Platonic/scientific canon. Knowledge is most artifactual and improvable where the 'referential ecology' (Campbell 1986) is most stable; and that is the case in the world of natural science; this same feature also makes the knowledge produced in natural sciences best suited for collaborative work. Many thinking people, such as the disciplinary 'pluralists' Feyerabend and Rorty, have given reasons for rejecting such a proposal. To make the Platonic/scientific canon so central unduly privileges a particular 'grand narrative' (Lyotard 1979), say such voices, one that has had its day and is anyway under suspicion of being nothing but an ideology for bourgeois male hegemony. Nonetheless, this section will defend Bereiter's proposal.

The most compelling case for it is practical. Children acculturated in the Platonic/scientific canon, it can be argued, have a higher potential lifetime income; i.e. making that canon basic will increase equality of opportunity. This is an entirely legitimate argument, and indeed it can be extended to the more general case for enabling children to acquire mental lives in the first place. Children at the age in question can't conceive of the investment involved to achieve such a thing, so the case is one for educators—parents, teachers, policy makers. It could certainly be argued (though there is not much empirical data; this would have to be the basis for a long-term research program) that nothing more valuable than a mental life could possibly be given to a child, and that the child who emerges from adolescence with a mental life will be better at anything he or she undertakes. In the economic terms we began with, in other words, acquisition of a mental life is the highest-return form of investment in human capital.

But this is not the place to make that case, even in outline (and even if there were better data). The worldly or practical justification for Bereiter's proposal is the most important, in the sense that it is best suited to promote it in a market society, in the political arena, among funding bodies, and everywhere it counts. But the focus of this paper is on the *values* of the Platonic/scientific canon, which are usually left by the wayside in these discussions.

What are those values? Isn't science supposed to be value-free? Few commentators who pronounce on such matters are still prepared to say that. Even those who are in favor of science now see it, like Kuhn, as a community with strong positive values of inquiry (Kuhn 1977), and on the other hand as "organized skepticism" (in Merton's words).[21] Can we spell out these values in a kind of hierarchy, as we did for Loyola's and for George Eliot's? Perhaps,[22] but that would, in a sense, be missing the point. The scientific canon is different from the others to the degree that it values just one single

---

21. Merton's description (1973) is developed by Donald Campbell (1986, p. 514), who comments, "Both features of the term are required, yet 'organized' and 'skepticism' are inherently at odds. Societal and institutional settings in which organized skepticism can be approximated are rare and unstable . . . the ideology explicitly rejects the normal social tendency to split up into like-minded groups on specific scientific beliefs, but at the same time it requires a like-mindedness on the social norms of the shared inquiry." This might be regarded as a latter-day, naturalized version of Max Weber's 'Wertfreiheit' (Weber 1918)—which social constructivists about science reject out of hand.

22. As Kuhn (1977) has done—only to be contradicted by Helen Longino (1995), who prefers a different set of values.

thing (just as George Eliot accuses it of doing!). And that one thing is very hard to describe (to call it 'the truth' or 'knowledge' is to beg the question).

The best-known metaphor for the attraction of science to its adepts is still perhaps Plato's story of the cave. In that famous metaphor, we humans are imagined as prisoners in a cave. We are held captive by some people whose campfire, some way off, between where we are kept and the entrance to the cave, is out of our sight. In fact, we are facing away from the campfire, we never see it; we see nothing but flickering shadows against a cave wall, thrown by the campfire against the wall facing our prison. We grow skilled in our ability to recognize these shadows and predict their movements; status in our community of prisoners depends on such skill. But what if I, a prisoner, were suddenly liberated, and stumbled toward the fire? It would hurt my eyes, I could only look at it sideways; only after some adjustment could I discern even the objects reflecting its light. And if someone told me *this* was reality, not the two-dimensional shadows I'd spent my life recognizing and analyzing, would I believe them? Wouldn't it seem dazzling and bizarre? Wouldn't the process of adjustment be painful and gradual? And then, as I progressed, and walked up the pathway beyond the campfire, out into the sunlight, wouldn't the shock be almost too much to bear? Colors, three-dimensional movement, distant horizons, the mackerel-crowded seas, heaven and earth, a whole unimagined universe more luscious and thrilling than anything I could have conceived in the prison where I grew up—only very slowly and agonizingly would I be able to assimilate this new reality, make sense of it, understand it, navigate it.

But could I then—Plato went on—once I had undertaken this short but arduous journey, return to my fellow-prisoners and convince them that there was something out there beyond their wildest imaginings? I would be handicapped because my eyes are not yet re-adjusted to the dark; I can hardly see, and anyway, I haven't kept up my skill at recognizing and analyzing the shadows on the wall. It no longer seems important to me, knowing what I now do. But to my former companions I seem ridiculous. The harder I protest about what I have seen outside, the more crazed and fanatical I sound to them. If I attempt to carry them off by force to the light, to see for themselves, they will think I am trying to drag them down to my level of imbecility, and they would kill me rather than follow.

Even in an age when people no longer believe in a separate, metaphysical 'realm of ideas', and when it is recognized that science is empirical as well as deductive, Plato's story describes something important about the scientific ethos that is hardly captured either in popular literature about science or in most philosophy of science. Certainly among the most intense members of the scientific professions (and those who contribute the most), the desire to be out of the cave, in the sun, regardless of the taunts and threats of the society they live in, is what motivates. This is a strong tradition, it has been around for millennia, and it will survive; it is in no danger from irrelevant criticisms from people whose scale of values is Loyola's or George Eliot's.

But the question here is: What is of *general* importance in scientific values? The cave story is just for a small elite of scientists, who by ordinary standards would be classified as neurotic or insane (since most psychologists share George Eliot's values, or something like them). How can Bereiter justify (apart from worldly or economic considerations, which we are bracketing here) making the Platonic/scientific canon the basis of a mental life for *everyone*?

There is actually a simple and straightforward answer to this. The scientific canon is basic to the self-image of humankind. It lies behind not just one, but a whole series of Copernican revolutions: First Copernicus took us away, counter-intuitively, from the center of the universe. Then Newton showed that even the heavens are nothing special; the same forces operate everywhere, on earth as in heaven, and they account for day and night, the seasons, the comets, the phases of the moon, the tides, much else. And Darwin showed that we too are a part of this nature (a final link in this Darwinian revolution fell into place only a few decades ago, with the discovery of DNA). The trend of this continuing Copernican revolution is clear: we humans are part of nature, we are nothing inherently special, and whatever we may do to *make* ourselves special is up to us. There is no one out there to ask, or to rely on. The predicament of the 'modern condition', in other words, is most acutely brought home—paradoxically—by assimilating one *particular* canon, the Platonic/scientific one.

For those who are concerned that children learn to think for themselves, that they are not merely slaves to fashion or the marketing efforts of pop culture, the Platonic/scientific canon has the further merit that it is further removed from the barnyard warmth of human conformity and unreflective common sense than other canons. It is therefore a better framework in which to imbue children with a critical view of their surroundings, and understand the power of reason as a subversive instrument, and as an instrument of moral and intellectual autonomy.

It will be objected that other canons see things differently. That is true. But it is also true that the scientific one has the highest intellectual prestige. Even those who most vehemently reject its hegemony organize their ideas around the threat it presents. The whole of romanticism could easily (and has been) portrayed as a way of warding off the implications of the continuing Copernican revolution (Berlin 1999). And even current thinkers who are most anxious to deny the Platonic tradition its merits nearly always accept its diagnosis of the modern condition; they accept that meaning comes only from ourselves, and not from some external agency. The Platonic/scientific tradition thus has a kind of centrality even for its opponents; to keep people ignorant of it is to keep them in the dark about where the action is.

The basic motif of this defense of Bereiter's proposal is this: The Platonic/scientific canon should be learned by everyone because it is better suited than any alternative as the basis for a genuinely autonomous mental life. More than other canons, it gives children the opportunity to improve their lives—not so much materially (that is not in question here) as in terms of their *overall* opportunity of becoming more the kind of person they would like to be. That is because it gives them the straight story about the modern agenda. They may elect to ignore it or look the other way, later on, but at least they should know. And they should learn to understand the radical skepticism built into its culture. The Platonic/scientific canon has both historically undermined all intellectual and spiritual authority (and thus inflicted on us the modern condition) and is, as a culture, more hostile to authority than others.[23] For all these

---

23. Of course it is a culture, so it has authority structures like any other culture; 'tribal' continuity needs to be maintained even in a community of 'disputatious

reasons, it is better suited than other canons to the pursuit of human self-betterment (i.e. to moral expertise) since it provides a framework in which that pursuit does not envisage an end-state of blessedness or perfection. In this framework, as in the cognitive-science account of expertise, there is no arrival, only continuous striving for improvement.

But, one might still object, isn't that just to reinforce the authority of what is already the most powerful canon? Isn't it just the *reverse* of skepticism, isn't it the utmost complacency, to brainwash children into accepting the mainstream scientific 'self-image of humankind'? But the scientific tradition, for all its prestige, is not as powerful as it may seem, as any political debate involving science, or weighing evidence for a scientific generalization, will easily show. Many of the books on American bestseller lists invoke the supernatural, and of course religious fundamentalism, complete with rejection of Darwin, is not a fringe movement here. But even much of the supposedly secular, educated minority harbors hopes of some larger meaning issuing from out there somewhere; not long ago the *New Republic* ran a cover article (Easterbrook 1998) that argued in all seriousness that the 'pessimistic' interpretation of science (i.e. the Copernican one) was going out of fashion (among scientists!). Popular expositions of quantum theory often suggest that Heisenberg's uncertainty principle somehow reverses the whole trend of the Copernican revolution, and puts human consciousness back at the center. One could easily multiply these instances. Very few people, it seems, have genuinely internalized

---

truth-seekers' (Campbell 1979, pp. 492–93): "A scientific community must recruit new members and reward old members well enough so that young recruits will be attracted to a lifelong commitment to the field and will justify the drudgery and the painful initiation rites. Journals must be published, purchased, and read. Members must remain loyal to the group and not 'defect' to other tribes. Jobs must be found for loyal followers. Social facilitators are needed to keep the group together and must be rewarded for this role, even if this means giving them scientific honors not earned by their cognitive contributions. The requirements of leadership for coordination and continuity may produce leaders whose decision-making power is used to protect their own social positions and their own scientific beliefs against internal challenge from young rivals. The deeply ingrained social customs of building ingroup loyalty by mobilizing hostility and disgust toward outgroups may be employed . . . in maintaining group cohesion and continuity. Without meeting these social-structural requirements, there can be no scientific community to serve as the vessel carrying scientific knowledge."

the ongoing Copernican revolution. Its effective power, out on the street, is pretty feeble. But it *is*, certainly, a kind of negative secret agenda that all the pop denials and rejections of it have in common. It occupies a secret centrality even in pop culture. Why should children not get to meet it first-hand before they join the others in the anti-scientific cult of their choice?

In fact, though, very few people actually have the *opportunity* of internalizing the Copernican revolution. How many have been taught a coherent picture of science in such a way that they have actually had the opportunity of understanding how it fits together? How many have an inkling of its power to explain not only the few examples they learn in textbooks, but nearly everything in the physical world around them, their own bodies included? And of those, how many have had the chance to think about its connections with everything else they do and think about, including its implications for larger questions about the meaning of life? Bereiter's proposal is that all people should have this opportunity.

In the end, there is probably no defense of Bereiter's position beyond the conviction (entertained, of course, only by those minimally enculturated into the Platonic/scientific canon) that the avoidance of its consequences is an avoidance of our responsibilities, among which the most basic (inherited from the Enlightenment) is to face up to what we know.

There is, perhaps, no way to communicate to those not enculturated into the Platonic/ scientific canon how dishonest it seems to conceal the full extent of the Copernican revolution, however destructive of cherished illusions, from anyone capable of absorbing it. A brief thought experiment, to conclude, may help. An astronomer, cataloguing the big rocks floating around in the asteroid belt, arrives at the conclusion that one of them will hit the earth in a year's time, most likely wiping out all life, and *in her judgment* no possible human effort could deflect or destroy it. Should she keep the knowledge to herself, on the grounds that a) nothing can be done anyway, and the rest of humanity may as well have a good time while it can; b) science is just a social construct, and what she's found out is true only relatively to her own canon's 'grand narrative', not for those outside her narrow culture circle, who have a different self-image of humankind?

References

Adams, M.J. 1990. *Beginning to Read: Thinking and Learning about Print.* Cambridge, MA: MIT Press.

Barzun, J. 1959. *The House of Intellect.* New York: Harper.

Becker, G. 1975. *Human Capital: A Theoretical and Empirical Analysis, with Special Reference to Education.* Second edition. Chicago: University of Chicago Press.

——. 1996 Preference and Values. In *Accounting for Tastes* (Cambridge, MA: Harvard University Press), pp. 3–23.

Bereiter, C. 1985. Toward a Solution of the Learning Paradox. *Review of Educational Research* 55, pp. 201–226.

——. 1990. Aspects of an Educational Learning Theory. *Review of Educational Research* 60, pp. 603–624.

Bereiter, C. and M. Scardamalia. 1987a. An Attainable Version of High Literacy: Approaches to Teaching Higher-Order Skills in Reading and Writing. *Curriculum Inquiry* 17, pp. 9–30.

——. 1987b. *The Psychology of Written Composition.* Hillsdale, NJ: Erlbaum.

——. 1989. Intentional Learning as a Goal of Instruction. In L.B. Resnick, ed., *Knowing, Learning, and Instruction: Essays in Honor of Robert Glaser* (Hillsdale, NJ: Erlbaum), pp. 361–392.

——. 1993. *Surpassing Ourselves: An Inquiry into the Nature and Implications of Expertise.* La Salle, IL: Open Court.

Berofsky, B. 1995. *Liberation from Self: A Theory of Personal Autonomy.* Cambridge: Cambridge University Press.

Brown, A.L., J.D. Bransford, R.A. Ferrara, and J.C. Campione. 1983. Learning, Remembering, and Understanding. In J.H. Flavell and E.M. Markman, eds., *Handbook of Child Psychology*, Vol. III, *Cognitive Development.* Fourth edition (New York: Wiley), pp. 77–166.

Brown, A.L. and J.C. Campione. 1990. Contexts of Learning and Thinking, or A Context by Any Other Name. *Contributions to Human Development* 21, 108–126.

Brown, J.S., A. Collins, and P. Duguid. 1989. Situated Cognition and the Culture of Learning. *Educational Researcher* 18, pp. 32–42.

Campbell, D.T. 1979. A Tribal Model of the Social System Vehicle Carrying Scientific Knowledge. *Knowledge: Creation, Diffusion, Utilization* 1. Reprinted in Campbell 1988, pp. 489–503.

——. 1986. Science's Social System of Validity-Enhancing Collective Belief Change and the Problems of the Social Sciences. In D.W. Fiske and R.A. Schweder, eds., *Metatheory in Social Science: Pluralisms and Subjectivities* (Chicago: University of Chicago Press). Reprinted in Campbell 1988, pp. 504–523.

————. 1988. *Methodology and Epistemology for Social Science: Selected Papers* Chicago: University of Chicago Press.

Case, R. and Y. Okamoto. 1996. *The Role of Central Conceptual Structures in the Development of Children's Thought.* Chicago: University of Chicago Press.

Collini, S. 1991. *Public Moralists: Political Thought and Intellectual Life in Britain, 1850–1930.* Oxford: Oxford University Press.

Damrosch, D. 1995. *We Scholars: Changing the Culture of the University.* Cambridge, MA: Harvard University Press.

Deaton, A. and J. Muellbauer. 1980. *Economics and Consumer Behavior.* Cambridge: Cambridge University Press.

de Vries, J. 1993. Between Purchasing Power and the World of Goods: Understanding the Household Economy in Early Modern Europe. In J. Brewer and R. Porter, eds., *Consumption and the World of Goods* (London: Routledge), pp. 85–132.

diSessa, A. 2000. *Changing Minds: Computers, Learning, and Literacy.* Cambridge, MA: MIT Press.

Donner, W. 1991. *The Liberal Self: John Stuart Mill's Moral and Political Philosophy.* Ithaca, NY: Cornell University Press.

Easterbrook, G. 1998. Science Sees the Light: How New Scientific Discoveries Have Made the Notion of Higher Meaning and Purpose Intellectually Respectable Again. *The New Republic* 219, pp. 24–29.

Eliot, G. 1872. *Middlemarch.* Harmondsworth: Penguin (1965).

Fox, A. *Oral and Literate Culture in England, 1500–1700.* Oxford: Oxford University Press.

Frankfurt, H.G. 1971. Freedom of the Will and the Concept of a Person. *Journal of Philosophy* 68. Reprinted in H.G. Frankfurt, *The Importance of What We Care About: Philosophical Essays* (Cambridge: Cambridge University Press 1988), pp. 11–25.

Goody, J. 1977. *The Domestication of the Savage Mind.* Cambridge: Cambridge University Press.

Greeno, J. 1993. For Research to Reform Education and Cognitive Science. In L.A. Penner, G.M. Batsche, H.M. Knoff, and D.L. Nelson, eds., *The Challenges in Mathematics and Science Education: Psychology's Response* (Washington, DC: American Psychological Association), pp. 153–192.

Griffin, J. 1986. *Well-Being: Its Meaning, Measurement, and Moral Importance.* Oxford: Oxford University Press.

Griffin, J. 1991. Against the Taste Model. In J. Elster and J.E. Roemer, eds., *Interpersonal Comparisons of Well-Being* (Cambridge: Cambridge University Press), pp. 45–69.

Hare, R.M. 1952. *The Language of Morals.* Oxford: Oxford University Press.

Harvard Committee 1945. *General Education in a Free Society: Report of the Harvard Committee*. Introduction by James Bryant Conant. Cambridge, MA: Harvard University Press.

Hirsch, E.D. 1996. *The Schools We Need and Why We Don't Have Them*. New York: Doubleday.

Hoffman, R.R., P.J. Feltovich, and K.M. Ford. 1997. A General Framework for Conceiving of Expertise and Expert Systems in Context. In P.J. Feltovich, K.M. Ford, R.G. Hoffman, eds., *Expertise in Context: Human and Machine* (Cambridge, MA: MIT Press), pp. 543–580.

Irvine, M. 1994. *The Making of Textual Culture: Grammatica and Literary Theory, 350–1100*. Cambridge: Cambridge University Press.

Kerr, C. 1963. *The Uses of the University*. Third edition. Cambridge, MA: Harvard University Press 1982.

Kimball, B.A. 1986. *Orators and Philosophers: A History of the Idea of Liberal Education*. New York: Teachers College Press.

Kintsch, W. 1974. *The Representation of Meaning in Memory*. Hillsdale, NJ: Erlbaum.

———. 1998. *Comprehension: A Paradigm for Cognition*. Cambridge: Cambridge University Press.

Kirshner, D. and J.A. Whitson, eds. 1997. *Situated Cognition: Social, Semiotic, and Psychological Perspectives*. Mahwah, NJ: Erlbaum.

Kuhn, T. 1977. Objectivity, Value Judgement, and Theory Choice. In T. Kuhn *The Essential Tension* (Chicago: University of Chicago Press), pp. 320–339.

Kuppermann, J. 1991. *Character*. Oxford: Oxford University Press.

Lave, J. 1997. The Culture of Acquisition and the Practice of Understanding. In Kirshner and Whitson 1997, pp. 17–35.

Lave, J. and E. Wenger. 1991. *Situated Learning: Legitimate Peripheral Participation*. Cambridge: Cambridge University Press.

Longino, H. 1995. Gender, Politics, and the Theoretical Virtues. *Synthese* 104, pp. 383–397.

Loyola, I. Of. 1548. *The Spiritual Exercises*. In I. of Loyola, *The Spiritual Exercises and Selected Works*. G.E. Ganss, et al., eds. (New York: Paulist Press 1991), pp. 113–214.

Lyotard, J.-F. 1979. *La Condition Postmoderne: Rapport sur le Savoir*. Paris: Éditions de Minuit.

Mandelbaum, M. 1971. *History, Man, and Reason: A Study in Nineteenth-Century Thought*. Baltimore: Johns Hopkins Press.

McKitterick, R. 1989. *The Carolingians and the Written Word*. Cambridge: Cambridge University Press.

———, ed. 1990. *The Uses of Literacy in Medieval Europe*. Cambridge: Cambridge University Press.

Metcalfe, J. and A.P. Shimamura, eds. 1994. *Metacognition: Knowing about Knowing*. Cambridge, MA: MIT Press.

Mill, J.S. 1859. *On Liberty*. Reprinted in J.S. Mill, *Utilitarianism, On Liberty, and Considerations on Representative Government* (London: Dent, 1972), pp. 63–170.

Nagel, T. 1986. *The View from Nowhere*. Oxford: Oxford University Press.

Olson, D.R. 1994. *The World on Paper: The Conceptual and Cognitive Implications of Writing and Reading*. Cambridge: Cambridge University Press.

Peterson, A.D.C. 1972. *The International Baccalaureate: An Experiment in International Education*. London: Harrap.

———. 1987 *Schools Across Frontiers: The Story of the International Baccalaureate and the United World Colleges*. La Salle, IL: Open Court.

Pinker, S. 1994. *The Language Instinct*. New York: Morrow.

Rorty, R. 1998. Against Unity. *Wilson Quarterly* 22, pp. 28–38.

Scardamalia, M., C. Bereiter, C. Brett, P.J. Burtis, C. Calhoun, and N. Smith Lea. 1992. Educational Applications of a Networked Communal Database. *Interactive Learning Environments* 21, 45–71.

Scardamalia, M., C. Bereiter, and M. Lamon. 1994. The CSILE Project: Trying to Bring the Classroom into World 3. In K. McGilley, ed., *Classroom Lessons: Integrating Cognitive Theory and Classroom Practice* (Cambridge, MA: MIT Press), pp. 201–228.

Scruton, R. 1998. *An Intelligent Person's Guide to Modern Culture*. London: Duckworth.

Skidelsky, R. 1983. *John Maynard Keynes: Hopes Betrayed 1883–1920*. London: Macmillan.

Snow, C.P. 1959. *The Two Cultures*. Reissued 1993 with an introduction by S. Collini (Cambridge: Cambridge University Press).

Sternberg, R.J. 1997. Cognitive Conceptions of Expertise. In P.J. Feltovich, K.M. Ford, R.G. Hoffman, eds., *Expertise in Context: Human and Machine* (Cambridge, MA: MIT Press), pp. 149–162.

Stigler, G. and G. Becker. 1977. De Gustibus Non Est Disputandum. *American Economic Review* 67. Reprinted in G. Becker, *Accounting for Tastes* (Cambridge, MA: Harvard University Press), pp. 24–49.

Weber, M. 1918. Der Sinn der 'Wertfreiheit' der soziologischen und ökonomischen Wissenschaften. In M. Weber, *Gesammelte Aufsätze zur Wissenschaftslehre*, 6th ed. (Tübingen: Mohr/Siebeck, 1985), pp. 489–540.

———. 1919. Wissenschaft als Beruf. In M. Weber, *Gesammelte Aufsätze zur Wissenschaftslehre*, 6th ed. (Tübingen: Mohr/Siebeck, 1985), pp. 582–613.

Williams, B. 1985. *Ethics and the Limits of Philosophy*. Cambridge, MA: Harvard University Press.

9

Artifacts, Canons, and the Progress of Pedagogy: A Response to Contributors

Carl Bereiter

How, other than through the occasional updating of content, ought liberal education to change to meet changing conditions? That was the question addressed in my target paper, 'Liberal Education in a Knowledge Society' (Chapter 2 above). The answer I offered is a radical one, radical in that it entails a change in goals and conception rather than only a change in method or content. Yet I see it as preserving rather than abandoning the essence of liberal education. Quite appropriately, most of the responses dealt with conceptual issues and underlying assumptions. Disappointingly, there was little direct questioning of my conclusion: that schools should change to become workshops for the production of knowledge. I fear that the reason this proposal escaped criticism is that I have not yet succeeded in making it intelligible.

Perhaps I can make the proposal clearer by moving away from generalities to focus on one topic, the teaching of evolution. This may be an unwise choice, because the topic has given rise to much impassioned debate that is irrelevant to the points I want to make. Most of the contemporary debate, however, including the notorious dispute over the demotion of evolution in Kansas, has concerned whether evolution is "just a theory" or whether it is established fact. In the Popperian terms that I adopted in my target paper, this is an argument about whether the teaching of evolution is teaching about a World 3 object, Darwinian theory, or whether it is teaching about World 1, what really happened over the course of life on earth. Obviously, it should be both, but the sad fact is that school teaching is likely to focus exclusively on Worlds 1 and 2, ignoring World 3. The textbook or some related kind of document will be the basis of study. The textbook treatment of evolution will typically be treated as a surrogate for World 1—as a stand-in for the flesh-and-blood reality of evolutionary history. Alternatively, it may be treated as a statement of beliefs, a window on the scientists' World 2. Or it may, with little regard for consistency, be treated as both. Uncertainties may be acknowledged, but they are uncertainties about what is *really* the case, not uncertainties about the status or qualities of a World 3 object. Although the term 'theory' may appear in the discussions, it is likely either to refer to personal opinions or else simply be used to indicate uncertainty. But Darwin's theory and competing or revisionist theories will not be dealt with *as such*, as objects of inquiry in their own right.

This focus on Worlds 1 and 2 and ignoring of World 3 leaves several serious gaps. There is a cultural gap: students acquire no sense of what a major intellectual leap Darwin's theory was over its predecessors and what a profound impact it had on nineteenth-century thought. There is an epistemological gap. Thomas Kuhn (1970, p. 77ff) has emphasized that scientists never evaluate theories solely by comparing them to the world but always also by comparing them to each other. Without this kind of World 3 analysis, students are unlikely to escape from naive empiricism in their scientific thinking. There is also a more specific comprehension gap: large numbers of students fail to grasp the idea of natural selection. Failure to grasp the idea leads to an intellectual gap: the idea of natural selection has applications far beyond explaining the origin of species (Ohlsson 1993). It applies to such diverse mechanisms as the immune system and operant conditioning. It explains why misuse of antibiotics produces resistant strains of disease germs and why cancers develop resistance over the course of chemotherapy. It is essential to understanding the difference between using knowledge of the genome to improve classical breeding practices and using it to produce genetic alterations directly (a difference with significant implications for what appears on our grocery shelves).

The idea has been used and misused in social theories, is basic to sociobiology and psychobiology, and is the basis for one of the more plausible explanations of creativity and genius (Simonton 1999). In short, the idea of natural selection—the World 3 object— should be part of the intellectual equipment of every educated modern, including those who for whatever reason reject some or all of the empirical claims of evolutionists.

According to Stellan Ohlsson (1991), who has studied evolution beliefs among university students, it is not that students acquire a wrong theory—a Lamarckian theory, as is commonly said. Ohlsson concluded that most students have no theory of evolution at all, that is, no explanation of how evolution works. They simply take species adaptation as a fact. This suggests that they have not visited World 3 and got things wrong; they have not visited World 3 at all. Their study has been confined to World 1 (albeit World 1 as represented in textbooks).

If you look at scientifically respectable biology textbooks, it is not apparent why the teaching of evolution should fail on so many counts. The necessary information and explanations are there. With normal instruction by teachers who understand natural selection themselves, half or more of the students will indeed grasp the idea, but a sizable minority will not. But of those who do grasp it, how many will be able to use it, and use it with proper care, as an intellectual tool for purposes other than explaining biological adaptation? I don't know, but I suspect the number is small, probably as small as the number who master algebra as an intellectual tool for purposes other than solving textbook algebra problems.

Something more seems to be required than clear explanations and careful instruction. My paper addresses what that something is. It is immersion in World 3, not just as a visitor but as an active participant—a knowledge worker, a producer of knowledge. Popper said that in order to grasp a theory you must first understand the problem that the theory was intended to solve and try out the obvious solutions to discover that they don't work (Popper and Eccles 1977, p. 44). Doing that means getting into the theory-building business yourself. According to this proposal, the biology class needs to become a workshop for developing, testing, and improving explanations of biological phenomena. Trying to develop an evolutionary theory of their own and testing it against facts—does it explain this? Does it explain that? Does it imply that apes should be extinct, which they obviously are not?—leads students to recognize the problems that a theory of evolution must solve. As they begin to see how Darwinian theory solves these problems they will not only grasp its core idea but they will appreciate keenly what a powerful idea it is, how it changes your whole outlook on nature. And, with encouragement, they may begin to apply the idea to other problems of understanding. Of course, they are likely to apply it simplistically at first (as many respectable nineteenth-century thinkers did), but that is liable to happen with any new tool. What is important is to sustain the effort at idea improvement.

The proposal, obviously, is a constructivist one. The phrase, 'production of knowledge', gives that much away. There are a lot education proposals in the air these days that carry the label 'constructivism', and there is also a mounting counter-reaction. In its most degraded forms, constructivism is distinguished by the absence of instruction. A slightly more coherent form goes by the name of 'project-based learning'. It is the almost universally favored way of putting information technology to work in schools (Moursund 1999). Although my proposal is compatible with 'project-based learning', it insists on a distinction that is not made by advocates of that approach—a distinction between projects aimed at creating a piece of knowledge and those aimed at producing a tangible object. The trouble with constructivism as generally practiced in schools is that, compared to traditional subject-matter instruction, it takes students even farther away from World 3, into an almost exclusive occupation with the palpable and observable.

My proposal is not, as Miller seems to suspect, a plot to pervert liberal education into "the production of knowledge that is useful in the global marketplace." Usefulness enters the picture only in the way that Whitehead intended when he said (1929, p. 14),"Of course, education should be useful, whatever your aim in life. It was useful to Saint Augustine and it was useful to Napoleon. It is useful, because understanding is useful." The most likely products of youthful knowledge building are explanations of physical and cultural phenomena, interpretations, historical accounts, and other more-or-less scholarly efforts. Thus the problem with my proposal is not to see what it preserves of liberal education but what it changes. Seeing what is different about it requires a distinction between learning and knowledge building; this distinction in turn rests on a distinction between knowledge in the head and knowledge that is in some reasonable sense independent of individual minds. These distinctions were the object of much of the criticism in response to my target paper.

The Constructedness of Knowledge

Everyone seems willing to recognize a kind of knowledge that in some sense exists independently of its authors or of individual knowers. Conceptions differ widely, however. There is the commonsense view, probably still dominant in schooling, of a body of truths of which personal knowledge constitutes a small and probably corrupt sample. Then there is the opposite view, enunciated by Nonaka and Takeuchi (1995) and seemingly taken up as the final word by business pundits. It sees 'explicit knowledge' as simply personal knowledge made public. Then there is a sociological view according to which certain beliefs and categorizations become certified as knowledge through the actions of institutions such as scientific societies and law courts (Bloor 1998). Philosophers over the centuries have produced a number of conceptions, from Plato's pure ideas to Reck's 'conceptual possibilities'. Semioticians and socio-cultural theorists have on the one hand rejected the idea of knowledge as an "immaterial object that... exists, independent of the linguistic formulation and argumentation through which it was constructed" while at the same time recognizing something like what Wells calls "semiotic artifacts," which "play a central role in the knowing of those involved" (Wells, this volume, p. 116).

It is tempting to leave the sorting out of differences to philosophers and to adopt some suitably vague notion like 'explicit knowledge' in order to get on with educational argument. But that will not work if the argument you wish to make is about changing the way knowledge is treated in schools. It then makes a difference whether you are talking about knowledge as a body of truths, as externalized personal beliefs, as institutionally certified beliefs, as hypothetical possibilities, or as semiotic tools. Rigor, though always desirable, is not of the first importance. Serviceability is. The most serviceable conception of knowledge-outside-the-head that I have been able to find is Popper's idea of World 3. Despite the criticisms, of which those by Reck and Wells are among the more charitable, and despite the general disdain that falls from some quarters on anyone who says a good word for Popper, I have not found an alternative that serves the purposes of educational modernization as well.

To be serviceable in the contemporary context, a conception of knowledge has to represent it as something that can be created and worked with, criticized and improved. Also—and this is essential for the proposal I presented—it needs to allow the work of scientific research laboratories and leading-edge scholars to share the same conceptual space as the efforts of school children to formulate problems and explanations, to conjecture and refute, and to interpret the products of those scientists and scholars. Popper's World 3 does all this. The immaterial objects composing World 3 are unequivocally human constructions, yet they have a certain autonomy that allows them to be studied, modified, adapted to new uses, and so on. Popper was also clear that creating a World 3 object and understanding one that already exists are essentially similar processes (Popper and Eccles 1977, p. 461). The great virtue of Popper's three worlds scheme from an educational point of view is that it provides the basis for a reasonable and practical constructivism.

There is another meaning of constructivism only tangentially related to the one I have been advancing. This is a meaning that has come to prominence in the sociology of knowledge. Much more controversial and inflammatory, it tends to drag the educational version of constructivism along with it. So it is important to separate them. The inflammatory version, commonly referred to as social constructivism or 'constructionism', asserts that *truth* is socially constructed (Berger and Luckman 1967). According to this view, the fact that most scientific theories are the work of European males is relevant to judging them. This is in contrast to the more traditional view (held by Popper, among many others) that the truth of a proposition is independent of its origins and of what people happen to think.

The confusion about constructivism is aggravated by the ambiguity of the term knowledge. If you take the traditional epistemological definition of knowledge as 'true or warranted belief', then to say that knowledge is constructed is the same as saying that truth is constructed. But if you hold the more workaday conception of knowledge as something like 'intellectual property', then saying that it is constructed is almost self-evident and it does not commit you to any position one way or another concerning the nature of truth. This latter is the position I have been trying to maintain.

When Reck (Chapter 7 above) criticizes constructivism he is apparently doing so on the basis of a 'true or warranted belief' conception of knowledge. The *truth* of the Pythagorian theorem, he seems to be saying, is timeless and therefore it should not be regarded as a human construction, with a history and all the other attributes that a constructed artifact may have. The credit due to Pythagorus (or whoever was actually responsible) should be credit for formulating the theorem, not for creating it. Referring as it does to ideal entities (sides of a triangle), the theorem does not carry a date stamp. There is not a time before which it was not true and after which it was true or at least arguably true. That sounds right to me, but if some postmodern theorist wants to dispute it, I don't (for present purposes) care; it has no relevance to the kind of constructivism I am advocating.

There is one point, however, at which the issue of timeless truth impinges on educational constructivism. If the present value of a World 3 object (its truth, applicability, or whatever) is independent of its origins and history, then why trot in all this baggage about knowledge being humanly constructed at all? Certainly if you are going to teach children that two plus two is four, it does not help the project along to explain that arithmetic is a human invention. Where the constructedness of human knowledge becomes important is in achieving what I called "enculturation into World 3" and which I have defined as "joining the ranks of those who are familiar with, understand, create, and work with the conceptual artifacts of their culture" (Bereiter 2002, Chapter 7). If students are to become enculturated into this world, it is essential but by no means sufficient that they become acquainted with the major intellectual products of past generations. 'Joining the ranks' means becoming part of the knowledge-producing subculture, identifying with its members, learning their skills, sharing their aims and their norms. Except for adding some well-motivated qualifications, I don't think many people would disagree with this as a prescription for graduate studies, nor would they doubt the wisdom of earlier preparation that would ease the shock and panic some graduate students experience when informed that getting good marks is no longer sufficient, that they are expected to 'make a contribution to knowledge'. The question is how early enculturation into World 3 should start. As Scardamalia's contribution (Chapter 4 above) suggests, the first grade is not too soon. Others have found this also to be the case. Even at the stage of learning two plus two equals four, children can begin producing generalizable mathematical ideas and learning the norms that apply to such knowledge production (Cobb et al. 1997).

Conceptual Artifacts

Popper's term for what populates World 3, 'objective knowledge', invites the sorts of criticisms Reck has made, and also criticisms by sociologists of knowledge and others who detect yet another European male declaring that his beliefs are 'objectively' true. That is why I have never used Popper's term except to criticize it. A preferable term, I believe, is 'conceptual artifact'. This captures the notion of human constructions that are created to some purpose, but it avoids the ambiguity of the term 'knowledge' and leaves it quite open to what purpose such artifacts are created, how successful they are in serving that purpose, and what other unplanned purposes they may come to serve.

The qualifier 'conceptual' is meant to distinguish these kinds of artifacts from a. material artifacts, such as ATM machines and ironing boards, and b. immaterial but nonconceptual artifacts, such as sonatas and jokes. As with most artifacts, rigorous definition is impossible and boundary problems are to be expected.[1] The distinction between cars and trucks used to be clear but now it is fuzzy—not because analysts have discovered ambiguities but because manufacturers have started producing ambiguous vehicles. Despite its growing uncertainty, we retain the distinction

---

1. Exceptions, of course, are theoretical and mathematical concepts. Note, however, that while the conceptual artifacts such as line, ray, angle, and triangle, as defined in Euclidean geometry, are (for instructional purposes, at least) precise, the conceptual artifact called 'Euclidean geometry' is not. It has boundary problems, problems of when it came into existence, problems of whether variations are still 'Euclidean geometry' or are something different, and so on.

between cars and trucks because it still serves to sort out cases warranting different treatment.[2] We should similarly expect a category like *conceptual artifacts* to be useful only insofar as it helps us sort out cases needing a certain kind of treatment. The point of my paper was that these objects making up World 3, which I now propose to call conceptual artifacts, do indeed warrant special attention in education, attention they have failed to receive partly because the two-worlds conceptual framework of educational thought has provided no place for them.

Culture and World 3

Students need to become knowledgeable about the important conceptual artifacts of their culture as well as other important cultural artifacts. I had no intention of playing down the arts and humanities nor other educational missions such as the development of values and virtues. The issue before us was what, if anything, needs to be changed to adapt liberal education to present and foreseeable circumstances. What needs changing, I have been arguing, is just that part of liberal education that deals with conceptual artifacts.

Cultural artifacts may be defined as artifacts of any kind that are preserved because of their meaning. An old household appliance may be preserved because of its historical interest or because of its artistic interest as an example of, say, art deco design. Statues and cave drawings are more obvious examples. Some cultural arftifacts are immaterial. Poems, myths, and musical compositions are examples of these. Copies of the first edition of an important literary work may be preserved as material artifacts of cultural value, but the literary work as an immaterial artifact persists through many changes in physical embodiment. When we discuss Milton's *Paradise Lost*, we are discussing the immaterial artifact rather than any material one. None of this should present any particular con-

---

2. Distinctions among artifacts not only lack the rigor some intellectuals demand, but they also shift depending on context and purpose. For determining license fees, the relevant distinctions between cars and trucks have to do with size, horsepower, and use. From the standpoint of highway safety, however, a truck is best defined as any vehicle built on a truck frame, for it is the frame that in a collision causes a truck to ride up over a sedan and kill the occupants.

ceptual problems. It is therefore uncontroversial to say that a major concern of liberal education has been to develop not only a knowledge of but also a deep intimacy with a range of cultural artifacts.

What I am calling conceptual artifacts would fall within that range. Students are expected to become familiar with Newton's laws and Plato's scheme for a republic, just as they are expected to become familiar with *Paradise Lost* and the Acropolis. So why make a special case of *conceptual* artifacts? One reason, advanced by Carus (Chapter 8 above) is that they include scientific theories and principles, and these are of exceptional importance in contemporary society. Although I agree, that is an argument that picks out only a particular subset of conceptual artifacts—those that assert something to be the case and, among those, assertions growing out of scientific methods (however those may be characterized). Conceptual artifacts cover much more ground than that. They are not limited as to subject matter and they include plans, problem formulations, proposals (like the one I have been advancing here), interpretations, and criticisms. Given this loose and generous inclusiveness, the question arises whether conceptual artifacts can be distinguished at all from the full range of cultural artifacts, leaving aside the question of whether there is any point in doing so.

Let me respond, however, by emphasizing that there is a point in making a distinction. With respect to most kinds of cultural artifacts, students necessarily take a rather passive, receptive role. Although, as part of their liberal education, they may engage in arts and crafts, do creative writing, put on plays and musical performances, and other such active pursuits, these are usually at some remove from the cultural objects they are studying. Their study of major works of art and literature, of historical and natural wonders, and of the lives of culturally significant people is focused on understanding and appreciation. The students are not prospective builders of new pyramids, and making models of the old ones is a questionable activity, often reserved for the less literate. With conceptual artifacts, students can and indeed should take a much more active role. The best way to understand a scientific theory, as Popper declared, is to reconstruct it, starting with trying to solve the problem that the theory was created to solve. Students can then set about actively using the theory, sometimes for practical purposes but more often as a device for explaining phenomena. The explanations they produce are also conceptual artifacts, and they can work collaboratively to improve them. Moreover, their interaction with other kinds of cultural artifacts can be enriched and enlivened by creating conceptual artifacts related to them—interpretations, criticisms, close readings, historical accounts, psychological or sociological analyses. Although there is a danger here of overintellectualizing things that should be experienced more viscerally, a good teacher should be able to ensure a healthy balance (and help students to experience Euclid's geometry and Newton's laws viscerally as well).

What, then, distinguishes conceptual artifacts from other cultural artifacts? Keeping in mind that, as with all artifacts, strict categorization is impossible because of the possibility of creating intermediate instances, I suggest the following rough distinction: Conceptual artifacts are distinguishable from other cultural artifacts by virtue of the logical relations that may obtain among them. One conceptual artifact may be derivable from or constitute a limiting case of another; one may contradict or support another; whether two conceptual artifacts are the same or different or whether one is a modification of or improvement on the other are substantive questions. Material artifacts cannot relate to one another in these ways, and neither can such nonmaterial cultural artifacts as songs and poems. An important part of mastering any intellectual discipline is grasping the relations among ideas; the more theoretically developed the discipline, the more interdependent the ideas tend to be and the more essential it becomes to grasp them as a system. This systematicity, based on logical relations among elements, is what sets World 3 apart from the larger world of cultural artifacts, which may relate to each other in many ways but not in the particularly powerful and difficult-to-grasp way of conceptual artifacts.

The educational value of work with ideas has long been recognized. We can see it in the medieval *disputatio*, in the recurrent popularity of debate and Socratic dialogue, and even in that contemporary travesty, the critical thinking skills program. But all of these are focused on but one aspect of intellectual work, the arrival at truths or the resolution of competing truth claims. Important as this is, it makes for a static and hide-bound mental life if it is detached from the formulation and elaboration of problems, the creation of ideas, the shaping of intuitions into discussible propositions, the exploration of what particular ideas and systems of ideas can and cannot do, and what is absolutely central to all the sciences and progressive disciplines: idea improvement. The narrow focus on issues of truth or validity also makes for an unhealthy separation of intellect from feeling. It denies to conceptual artifacts the opportunity that is allowed to all other kinds of artifacts: the opportunity to become objects of passion, to become part of the inner core of things that people really care about.

The preceding paragraph does not say anything glaringly controversial. Indeed, it is vulnerable to the death sentence that practitioners so often pass on novel educational ideas: 'we already do that.' Without a different epistemology, it is difficult to appreciate the gap between what actually goes on in even the most intellectually alive classrooms and what would ideally go on in what I am proposing the classroom of tomorrow should become: a workshop for the production of conceptual artifacts. Although commonsense epistemology can undergird quite a lively program of inquiry and analysis, it leaves two questions unaddressed, virtually unaddressable:

> What is this idea (concept, theory, principle) good for?
>
> How could it be improved?

As far as I can recall, I never in my years of schooling, including university and graduate school, heard these questions raised. Only in the knowledge-building classrooms Scardamalia refers to have I ever encountered them since. Unless you hold some notion of ideas as real things, and recognize work with ideas as real productive work, these questions will not arise. If there is anything to the claim that we are entering a new phase of civilization, a knowledge age, then these questions are ones that students must learn to ask and ponder.

Is The Knowledge Society a Fiction?

But is there anything to the claim that we are entering a new age? Edwards and Ogilvie cite data that raise doubts whether there is any general rise in demand for knowledge workers or that society is undergoing a massive shift comparable to the shift from an agrarian to an industrial economy. Instead, they say, what is going on is a shift from manufacturing to service jobs and a general rise in the level of schooling required for good jobs. Their educational message is to concentrate on raising the educational floor rather than striving to extend the high end of educational attainment.

One could dismiss their arguments by saying that the present discussion is not about increasing employability but about increasing the capacity of society to take advantage of the new opportunities offered by the explosion of information and communications technology. There is a factual basis for the futuristic business literature, but it is not in labor statistics. Most of its authors are management consultants or business magazine journalists, and the material they draw on consists mostly of cases in which companies, large and small, are reorganizing in ways that make knowledge creation and innovation more central to their business. These companies are not claimed to be typical but to be front-running and therefore likely to force other companies to follow suit in order to remain competitive.

Nevertheless, the challenge Edwards and Ogilvie raise does strike close to the core of the issue with which this volume deals. For if there is not a major economic transformation taking place, then perhaps there is no need for liberal education—or any other variety of education, for that matter—to change. See to it that kids learn to do something with computers beyond playing video games and otherwise go ahead with normal efforts to do a better job of what schools already do. That is probably a fair description of the present state of educational reform in North America and the U.K., and so it can stand as the default position on the question of educational change.

It is not evident to me, however, how the kinds of economic indicators Edwards and Ogilvie consider could confirm or disconfirm the millennialist claims. Suppose the most radical claim is right, that there is a shift underway toward a society organized around the production of knowledge, and that this is as profound as the earlier shift from a society organized around agriculture to one organized around manufacture. The earlier shift was marked by massive movement of people from the countryside into the cities and by an accompanying change in occupation. Nothing of this scale is in the offing. The supposed changes are internal to firms and occur within rather than between large occupational categories. One of the skeptical arguments is that if knowledge workers are so much in demand their incomes ought to have risen more rapidly than they have. But this argument does not reckon with the strategies large companies now have available for holding down labor costs, which include hiring younger workers, offering non-salary incentives, and outsourcing knowledge work to cheaper labor markets.

In short, something quite complex is going on. In the face of uncertainties, we need education policies that make sense under a variety of possible scenarios. Although radical predictions, such as Rifkin's 'end of work' (1995), may prove mistaken, so may advice such as 'Stay in school and you will earn a higher income.' Perhaps the sounder advice would be, 'Learn to do work that cannot be outsourced.' The kinds of work that cannot readily be outsourced to distant places include on one hand personal services, most of which are poorly paid, and on the other hand ill-structured tasks in knowledge-rich domains (Bereiter 2002, Chapter 7). Serious reform in education systems ought to be aimed at qualifying more people for the latter. That is what they are trying to do in Singapore and Hong Kong, for instance, while the U.S. is preoccupied with 'raising the floor'. The question to which educators the world over lack sound answers, however, is *how* to equip students to handle ill-structured tasks in knowledge-rich domains. They may opt for well-structured tasks in knowledge-rich domains (for example, memorizing facts) or ill-structured tasks in knowledge-poor domains (the stuff of thinking skills programs) or, the favorite these days, 'project-based learning', which gives the impression of creative knowledge work without actually requiring that students do any. Knowledge building, the creation and improvement of useful conceptual artifacts, is intended as a fourth option that more directly addresses the need.

Canons to the Right of Us, Canons to the Left of Us

Demonstrating that it often takes a radical to be a true conservative, Miller eloquently argues two points:

1. That what students need to learn does not necessarily coincide with
what they want to learn—or with what they want to do, which may be
only incidentally productive of learning.

2. That teachers ought to know better than the students what students
need to learn.

These, the pillars of 'basic education', have often been challenged
by child-centered educators, but I believe they should be allowed to
stand, provided they are augmented by two additional principles:

3. That understanding, in particular, cannot be received but must be
constructed or reconstructed by each person who would possess it.

4. That, as Dewey and Whitehead both insisted, subject matter should
have value to students at the time they learn it; it should not merely be
banked against future needs.

In my target article (Chapter 2 above), I assumed the first two
principles—acknowledging the first and taking the second for
granted—in order to concentrate on the latter two, toward which I
thought I had something to offer. It seems I miscalculated. If you
do not emphatically proclaim the first two principles, then anything you say in favor of the latter two is liable to be taken as a
rejection of the first two. More seriously, however, I did not deal
with the tension that exists between them, a tension that any educator must live with who tries to do justice to all four principles.

Miller discusses, with a good deal of wisdom and charity, the
tension between what students ought to learn, for their own and
society's good, and what their peer culture disposes them toward.
His optimistic conclusion, based on experience, is that if you offer
what students need, some at least will come. Carus's discussion represents, among other things, a creative response to the tension
between the need for a shared body of knowledge and the need for
students to construct their own understanding of the world. An
interesting way to think about this tension is introduced by
Edwards and Ogilvie and taken further by Carus. It is to see it as a
tension between education for consumption and education for production. There is no doubt that the average person has more
impact on society as a consumer than as a producer. Schools invest

considerable effort in trying to discourage bad consumption, with their anti-drug and other 'just say no' campaigns. But where is the effort to encourage good consumption—that is, socially beneficial consumption? Isolated in those few remaining bastions of traditional liberal education, it would seem. But Carus's point is not about the social value of education for consumption, it is on its value in helping students to develop a personal mental life.

Carus's chapter, as I read it now, addresses a question that I raised at the beginning of my target article but that neither I nor any of the other participants addressed directly: "What should it mean to be an educated person in the twenty-first century?" That is, what should it mean *on the whole* to be an educated person under the rapidly changing conditions of twenty-first-century civilization? This is not a question that can be answered by citing specifics of what is to be learned or indicating changes that need to be made. It is a question about what holds all those separate learnings together.

We do not expect students on their own to discover universal gravitation, the circulation of the blood, or the rise and decline of feudalism; but it seems that we expect them to discover Western thought (or whatever is the leading thought of their culture) on their own. Thus the implicit belief, shared by traditionalists and constructivists alike, is that students need help with the pieces but the whole will take care of itself. Carus challenges this belief. There has to be a canon, he argues, but it cannot in this century be the canon of an all-encompassing religion or of an institutionalized and static world view or body of wisdom. It needs to be a canon that itself embraces the continual advancement of knowledge, the continual breakdown of established beliefs, and the unending clashes between world views. Science, he somewhat reluctantly concludes, provides the closest things we have to such a canon, and so fostering scientific thinking should be central to modern liberal education.

I pretty much agree with all of this. Somehow schooling needs to embody the modern canon, which is one of sustained effort to advance the frontiers of knowledge. Despite considerable differences, I think there is a common impulse in the contributions of Carus, Wells, Scardamalia, and myself, toward a kind of education attuned to the modern dynamism. We have provided different perspectives—philosophical, semiotic, psychological, anthropological—on what may or may not prove to be the same object. We cannot tell for sure from the accounts given, much less synthesize a coherent description of the whole object. It is early days, but it does look as if an important shift is taking place in what it means to be an educated person. First there was the educated person as the embodiment of an inherited high culture. Along about the time of Sputnik came the realization that education must adapt to the continual advancement of knowledge. 'Lifelong learning', which earlier meant a lifetime devoted to absorbing the riches of the past, now took on the added (or alternative) meaning of keeping up with progress. With the coming, whether imaginary or not, of the 'new economy' driven by innovation, a whole new level of expectation is introduced: The educated person of the twenty-first century is one who can help create progress, not merely keep up with it.

Making It Happen

My target article had little to say about how to bring about the educational change it advocated or indeed what a knowledge-building approach to education would be like. The chapters by Wells and Scardamalia partly remedy this lack, but they too stop well short of how-to-do-it advice. What they do convey, however, is how formidable a job of change is required.

'Systemic change' is the well-chosen label for what is required (Smith and O'Day 1991). There is an interlocking, self-perpetuating system comprising regulations, curriculum guidelines, textbook adoption procedures, achievement tests, credentialing, teacher education, and teacher development that constitute institutionalized stupidity, or what Harriet Tyson-Bernstein (1988) more charitably termed "a conspiracy of good intentions." In order to succeed, systemic change has to reach down into the classroom, and in order for systemic change to occur there, a radical shift has to occur in how teachers conceive of their jobs. From their earliest preservice training to the workshops and teacher's guides that are supposed to advance their professional development, teachers are encouraged to believe that their job is to enact procedures that result in learning. Procedures become the focus. Ideas serve to justify procedures rather than procedures serving to implement ideas.

Project-based learning, hands-on learning, process-writing, strategy instruction, whole language, cross-curriculum integration, and teaching for multiple intelligences are all currently degraded practices that came about when an idea of some merit was reduced to procedures. Once the idea is reduced to procedures, two things happen. The procedures take on a life of their own, come to be valued in their own right, and evolve in ways that drift away from the original idea. The more serious consequence, however, is that criticism and efforts at improvement focus on the procedures and the original idea fails to undergo criticism and improvement. That can happen with knowledge building as much as with any other idea, unless it can somehow be saved from the degenerative effects of proceduralization.

Wells's quotations from teachers show how much has to be overcome in order to break loose from procedures, including supposedly progressive ones, and to confront the realities of the intellectual life of a classroom community. The fundamental shift, as I see it, is from managing the activities of the classroom to transforming its intellectual life. Of course, teachers must continue to manage classroom activities. Much of what has gone by names such as progressive education and child-centered education 'consists of changing the style of management so as to provide more scope for student initiatives. Such loosening of authority has proved troublesome enough, but it is nothing compared to turning the classroom into a community in which the students themselves begin to assume responsibility for its intellectual life—for raising its collective intelligence, as Scardamalia says; for advancing the 'state of knowledge', as that term is understood in the learned disciplines.

The teachers in DICEP perceptively pointed out to Wells the difficulty they were having in creating knowledge building communities because they had never experienced such a community themselves. This is the basic 'can't get there from here' problem of all utopian schemes, and we must face up to the fact that the idea of schools as knowledge building communities is utopian. In order to 'get there', people need, first of all, concepts that make the utopian ideas discussible in realistic terms. That is what much of the discourse in this book is about. Secondly, they need images—images of the possible that are strong enough to hold firm against the degenerative forces of reduction to procedures. Wells and Scardamalia provide glimpses; but compelling images would require a different kind of book from this—or, better perhaps, a multimedia document devoted to making such images clear and memorable.

Finally, teachers need something concrete to take the place of recipes. Scardamalia's chapter offers reason to believe that the right kind of technology may provide this. That is, the technology may provide tools, supports, channels of communication, a kind of environment in which teachers and students can bootstrap a classroom culture different from anything they have previously experienced. An important question is the extent to which software to support a new educational vision needs to embody that vision. There is no logical requirement that it do so. The sculptor's chisel does not have to embody a vision of the statue. However, it seems to me that a if a technology is to stand a chance against the 'conspiracy of good intentions' it has to consist of more than neutral tools. Like Knowledge Forum, it needs to have a very strong pedagogical bias—yet it must not proceduralize or micromanage the learning process, lest it become itself part of the 'conspiracy'.

The idea of 'collective cognitive responsibility' advanced by Scardamalia can help to clarify some of the ideas at issue in this conference. When I suggest that classrooms should become "workshops for the production of knowledge," this may bring to mind the image of children at their desks stitching away like so many little tailors in a garment factory. That is an altogether wrong image, and it is not much improved by introducing notions of co-operation or collaboration. What is missing is a common mission, shared by teacher and students alike, the success of which counts for something beyond the achievements of individual students. Although it may be expressed differently for different audiences, what the knowledge-building mission comes down to is making the world more intelligible. Improving one's personal knowledge and competence is a different, though complementary task, and one that can benefit from participation in collaborative knowledge building. It is work in World 2, whereas collective cognitive responsibility, as I construe it, has to do with work in World 3. Both are important in education, but traditionally no distinction is made and the result is an often dreary amalgam in which the student's responsibility is limited to carrying out tasks that the teacher believes will result in the desired learning. Scardamalia and I discuss the World 2 aspect of cognitive responsibility in an article on 'intentional cognition', attached as an appendix to this volume. Its concern is with the student's development of a mental life. The work Scardamalia reports on collective cognitive responsibility is concerned with students' contributions to advancing the state of knowledge in their community. Both of these figure in Carus's treatment of moral expertise and the canon. You can, as you prefer, regard them as two sides of the same coin, as the same task carried on at two different levels, or as complementary work in two worlds; what matters is that the two not be allowed to settle into the conceptual sludge of turn-of-the-century pedagogy.

Extending the Limits

One legitimate concern about liberal education is that it seems to represent a timeless pedagogy, which is from time to time applied to new content. The tacit assumption, accordingly, is that pedagogy is not one of those disciplines, like medicine and engineering, that has a leading edge, that keeps advancing the limits of what it is able to do. Rather, education is like politics and law, professions that do their work well or badly and that are sometimes in need of reform, that occasionally sport innovations, but that have no internal dynamic that generates progress.

The past century has seen wave after wave of educational reforms that gathered energy for a while and then lost it. If we ignore the counter-reforms and look at those that struck people as new and exciting, we find that almost always the perceived novelty lay in a more enlightened and humane way of carrying on the process of education. It was not perceived as extending the limits of the possible. Yet what we find and indeed have come to demand in most other aspects of modern life is a continual expansion of the possible. We expect cures for the previously incurable, travel to the previously unreachable, explanations of the previously incomprehensible, and low-cost versions of the previously unaffordable. To a large extent these expectations are being met. But not only has this failed to occur in education, it has not even occurred to people to look for it. People cannot imagine what an extension of the limits of the possible in education would mean. I believe the work that casts students as legitimate creators of knowledge is the first in a very long time to be seriously trying to extend the limits. If it succeeds—and the indications so far are positive—this may finally herald a reform that can survive.

References

Bereiter, C. 2002. *Education and Mind in the Knowledge Age*. Mahwah, NJ: Erlbaum.

Bereiter, C. and M. Scardamalia, M. 1993. *Surpassing Ourselves: An Inquiry into the Nature and Implications of Expertise*. La Salle, IL: Open Court.

Berger, P.L., and T. Luckmann, T. 1967. *The Social Construction of Reality*. Garden City, NY: Doubleday.

Bloor, D. 1998. The Strong Program in the Sociology of Science. In R. Klee, ed., *Scientific Inquiry: Readings in the Philosophy of Science* (New York: Oxford University Press), pp. 241–250.

Cobb, P., K. Gravmeijer, E. Yackel, K. McClain, and J. Whitenack. 1997. Mathematizing and Symbolizing: The Emergence of Chains of Significance in One First-grade Classroom. In D. Kirshner and J.A. Whitson, eds., *Situated Cognition: Social, Semiotic, and Psychological Perspectives* (Mahwah, NJ: Erlbaum), pp. 151–233.

Kuhn, T. 1970. *The Structure of Scientific Revolutions*. Chicago: University of Chicago Press.

Moursund, D. 1999. *Project-based Learning Using Information Technology*. Eugene, OR: International Society for Technology in Education.

Nonaka, I. and H. Takeuchi. 1995. *The Knowledge Creating Company*. New York: Oxford University Press.

Ohlsson, S. 1991. *Young Adults' Understanding of Evolutionary Explanations: Preliminary Observations*. Tech. Rep. to OERI. Pittsburgh: University of Pittsburgh, Learning Research and Development Laboratory.

———. 1993. Abstract Schemas. *Educational Psychologist* 28(1), 51–61.

Popper, K.R. and J.C. Eccles. 1977. *The Self and Its Brain*. Berlin: Springer.

Rifkin, J. 1995. *The End of Work: The Decline of the Global Labor Force and the Dawn of the Post-Market Era*. New York: Tarcher/Putnam.

Simonton, D.K. 1999. *Origins of Genius: Darwinian Perspectives on Creativity*. New York: Oxford University Press.

Smith, M.B. and J. O'Day. 1991. Systemic School Reform. *The Politics of Curriculum and Testing*, 233–267.

Tyson-Bernstein, H. 1988. *A Conspiracy of Good Intentions*. Washington, DC: Council for Basic Education.

Whitehead, A.N. 1929. *The Aims of Education*. New York: Macmillan.

Appendix

Schooling and the Growth of Intentional Cognition: Helping Children Take Charge of Their Own Minds*

Carl Bereiter and Marlene Scardamalia

The following essay was composed during the early 1980s and is presented unaltered, except for the updating of references. The ideas set out here were developed under the happiest conditions of anything we have written together—sitting in the garden of a beautiful and almost empty hotel in Fortin de Los Flores, Mexico. Bushels of gardenias were scattered over the pool every morning and raked out when they wilted. In addition to the delights of tropical flora, we also had a ready supply of research subjects in the form of children who would climb over the wall at our beckoning and respond eagerly to questions that occurred to us as we deliberated.

We were trying to solve a specific, though large, educational problem. In our research on writing and reading we had become impressed with how reliably most students settled on strategies that minimize thinking. These are fine strategies for meeting the immediate demands of schooling, but unfortunate from the standpoint of educational development. Some students, however, appeared to have a higher agenda of their own that took them beyond the demands of

---

*This paper, originally published in Hebrew as Bereiter and Scardamalia 1983, is published here for the first time in English.

schooling. They displayed what we came to call 'intentional cogni-tion'—something more than 'self-regulated learning', more like the active pursuit of a mental life. The problem we were trying to solve was how to foster intentional cognition. This is the problem that sub-sequently motivated the design of CSILE—Computer Supported Intentional Learning Environments—the source of the Knowledge Forum *software described in Chapter 4 of this volume.*

The addition of the word 'environment' is important, because it was this idea that led us into the unfamiliar world of software devel-opment. The focus of 'Schooling and the Growth of Intentional Cognition' is on individual cognition. The importance of the social environment is considered, but only as it affects the individual learner. The development of CSILE grew partly out of recognition that the structure of classroom life and particularly of classroom dis-course militated against intentional cognition. But it also grew out of the belief that the students themselves represented a resource that was largely wasted and that could be brought into play through network technology. This proved true beyond anything we had imagined. As we observed what was happening, we began to realize that the class-room, as a community, could have a mental life that was not just the aggregate of individual mental lives but something that provided a rich context within which those individual mental lives took on new value. That is not an original concept, of course. It is what people talk about when they talk about the intellectual life of ancient Athens or Bloomsbury or the Vienna Circle. Intentional cognition in individual students remains a focus, because it is as individuals that students go out into the world; but collective responsibility for the creation of community knowledge has proved to be a powerful way of fostering this individual trait, as well as generating knowledge of value to the group. We now see signs of a larger effect: the development of a desire in students to recreate a knowledge building culture in new settings. It is on this that we might base the hope of someday having a knowl-edge-building society.

Between the dependent state of infancy and the autonomous state of the free adult lies a process of internal development in which schooling is supposed to play a role. That role remains ambiguous, however, partly because we still have such a weak understanding of the internal development process by which children become able to function as adults in the full psychological sense. We understand in some depth what happens in the course of development to children's knowledge and to their capacities for reasoning and comprehension, but we do not yet have a coherent understanding of what regulates the use of these capacities. Certainly there is a difference between being able to think logically about a problem that happens to capture one's interest and being able to think logically about a problem that one has autonomously *decided* warrants attention, and this difference would seem to have a great deal to do with intellectual maturity—but it is precisely this dimension of intellectual maturity about which so little is understood. This is the dimension which, in this paper, we shall refer to as the development of *intentional cognition*.

We see the development of intentional cognition as a profound, even revolutionary change, altering one's whole relationship to the external environment. Its importance shows up most dramatically if we consider adults who have failed to achieve intentional cognition. They go through life looking for the thing that will interest them, that will give meaning to their lives. They may look outside, search for places, activities, people that will bring meaning to them, or they may look inside, searching for meaning and purpose in the ideas that rise spontaneously from memory. But in any case they are trying to *find*, not create. Life is altogether different to people who have succeeded in taking charge of their own minds. To them the world presents conditions ('boundary' conditions) within which it is their job to construct meanings and to formulate and pursue goals. Thus, objective conditions in the world are neither meaningful nor meaningless to the intentionally cognizing person. They are simply sources of constraint on the meanings that are created through one's own mental efforts.

In the absence of a clear understanding of what intentional cognition is and how it develops, opposing viewpoints of a more-or-less philosophical nature have grown up. In educational thought these appear as, on the one hand, a traditional viewpoint that emphasizes the building up of knowledge and skills for future intentional use and, on the other hand, what is most commonly called the child-centered viewpoint, which emphasizes the direct experience of autonomy.

Both of these are reasonable approaches so long as one is obliged to treat the child's developing mind as a black box. We know what we want to come out of the box—independent thought, self-directed learning, willingness to tackle problems, and so on. We want to feed things into the box that will yield these desired outputs. Knowing nothing about the mechanism that converts inputs to outputs, we have two reasonable choices. One is to feed in constituents of the desired product. In this case, this means feeding in general knowledge, logic skills, moral principles, etc.—all the elements that may be discerned in the mental activity of mature adults. The other choice is to nurture whatever appears to be an embryonic form of the desired outcome. In this case it means nurturing the child's curiosity, interests, self-assertiveness, and the like.

During recent years cognitive science, neuropsychology, and developmental psychology have been making advances toward understanding the workings of the black box, including its developmental workings. By developmental workings we mean the internal processes by means of which the functioning of the black box itself evolves over time. Only a small part of research has been focused on how the mind gains voluntary control over its own workings. Nevertheless, this research, taken together with research on related topics such as the growth of metacognition (Brown 1978; Flavell 1979), provides enough substance that we can begin to construct a picture of what intentional cognition is and some plausible conjectures about how it develops.

On the basis of this growing knowledge, it is becoming clear that neither the traditional nor the child-centered approaches are very satisfactory, that in fact they share common and serious faults. Our aim in this paper is to give a provisional account of intentional cognition and its role in human development. On the basis of this account we will then offer a critique of current educational practice and sketch the outlines of a new kind of education which has as its main goal helping children develop a mental life constructed by their own intentional cognitive efforts.

What is Intentional Cognition?

Intentional cognition may be defined in brief as *the voluntary direction of mental effort*. Both of the main terms in this definition need elaboration in order for the concept itself to come alive. Let us start with *mental effort*. Although what mental effort actually is remains quite a speculative issue in psychology (see, for instance, Kahneman 1973 and Pribram 1976), we can, for a start at least, be content with the everyday meaning of the term. Mental effort is perceptible and even schoolchildren appear to be able to judge how much effort they have had to exert in performing deductions of differing complexity (Osherson 1975). You can easily detect the difference in effort between mentally adding 79 to 79 and mentally multiplying the two numbers. You may even fail at the latter task, not because you don't know how to multiply but because the task of keeping all the operations and intermediate results in mind gets to be too much.

The direction of mental effort can be voluntary or involuntary, much like the blink of an eye. That is, we can decide to exert mental effort or it can be engaged by events outside our control. Suppose you are involved in a mental task such as trying to compose an essay. You are exerting considerable mental effort, which is being voluntarily directed to the task. Then someone nearby turns on the radio to a newscast. Even though you have no intention of listening to the news report, you find your attention being drawn to it involuntarily. The proof that it is usurping mental effort is that you are no longer able to focus as much effort on the writing task. You may even find yourself exerting mental effort to *ignore* the radio.

There is a difficult conceptual problem in understanding intentional cognition. By the end of this paper we hope the problem will be overcome. At this point we shall only try to signal what the problem is and offer a few leads in the direction of clarification. The problem is to understand that intentional cognition is not simply concentration or thinking hard. It involves concentration and thinking, but it is special in two ways:

1. Intentional cognition is concentrating or thinking as a voluntary act *separate from or in addition to other voluntary acts in which one may be engaged at the same time.*

2. Intentional cognition involves the allocation of *spare mental capacity*—capacity not automatically engaged by ongoing activity.

That intentional cognition is not simply concentration is easy to show. Someone captivated by a spectacle is concentrating, but the concentration is obviously not directed voluntarily. 'I couldn't take my eyes off it', or words to that effect, express the involuntary nature of such concentration. That intentional cognition is not simply thinking hard is more difficult to show because now the contrast is between two kinds of intentional behavior rather than between one kind that is intentional and one kind that is not.

Let us try one example and then leave the idea to gestate for a while. Imagine a salesman trying very hard to make a sale. He is concentrating and he is thinking intently. But we say he is not engaged in intentional cognition. His thinking and his concentrating are in no way separate from or additional to his trying to make the sale. Trying to make the sale totally consumes the salesman's mental capacity, just as the exciting spectacle totally consumes the mental capacity of the person in our other example. Neither person has any leftover capacity for mental effort that can be directed voluntarily. It is this discretionary mental capacity, not taken up by ongoing activities, that creates the possibility for intentional cognition.

Intentional cognition is only possible, therefore, when mental capacity is not fully occupied by other activities. Idleness and routine tasks make it possible, but so do many other activities that take up some but not all of our mental efforts.

Most activities of daily life seem to be of this latter kind. Whether driving a car, waiting on customers, or even teaching a class, we usually have at least some mental capacity left for discretionary use. We may exert no intentional control, thus leaving the spare portion of our attention free to be captured by external stimuli or stray associations. Perhaps we may direct our mental effort toward something entirely apart from the ongoing activity, but this is usually possible only with mentally undemanding tasks like driving a car or digging a garden. A third and very important option is to direct surplus mental effort back to the task itself. Such effort may go either into extracting general knowledge from the particular experience or into transforming one's task performance to a different plane.

In every skilled activity from tennis to operatic singing, one finds the top-level performers saying that concentration is everything and that a performer has to be thinking quickly all the time. These are people skillful enough that even without special concentration and thought they would far excel the struggling amateur. But they are directing mental effort into doing still better and they have to direct that effort intentionally. The task itself—playing the tennis match or singing the aria—does not automatically mobilize those mental efforts. In fact, these top-level performers are subject themselves to periodic losses of concentration, when they slip back into responding to demands of the context rather than superimposing their intentions on those demands. In more ordinary context we may all be aware of the sense of being 'on top of' some activity, meaning that we have successfully invested spare mental resources in planning ahead, anticipating problems, attending to details and nuances, or keeping in mind the extended context of the activity. This sort of intentional cognitive activity not only enhances our performance at the moment but, perhaps more importantly, leads to further growth in competence. Tennis stars and opera stars, we may assume, do not adopt intentional cognition as a finishing touch to their expertise. Rather, they became stars in part because of intentional cognition—through continually investing spare mental capacity back into the performance.

We suspect that a similar principle may be involved in the normal course of cognitive development. In learning to add, for instance, children will normally proceed, without instruction from a teacher, through a series of increasingly sophisticated methods. At the start they will use a primitive method of finger-addition in which they add four and three, for instance, by counting out four fingers, counting out three fingers, holding them together, and then recounting the combined set. Later they will move to a more efficient but mentally demanding method in which they don't recount, but simply count on from four ('five, six, seven'). Neches (1979) has asked what causes children to move from one method to another, given that the more primitive method works. Neches suggested that the child may work according to a principle of least effort, favoring strategies that involve fewer operations. There is a problem with this explanation, however, since typically the new strategy requires more, not less effort during the early stages of its adoption. It seems that an essential element in children's progress toward more sophisticated strategies must be the reinvestment of mental effort back into activities that have started to become habitual. Thus, the child who becomes practiced in the primitive count and recount method of addition soon becomes able to do it without a total commitment of mental resources. If the spare resources are allowed to remain idle, then of course the child will not progress but will continue—as a few do—to use the primitive method. But if the resources are turned back into examining the activity, then it is likely that sooner or later a child will notice, when recounting fingers, 'Hey, I've already counted this first bunch of fingers once. There were four last time and I know there will be four again. I shouldn't have to do this part twice.' From this insight the child proceeds to experimentation that leads to the more streamlined counting-on method. But the implicit 'logic' of the child's behavior is not guided by the principle of minimizing effort. It is guided by a drive to put spare mental resources to use. Since the primitive method of counting, though simple, does not allow mental resources to be directed to something altogether different, they get directed back to the activity and finally lead to transforming it.

Intentional Cognition and Metacognitive Knowledge

In a landmark cognitive study, Bloom and Broder (1950) examined university students who were generally capable at academic work buy who were poor at solving test problems. They found that most of these students took a passive stance toward the problems. They would read a problem and then wait for something to occur to them. If nothing did, they would declare they didn't know how to solve the problem. A similar finding comes from Flower and Hayes's (1980) comparisons of expert and novice writers. Given a writing assignment, the expert writers would set about planning what they wanted to do, considering what difficulties the assignment entailed and how to overcome them. On the whole they directed their own behavior in a vigorous and purposeful way. The novices, on the other hand, appeared to depend on the assignment to tell them what to do; when they were stuck they would go back and reread the assignment, hoping it would give them some further direction.

In both of these studies we see the less competent people relying on the context to direct their behavior—the context in each case being some written assignment—whereas the more competent people appear to be directing their own cognitive behavior, using the context merely as an information source. Thus one aspect of the behavior of the less competent people was a lack of intentional cognition.

But another dimension stands out in these adult examples. The novices truly don't know what to do. It isn't just that the novice writers don't know what to write. They don't know what to *think about* in order to figure out what to write. Similarly for the problem-solvers studied by Bloom and Broder. We have posed problems to early adolescents and watched them go through the facial contortions normally associated with intense thought, only to find that on subsequent questioning they could not report anything having gone on in their minds. By their own accounts, thinking was synonymous with waiting—waiting for an insight or an idea or a pertinent recollection.

Evidently these 'novice thinkers' suffer under two related handicaps. First, they lack conscious awareness of their mental processes—and some awareness would seem to be essential if one is to direct the processes intentionally. Second, they lack strategies, conscious or unconscious, for carrying out mental tasks.

These lacks are ones which, in current psychological language, may be termed *metacognitive*. Metacognition in its broadest sense has been defined as "knowledge that takes as its object or regulates any aspect of any cognitive endeavor." (Flavell 1978). Thus the 'novice thinkers' could be said to lack, on the one hand, metacognitive knowledge *of* thinking and, on the other hand, metacognitive skill or *know-how* related to thinking.

Many of the issues we have dealt with under the rubric of intentional cognition have been approached by other investigators via the concept of metacognition (see especially Brown and Campione 1981, which intersects the present discussion at numerous points). When approached in this way, the development of intentional cognition is seen as a matter of acquiring strategies for directing cognitive activity. The passive learner or thinker is not thought of as lacking drive or inclination but as lacking knowledge necessary for self-directed learning or thinking.

Metacognition is a label for one aspect of intentional cognition, the knowledge aspect. While it is possible to do important work on just this one aspect, we believe that an educationally useful theory will have to embrace other aspects of intentional cognition as well. These include the motivational aspect, the affective aspect, the allocation-of-resources aspect, and the ecological aspect. In this paper we try, in a preliminary way, to show how all these aspects are related and how they form the facets of what could develop into a coherent theory of intentional cognition.

Within a coherent theory of intentional cognition, metacognition will stand, not as an explanation, but as something to be explained. How do we acquire knowledge of our own mental processes? Without wishing to diminish the importance of this question, we must say that it is only a part of the larger question of how we develop a mental life—a conscious life of mental activity superimposed on the life of action in concrete contexts. It is to this larger question that we turn, therefore, in the following sections.

Mental Life as Super-Context

Human beings learn through participation in various contexts and spheres of action. Home, street, workplace, supermarket, bank, airliner, the faceless but nonetheless real world of bill-paying—these are a few of the many contexts with which one must become intimate in order to function as a modern adult. People caught in unfamiliar contexts, such as a person taking an airline trip for the first time, will blunder, hesitate, and act not quite right in a dozen ways that people familiar with the context never even think about. Newcomers to a behavioral context are therefore liable to be judged as stupid. By the same token, people behaving in a context that is much more familiar to them than it is to the observer are likely to be admired for their mental powers. The natives who know just where the fish are, the bank clerk who can talk to someone while counting bills, amaze us with their virtuosity. No doubt a Rip van Winkle, awaking after 80 years, would find the ability of ordinary citizens to propel automobiles along crowded traffic ways at high speeds equally amazing.

It is virtually axiomatic that learning tends to be tied to the context in which it was acquired. Psychological research on mental set, functional fixedness, and transfer has documented the frequent failure of people to take knowledge gained in one context and apply it in another where it would be useful. Numerous educational experiments have shown the same for school learning. Students who had studied scientific method demonstrated a grasp of it on test problems given in the class where they had studied it, but failed to demonstrate it if similar problems were given in a different class (Price 1968).

Still, as educated moderns we would like to think that we have a great deal of knowledge that we can apply in varied contexts—scientific knowledge, mathematical knowledge, social knowledge, and even just a kind of common sense that seems to provide us with guides to reasonable action in most situations. How do we acquire such generalizable knowledge? Schools are often given the credit, but there is nothing automatically generalizable about school learning. School itself is a behavioral context and what is learned there, though universal in theory, is in fact often of little application outside the school context itself.

We want to argue that our attainment of generalizable knowledge is not a simple matter at all but that it depends on a great deal of mental effort *expended in a context created by that effort itself*. To explain this idea we need to develop further the notion of behavioral contexts or spheres of action.

Contexts overlap, so that a person is normally functioning in more than one context at a time. The factory context is also a social context, so that when one is learning to function in the factory one is also learning something about getting along with other people, and this knowledge will have application outside the factory because the social context is larger than the factory context. It seems that, in order to give coherence to their lives, people need a super-context that embraces all the other contexts in which they function. In traditional cultures this super-context has been the life of the community, typically actualized in the form of religion. Thus in traditional cultures it was often the case that everything a person did was, at one and the same time, a practical action in some concrete context, and a religious act within the all-encompassing super-context. (See, for instance, Huizinga's *The Waning of the Middle Ages* [1954] for a portrayal of this kind of life in medieval Europe.)

While this traditional super-context provided coherence it did not provide for transfer of knowledge across contexts, except perhaps for moral knowledge. But it is in the nature of traditional societies that such transfer was little needed. Social contexts and people's roles within them remained stable enough that there was seldom danger of finding one's self in a novel situation where knowledge would have to be drawn from remote contexts.

In such stable situations intentional cognition is not needed either. In familiar contexts, as Cole (1979) points out, the structure of the ongoing activity and the actions of other people in the situation structure your cognitive behavior for you. You do not have to direct your own mental effort. This is not to say that problems never occur, but that they occur as part of the activity that one is familiar with. You may have to think, perhaps even think very cleverly and hard, but you don't have to think about thinking. You don't have to pay attention to how your mental resources are being used.

All this changes when we enter the fragmented and unstable life of modern societies. First of all, there is no over-arching community or religious life in which all other contexts are embedded. (There are exceptional communities and exceptional times, when people join in a common cause, but these serve to point up the more typical fragmentation.) Thus there is no external structuring to relate action in one context to action in another. At the same time, the need for knowledge that can be transferred from one context to another is acute. There are so many contexts that a modern person must be able to function in, and they are so changeable, that it is quite impossible for a person to develop sufficient expertise in a natural way, by 'growing into' behavioral contexts. One has to develop a general sort of sophistication that allows one to function with some competence from the beginning and to learn quickly in new contexts. How is this generalizable competence attained?

The modern adult, we believe, creates his or her own super-context, a super-context which performs the integrating function of the communal super-context of traditional societies but which in addition makes possible flexible adaptation to new situations. This super-context is the person's own mental life.

We do not intend the term 'mental life' to be taken as a mere figure of speech. We see the mental lives of people as being perfectly real, though immaterial, just as the religious lives of traditional people were perfectly real to them, though immaterial. Just as, to the traditional villager, every practical act was at the same time an act with a different kind of meaning in the person's religious life, so to the modern adult events in concrete contexts are at the same time events with a different kind of significance in the person's mental life.

Take a concrete example. You go to sharpen the blade on a rotary lawn-mower. You notice that the blade is only sharpened near the ends. This fact becomes part of your lawn-mower knowledge. The fact makes sense in relation to your other lawn-mower knowledge because you reason that when you push the lawn mower ahead it is the ends of the blades that first come into contact with the grass, and so they are the only part that needs to be sharp. At the same time, however, you connect the fact to a rather vague idea you have to the effect that the outer points on a spinning body move faster than the points nearer the center. This idea applies to the lawn-mower blade, suggesting that the inner portions of the blade might be moving too slowly to cut effectively even if they were sharp. Thus you understand the lawn mower better. But at the same time the general idea about points on spinning bodies is clarified and made firmer in your mind so that it is more likely to be invoked another time. You might, for instance, at a later time see that it applied to phonograph records and thereby figure out, by drawing in yet other general principles, that fidelity should be greater in the outer bands than in the inner bands of a disc recording. But you might not have been able to figure this out, your hold on the general principle might have been too weak, if you had not had the prior experience with the lawn-mower blade.

This is a mundane example of the workings of intelligence. Our contention is that these things do not happen automatically. If they did they would occur more frequently and would not strike us as intelligent. Over and above the effort involved in dealing with the lawn-mower in its practical context was an effort that had nothing to do with lawn-mowers as such but that had to do with the construction of a general understanding of the world, framed in terms of scientific and logico-mathematical principles.

We call mental life a context because it is a sphere of purposeful action. The main activity that goes on in this context is building up and operating upon the store of generalized knowledge. Work is required to extract this knowledge from activity in concrete contexts, work is required to develop it into a self-consistent whole, and work is required to bring it into use in other concrete contexts.

As is true of any other context, work within the context leads to your coming to know the context intimately and to becoming skillful and clever at operating within it. Coming to know the context means acquiring metacognitive knowledge. You come to understand your own thought processes, to recognize when you are comprehending something and when you are not. Becoming skillful in the context means developing strategies for analyzing, planning, solving problems, etc.—strategies that are tied to abstract characteristics rather than to concrete cues. Thus, for instance, you become able to recognize and solve proportionality problems in all kinds of concrete contexts. Ability of this kind is what Inhelder and Piaget (1958) call formal operational thought, and which Donaldson (1978) argues is distinguished, not by the mental operations involved but by the fact that these operations can be performed without support from a concrete context. That is, the thinking that goes on within the mental life context is not fundamentally different from that which goes on in other contexts, it is simply applied to different objects and tasks.*

Consequently, people can be quite competent and clever in spheres of activity with which they are familiar and yet be quite inexperienced and inept in the context of mental life. Two major groups of people who fit this description are adults with little schooling or exposure to modern life and children of all kinds. Both groups demonstrate impressive competence in familiar situations and a great deal of recent cross-cultural and child development research shows that both groups demonstrate a full range of logical capabilities when tasks are put into a concrete form suitable to their habits (Cole and Scribner 1974; Donaldson 1978; Odom 1978). But both groups appear unable to handle problems removed from a familiar concrete context. Both unschooled adults and young children, in fact, show a distinct unwillingness to treat general statements as truly general, so that their reasoning is not only context-bound, but is focused on particular instances (see Piaget 1928; Scriber 1979).

---

* [Note added in 2002] A further development of the idea of a mental context or 'contextual module' and the mental resources it employs, as well as the role of such contexts or modules in learning and cognition, is to be found in Bereiter 1985; 1990.

We call mental life a super-context because it extends over most of the other contexts of life. You function in this context at the same time that you function in other contexts.

It appears that many people, even schooled adults in modern societies, do not develop much of a mental life. They acquire knowledge and skills in various contexts, but their competence and understanding are largely confined to particular contexts. Evidence for this belief comes from research showing that many adults (possibly a majority) do not achieve the generalized competence represented in Piaget's stage of formal logical operations, even though they manifest various of the logical operations involved in some situations (Gallagher and Mansfied 1980). Kitto (1951) would have it that a conscious mental life, in which thought is deliberately applied to knowledge and to thought itself, was an invention of the Greeks. Whether or not this is true, it seems clear that a conscious mental life is not an automatic consequence of possessing human intelligence but is a construction achieved through directed effort. Throughout much of human history it was possible to live a successful and well-integrated life without paying much attention to the contents and operations of one's mind. Now, when it becomes important for people to make of their own minds a workplace, we find many failing to do so, and we find educators unable to help them.

Intentional Cognition, Affect, and Creativity

"Nothing great in the world is achieved without passion," said Hegel. One of the weaknesses of cognitive process theories in general is that they have trouble accommodating notions of affect and motivation. They thus convey the impression of human beings as dispassionate information processing machines. Everyone— including cognitive psychologists, of course—knows that we aren't like that.

Introducing the idea of intentional cognition is a step in the direction of humanizing the entity created by cognitive theory. It attributes to the human being a purposefulness that is not the purposefulness of a programmed robot, but rather a purposefulness that is learned and that is achieved only with effort. As we have seen, it leads to the conception of a mental life superimposed on the life of context-bound activity. This notion of a mental life in turn attributes a wholeness to human cognition which is quite different from the picture we may otherwise get of a creature that acts one way in one context, another way in another, much like a computer which, when it switches from one program to another, shows no trace of its former behavior.

We have, however, been emphasizing the ideational side of mental life and it is time now to expand the picture. Action within the mental life context is not an abstraction from experience but is real human experience, which is always emotional as well as rational. To present a fuller picture we must shift our focus to a more biological level and see how affect is involved in cognition.

Any understanding of cognition at the biological level has to start with the issue of selective attention. The body is a mass of sense organs sending continual messages to the brain. Only by a highly selective attention to these messages can the mind possibly function in an organized way. This is as true of the mind of the infant as it is of the mind of the adult. When William James said the world of the infant is a "booming, buzzing confusion," he was making a plausible guess from an adult point of view, but mountains of research have since shown him to be wrong. From day one children are selective in what they attend to. What changes as they mature is the basis for selection.

Selective attention appears to go on at three different levels.[1] The first is instinctual, depending on response patterns built into the nervous system. Thus we have attention to touch, loud noises, and looming movements occurring even in early infancy. The second is the level of learned significance, and this is the level where affect comes in. This level depends on a brain system that compares the incoming messages to stored memories. But just as there are many messages, there are also many memories, and so a selection on the basis of relative significance still has to be made. We are talking here about a nearly instantaneous selection, however, not one arrived at through a slow process of judgment. The basis of selection at this level appears to be affect. The messages that com-

---

1. This discussion of selective attention draws on Luria 1973, Pribram 1976, and Wilke 1977.

mand immediate attention are messages that produce strong emotional reactions, positive or negative. Thus, a message associated with something we have learned to fear or like will be attended to before a message associated with something that is emotionally more neutral. The third level is the level of intentions and readiness. This level, which involves the highest brain systems, enables us to attend to messages that we have decided to attend to or ones which are part of some larger message complex which we have already started to attend to. As an example of the latter, this system allows us to attend to the end of a sentence that someone is uttering when we have already attended to the beginning, even though other people may be speaking at the same time (the 'cocktail party phenomenon', analyzed at length in Norman 1976).

Intentional cognition enters at the third level. We are most aware of it when it is competing with the emotionally-dominated attention at the second level—as when we resolutely try to attend to a lecture while affect keeps pulling our attention toward some person in the next row or toward some worry that keeps rising up out of memory. In such instances intentional cognition provides a check on emotionality, thus making possible a more rational control of behavior.

Equally important, however, and perhaps more common is *co-operation* between levels of selective attention. Co-operation is nowhere better demonstrated than in the realm of creativity. This is where Hegel's maxim applies, that nothing great is achieved without passion. Genuine creative endeavor seems to be marked by a maximum *both* of intentional cognition *and* of emotional involvement in the objects of cognition.

As it can be distilled from numerous personal reports, an extended process of creative thought goes like this: you decide on a project, which may be a problem to solve, an idea to develop, a novel to write, etc. You voluntarily direct mental effort to this project, overriding other concerns that might have an immediate affective appeal. This is intentional cognition of an obvious kind. But soon the project acquires an affective appeal of its own. Now you can't help thinking about it. Sometimes you wake up thinking about it. Chance events keep reminding you of it or suggesting ideas relevant to it. You become, to a degree, obsessed. Now the creative endeavor no longer sounds just like intentional cognition. Indeed, it may be out of voluntary control, so that even if you decide you should put the project aside and concentrate on something else for a while, you may find you can't stop thinking about it.

This obsessive character may mark the extreme case, but still it is important in raising the question of how intentional cognition, which at one point represents the ascendancy of reason over affect, can itself become emotionally driven to the point where it outweighs practical reason. The paradox disappears if we allow that any sort of mental context can acquire affective loading, including intentions and processes. We may deliberately set out to pursue a cognitive goal but our experiences along the way may be so aversive that eventually the negative affect becomes overwhelming and we can no longer succeed in directing mental effort toward the goal. This might be the case with mathematics phobia, for instance. On the other hand, experiences might be so positive (or the course of thought might bring together mental contents of such positive significance) that the project or process as a whole will become charged with favorable emotion. The benefits then become enormous. We no longer have to invest mental effort in staying "on task." Affect takes care of that. Therefore we have mental effort to spare for sub-goals that do require intentional cognition. Furthermore, the affect provides a continual sentinel ready to respond instantly to any message—whether from the environment or from the recesses of memory—which is associated with the project. It is by this means, we suspect, that the 'Eureka!' experiences, the sudden insights that appear to arise spontaneously without effort, come to the creative thinker (Hadamard 1945; Wallas 1926). Co-operation between affect and intentional cognition has the further advantage that the affective 'sentinels', since they respond to emotional rather than to rational connections, are likely to catch ideas that a purely rational search would overlook. Hence the unpredictable and seemingly inspired character of creative thought.

The idea of co-operation between affect and intentional cognition has implications beyond accounting for creativity, however. It has implications for why we have intentional cognition at all. We have over and over emphasized that intentional cognition involves exerting mental effort beyond what the immediate behavioral context requires or calls forth. Why do people exert this effort? The tangible rewards, if any, are remote and hard to predict.

Motivation is generally complex and we must seek its explanation not in simple variables but in the whole structure of the behavioral context. In the case of intentional cognition, this means looking for its motivation in the mental life context as a whole. We doubt if intentional cognition would persist were it not that its daily effect is perceptible growth in the richness and interconnectedness of the context in which it takes place. It is rather like building the house you are living in, which many people do with seemingly endless devotion. Building your own house of intellect is similarly a labor of love, and its daily increments are a source of joy even if the end never comes in sight.

We have been resorting to figurative language here, but we want to emphasize again that the mental life is a real context and the experiences one has in it are real experiences. Not in a simple way, but in the complex way that it suffuses all experience, affect becomes attached to all parts of our mental lives—to the contents and the processes, to everything from our highest purposes to the lowliest idea that we have forged through effort. The quality of this emotion-tinged experience will in the end determine for each of us the extent to which the mental life is a life worth living.

Meaning as Constructed versus Meaning as Given

The topic on which we do most of our empirical research is children's writing (see, for instance, Bereiter and Scardamalia 1982; Scardamalia 1981).* In the productions of serious and able writers one sees impressive evidence of intentional cognition at work, but for the most part the writing of school students shows little such evidence, even when the process is examined closely (Bereiter and Scardamalia 1982). Instead, school writing appears to be a kind of job carried out within the school context, which students gradually get better at doing, but the activity remains strictly context-bound and plays no part in their mental lives. Something of this sort is widely recognized by educators, and for years a main theme of edu-

---

* [Note added in 2002] Our many years of research in this area resulted in the book *The Psychology of Written Composition* (Bereiter and Scardamalia 1987).

cators concerned with writing has been the need to make school writing a more 'meaningful' activity for students (see, for instance, Moffet 1968 and Muller 1967).

Recently we began asking adults who are able (not necessarily gifted) writers to recall their school experiences. It was amazing, first of all, how vivid their recollections were. They remembered specific writing assignments, could recount the mental struggles they went through in figuring out how to approach the assignment, and some even claimed to recall verbatim passages of text they had created 25 years ago.

The assignments were nothing special and were certainly not ones that would qualify as 'meaningful' by present-day standards. One assignment, for instance, was simply to choose some species of bird from a list and write a paper about it. Yet doing this assignment was recalled by our informant as a meaningful, enjoyable, and significant experience in his development as a writer. How could this be?

What has emerged from our interviews so far is surprisingly consistent. The writing assignment was neither meaningful nor meaningless to these people as students. They did not look for meaning to reside in the assignment, nor did the assignment define their purpose. The assignment merely constituted one boundary condition on the task, just as for a professional writer the requirements that an article be no more than 4,000 words long or that it be completed by a certain date constitute boundary conditions which limit what can be done but do not in any way constitute the meaning of what is to be done. For these people *meaningfulness does not depend on external circumstances but instead is something constructed by themselves within limits set by external circumstances.*

Another way of saying this is that writing a composition is an activity that takes place within the context of school work. For students who are on their way to becoming able writers, however, the real purpose and meaning of composition do not come from this context but rather from the super-context of their mental lives. For students destined to remain poor or indifferent writers, writing is carried on only at the level of the school context and the only meaning it has is what comes out of that context—a meaning dependent, therefore, on the nature of the assignment and on the motivational conditions surrounding it. Critics often complain that school writing tasks have no authenticity, the only purpose in the eyes of students being to produce work that will please the teacher. That is clearly true of most students we have interviewed. It was apparently not true of the able writers we interviewed. They reported taking quite seriously the need to please the teacher, but again this did not define the meaning of the task, it was simply another boundary condition—a tacit part of the assignment, as it were. Curiously, this seemed to permit them to treat the teacher's needs more caringly than do students who see the teacher as defining the whole point of the activity.

We suspect that the same difference found in writing can be found in other school activities. Most students will address the activity only within the behavioral context of the school and so its meaning for them will be only the meaning it has within that context — as work to be done, as recreation, as a competition among classmates, as a significant sharing of experience, or whatever. We want to emphasize that within this school context—that is, within the school viewed as a little world of its own—the daily round of school activities may be very meaningful and satisfying to the participants. But the meaning arises directly from the participation. It requires no active construction, no special investment of mental effort on the part of the students.

At the same time there will be other students who, while participating in the social and work life of the school, are also continually at work constructing their mental lives. When a new fact or idea is encountered, its main significance does not lie in its relation to the ongoing lesson or 'project' or to a forthcoming examination. Its significance lies in its relation to what the student already knows and believes, to the structure of generalized knowledge which the student is daily revising and augmenting. For simplicity, let us call students of the first kind, for whom the meaning of school activities lies entirely in the school context, *participant learners*. Let us call students of the second kind, for whom the meaning of school activities lies mainly in how they relate to the students' active mental life, *intentional learners*.

Research by Karmiloff-Smith and Inhelder (1976) provides a graphic distinction between the two modes of learning. they engaged children in trying to balance blocks on a rail, some of the blocks being weighted in unusual ways so that the balancing point was not obvious. One approach of children was to focus totally on accomplishing the task, discovering and remembering the balance point of each block. This we would call participant learning: what is learned arises naturally out of the activity and its meaning resides in the block-balancing activity itself. Some children, however, became involved in constructing and testing theories about balancing points, so that the task of getting blocks to balance began to take a back seat to the task of discovering general rules that would work for all blocks. This kind of learning, which is not called for by the behavior context and which acquires meaning only in the context of the child's mental life, is what we call intentional learning.

We must now confront an alarming irony. Educational thought, along with contemporary culture in general, glorifies intentional learning and cognition. The 'inquiring mind', 'going beyond the information given', 'reflective thinking', 'self-motivated learning'— these and many other terms testify to the high place given to this sort of mental activity. And yet virtually the whole thrust of modernization in schools throughout this century has been directed toward enhancing participant learning instead!

Progressive education, under the intellectual leadership of John Dewey, was explicitly aimed at making all school learning arise as a consequence of natural behavior in the social environment of the school. Although this aim was never fully realized and was probably most of the time not even apprehended by practitioners, the major reforms that have occurred have tended in this direction. The social atmosphere of the school has been made more congenial. Activities are designed to have more immediate appeal to students. Fear of failure and avoidance of punishment have as much as possible been removed in favor of positive incentives for participation in the school enterprise. Above all, teachers have more and more taken on the responsibility of making school activities meaningful for students. Gone is the justification of 'because I say so', and in its place is justification of school activities that can be immediately appreciated by the students or, better yet, that will occur to them spontaneously. The result of all these reforms is to maximize participant learning, learning that comes about as a natural consequence of active involvement in the life of the school.

These reforms were certainly desirable, on both humane and practical grounds. It is hard to think seriously about turning any of them back. But what they add up to is an educational system that has very serious limitations. The following are four major limitations:

1. Participant learning makes intentional cognition unnecessary. Because the context provides directives to mental effort, students don't have to learn how to direct mental effort themselves. Consequently they don't really 'learn how to learn' or to take active control of their own minds. Children do learn how to memorize (Brown 1978; Rohwer 1973), which some people might take to indicate that memorizing is the main intellectual activity that goes on in schools. Instead, we would conjecture that of the many intellectual activities going on in schools, memorizing is the one intellectual activity that modern teachers are most likely to give the students the responsibility of accomplishing for themselves. When it comes to comprehension, criticism, application, composition, etc., the thrust of modern pedagogical technique is to arrange conditions that 'stimulate' and facilitate these processes as much as possible. This tends to take them outside the realm of processes that students can initiate and manage by themselves (Pascual-Leone et al. 1979, Scardamalia and Bereiter 1983).

2. Participant learning tends to be bound to the behavioral context in which it took place. This means that school learning of the participant type tends to be useful only in the school context. School learning has a great deal of *potential* generalizability, of course: that is the premise on which the very existence of schools is based. But in order to be generalizable in different contexts it needs the work of intentional learning. Students need to become familiar with and skillful in manipulating their own knowledge, and this is something that participant learning doesn't prepare them to do.

3. Meaningfulness that grows entirely out of the context of school life is precarious. Young children seem willing to accept almost any kind of school situation and school activity as 'real' and to participate wholeheartedly in it. If it is at the right level of difficulty for them and not too obnoxious, they will find almost any kind of school work meaningful. But as children grow up the contrived nature of the school world becomes more and more evident to them and it becomes increasingly difficult to convince them of the meaningfulness of what they are expected to do. Consequently they are likely to become rebellious or

indifferent. The fact is, of course, that school work isn't like other kinds of work. The garment worker produces a shirt that someone will wear. The student produces a page of worked exercises which, after being checked, will be thrown in the wastebasket. The only enduring meaning of school work is that which it has in the context of the student's mental life. But this kind of meaning is one which the teacher cannot bestow; it must be constructed by the student's own mental effort.

4. This brings us to the most important limitation of an educational system that strives always to manufacture meaningfulness for students. It deprives students of the chance to learn how to make things meaningful for themselves. A university student, discussing the dreariness of school writing assignments, recalls with gratitude one teacher who assigned an essay about bushmen, thus giving him the chance to do something 'creative'. We have found this passive attitude toward meaningfulness to be shared by most students. They are surprised and a bit frightened at the thought that meaning and creativity are for them to bestow on the task, not the task to bestow on them. The inability to create meaning seems to be crippling millions of young people today. Many of them become wanderers—from job to job, college to college, country to country—looking for the context in which action will become meaningful for them. A good many join fanatical religious or political sects in which they give over their whole intelligence to externally defined meanings. Many others simply acquiesce into a conventional role and try to rest satisfied with whatever meaning it bestows on their lives. But whether they rebel or conform, it is still meaning emanating from the external context that dominates their lives.

It would seem that the first responsibility of schools in the modern age should be to help students acquire the ability to construct meaning. But how can this be done in a positive and supporting way, so that all students benefit and not just the few who have managed to acquire elsewhere the necessary tendency toward intentional cognition? It seems that a new kind of schooling is required, and it is to this possibility that we now turn.

A New Progressivism

For decades educators have been talking about the need to prepare students for a world of rapid change, yet it is hard to imagine a worse way of going about it than the one that has prevailed.

Schools have evolved into little villages where a kind of work-play goes on which is its own reason for being. In this environment children do learn and think, but the learning and thinking depend on the work-play for guidance and motivation. We spend twelve years creating a sort of peasant and then catapult him into the modern world.

What a world of rapid change requires is knowledge that can be readily transported from one situation to another, an ability to direct our own mental processes instead of having them led hither and thither by external events, and an ability to construct goals and meanings of our own within boundaries set by external conditions instead of letting external conditions determine goals and meanings for us. Such a world, in short, requires an active, autonomous, well-developed mental life constructed through our own intentional cognition.

An education system that could foster such knowledge and abilities would truly deserve the label 'progressive'. But what kind of system would do this? We see all the current approaches to education as defective and, moreover, defective in essentially the same way. Whether child-centered or traditional in curriculum, whether emphasizing work for extrinsic rewards or emphasizing activity motivated by children's own interests, all the approaches aim to create some kind of behavioral context where meaning, purpose, and direction will inhere in the context. They all tend to minimize the need of children to construct mental lives of their own. But is there any other way by which schools can actually work?

Let us stop and remind ourselves that the main thing schools are suited for is imparting knowledge of high potential generalizability—the knowledge involved in literacy, mathematics, science, etc. Being isolated from the practical contexts of life, they are not very well suited to developing skills in the application of knowledge. Appreciation of this latter fact has led to a widespread movement in recent years toward getting students out of schools and into other contexts for learning (Bremer and von Moschzisker 1971; Coleman 1974). We endorse this movement, not only as beneficial to students but also as freeing the schools to focus effort more directly on that which they are equipped to do well (Bereiter 1972). But the movement could backfire, could lead to the creation of an urbanized peasantry, if the locus of all meaning gets shifted to the world 'out there'. We have seen this happen with student teachers who, for a while, judge every idea according to its immediate application in their teaching and thus become essentially ineducable.

The ideal situation would see a two-way relationship between the school and other behavior contexts. Students would bring experience in from other contexts and at school, through both private reflection and social interchange, they would process this experience into generalized and interconnected knowledge. At the same time, the mental life developed mainly at school would be extended as a super-context over all their other life, allowing them to bring greater knowledge and meaningfulness to all their activity in the world.

Although mental life is a private construction within the mind of each person, it has always been the case that it can only thrive in a social setting. Be it the school of Socrates, a medieval university, the salon of a wealthy patron of the intellect, a cafe frequented by thinkers, or simply a friendship involving a meeting of minds, some kind of social milieu seems to be required in which the context and processes of mental life are focal. The *autodidact*, alone in a library amassing evidence in support of his grandiose and logically flawed private theory, is a pathetic and familiar anomaly of mental life. (See, for instance, Sartre's portrayal of such a person in his novel *La Nausée*.) Even the most mindless classroom probably has some value as a milieu in which the development of mental life can go forward. At the very least, if teachers acquired an understanding of intentional cognition and its role in developing a mental life, they might help to provide a social atmosphere that was more supportive, in which individual efforts to construct meaning were made matters of mutual concern.

Right now the research worlds of educational psychology, cognitive science, and child development are in ferment, and much of the excitement has to do quite directly with people's abilities to direct their own mental processes and to operate on their own knowledge bases. Out of this ferment are beginning to emerge ideas about how schooling could foster development of an active mental life, but the ideas are not yet consolidated. Moreover, it seems that we should resist prematurely consolidating the ideas into a new educational 'ism', although we believe that a new 'ism' is definitely in the making.

Let us therefore look at the educational problem in miniature rather than on a grand scale. Davis and McKnight (1979), studying gifted young mathematical problem solvers, found that they tended to sit and think for some time *after* they had solved a problem. It seems likely, as Davis and McKnight conjecture, that during this period the students were converting the particular knowledge gained in the situation into generalized insights or strategies that they could use in other situations. Here, in miniature, is precisely what schools should be trying to foster. It is intentional cognitive activity. Nothing in the external context calls for it. Rather, its motivation and meaning come from the context of the student's mental life. And it leads to the kind of flexible and self-directed competence needed for a world of rapid change.

The difficulty of fostering this kind of mental behavior is immediately evident. That old stand-by, 'challenging students to think', will not work, because we are talking about something that goes on after or in addition to meeting the challenge. Exhortation cannot be expected to help much either, because students who have not experienced intentional cognition will have no way of knowing what they are being exhorted to do.

The educational task would probably look impossible were it not for evidence that children's natural inclinations dispose them toward intentional cognition. In our research on writing, an activity for which schoolchildren's motivation is typically not very high, we have been continually surprised at the eagerness with which children seize on any opportunity to gain a higher level of cognitive control over the process. This has encouraged us to believe that if ways can be found to put children in touch with intentional cognition they will show a readiness to use it.

One way of putting them in touch with unknown processes is by modelling them, through having people think aloud. Mardi Bird (Bereiter and Bird 1985) has obtained impressive results with this approach in getting adolescent students to employ more active cognitive strategies in their reading. She found, however, that simply demonstrating intentional cognition in reading and having students practice it by thinking aloud themselves was not effective. Direct instruction was also required to make students conscious of particular strategies and able to identify them. As cognitive processes come to be better understood, direct instruction ought be to become increasingly applicable.

Another method of promise is procedural facilitation (Bereiter and Scardamalia 1982; Scardamalia and Bereiter 1983). The idea of procedural facilitation is to help children gain voluntary control over their mental effort by providing them with simplified executive procedures that allow them to switch their attention between different levels of processing without losing hold of the task as a whole. This approach is very new and its further development will depend greatly on advances in our understanding of cognitive processes underlying intellectual abilities and how these processes change with learning.

Another, and perhaps the boldest, approach is a knowledge-based method developed and tested over a period of years by Floyd G. Robinson (1972). Robinson's approach amounts essentially to explicitly teaching students a structure for different kinds of mental tasks. This approach gives the student a virtual blueprint for the voluntary direction of thought, according to which every task is approached first at the highest possible level, with the question, 'What kind of problem is this?'

We think it is premature to advocate or condemn any of these approaches. They all need further development and investigation. Developed the wrong way, any of these approaches could turn into rituals that hamper rather than encourage intentional cognition. Developed the right way, they all hold promise of giving students added power to shape their own destinies. Finally, none of these approaches can be expected to amount to much in isolation. They must somehow be integrated into a context of school life where they support the whole and the whole supports them. Finally, that is, school life as a whole and not just some portion or aspect of it must encourage intentional cognition and all it entails.

Although this paper focuses on the process aspect of mental life, it is important to recognize that the school's main job is providing content. As we have been saying, a person's mental life consists of building up and processing generalizable knowledge. Schools are uniquely situated for helping in the build-up of such knowledge, having no practical function to which the student must contribute. Generalizable knowledge can be extracted from practical activities, of course; the mark of an active mental life is continual conversion of the immediate experience into generalizable competence. Schools, however, provide access to the fruits of other people's knowledge-building—to the knowledge of the teacher, for one thing, but more broadly to accumulated cultural knowledge as it is regularized in disciplines, expressed in books, and so forth.

Given the richness of accumulated knowledge and the impossibility of a person's extracting even an estimable fraction of it from practical experience, it is self-evident that schools have an enormous job to do in helping students take advantage of this accumulated knowledge. Yet educators frequently disparage this function and seem to regard every other thing that schools can do as being more valuable. How could this be?

The problem seems to be that schools have never discovered a way to present codified knowledge so that it will be actively taken up in students' mental lives. Early reformers pointed out that what went on in the name of humanity's intellectual wealth was often nothing but senseless memorization. It is always shocking to see how much memorization still goes on in schools and universities. Teachers today may be more careful to ensure that memorization is accompanied by some degree of understanding; but, still, packing away in memory facts and principles organized in the manner of encyclopedia entries is not much of a way to build a mental life.

There is hope that cognitive science will light the way to psychologically more useful ways of imparting knowledge. A good deal of current research is specifically concerned with how knowledge is stored in memory and with how it is brought to use in ongoing processes of thinking and comprehension (see, for instance, Anderson, Spiro, and Montague 1977; also, in a different research tradition, Piaget 1977). In the past researchers have tended to focus on differences in how knowledge is acquired—whether by lecture, by 'discovery', whether by rule followed by examples or the reverse. It is now apparent that these differences are superficial. What counts is what the knowledge actually consists of—its scope and its relatedness to prior knowledge (Ausubel 1963; Scandura 1973)— and what processing is done to it *by the learner*.

We foresee a new approach to education in which the main concern will not be with how knowledge gets into students' heads but with what happens to it after it is there. From an early age children will be made aware of their knowledge as a prized possession, to be developed, revised, and worked into forms that can be readily drawn on when needed. The curriculum will be geared to develop-

mental trends in the form as well as the content of children's knowledge. Little is known about this now. One possibility, by way of
illustration, is that knowledge at first is organized around memorable high points which themselves are unconnected and that gradually it becomes reorganized according to inferential links. Piaget's
genetic epistemology, which up until now has had little educational
significance except as a prop for advocates of discovery methods,
will be mined as a source of ideas for helping children free their
knowledge from its particularity and give it logical interconnectedness (compare Piaget 1970 with Piaget 1977).

Learning will become 'progressive' in a new sense, in the sense
of Lakatos (1970) when he calls a healthy scientific research program 'progressive'. It means developing knowledge that becomes
increasingly powerful in its ability to handle new experience,
instead of disintegrating into a mass of exceptions and special
cases.

As soon as they are able, children will be given to understand
that the real work of students goes on inside their heads and is
directed only by themselves. Of course there will be overt school
activities and school 'work', which at a superficial glance may not
look much different from what goes on now. The difference will be
in the extent to which the activities encourage and repay mental
effort. There will also be plenty of overt discussion and criticism of
ideas, for the intention is not that each student develop a private
knowledge store isolated from the incommunicable to others.

Teachers will lead and help in many ways, but what present-day
teachers try hardest to do these teachers will try hard to avoid. That
is, they will avoid manufacturing meaningfulness for their students
and avoid contriving activities so that learning goes on without
intentional cognition. Instead they will see their responsibility as
helping students work to generate meaning out of the context of
their mental lives, thus helping them in the fullest sense to take
charge of their own minds.

References

Anderson, R.C., R.J. Spiro, and W.B. Montague, eds. 1977. *Schooling and
the Acquisition of Knowledge*. Hillsdale, NJ: Erlbaum.

Ausubel, D.P. 1963. *The Psychology of Meaningful Verbal Learning*. New York: Grune and Stratton.

Bereiter, C. 1972. *Must We Educate?* Englewood Cliffs: Prentice-Hall.

————. 1985. Toward a Solution of the Learning Paradox. *Review of Educational Research* 55, 201–226.

————. 1990. Aspects of an Educational Learning Theory. *Review of Educational Research* 60, 603–624.

Bereiter, C., and M. Bird. 1985. Use of Thinking Aloud in Identification and Teaching of Reading Comprehension Strategies. *Cognition and Instruction* 2, 131–156.

Bereiter, C., and M. Scardamalia. 1982. From Conversation to Composition: The Role of Instruction in a Developmental Process. In R. Glaser, ed., *Advances in Instructional Psychology* (Hillsdale, NJ: Erlbaum), Vol. 2, pp. 1–64.

————. 1983. Schooling and the Growth of Intentional Cognition: Helping Children Take Charge of Their Own Minds. In Z. Lamm, ed., *Zeramim hadashim be-hinukh* (New Trends in Education) (Tel-Aviv: Yahdev), pp. 73–100.

————. 1987. *The Psychology of Written Composition*. Hillsdale, NJ: Erlbaum.

Bloom, B.S. and L.J. Broder. 1950. *Problem-Solving Processes of College Students*. Chicago: University of Chicago Press.

Bremer, J. and M. von Moschzisker. 1971. *The School without Walls*. New York: Holt.

Brown, A.L. 1978. Knowing When, Where, and How to Remember: A Problem of Metacognition. In R. Glaser, ed., *Advances in Instructional Psychology*. Vol. I. Hillsdale, NJ: Erlbaum.

Brown, A. L., and J.C. Campione. 1981. Inducing Flexible Thinking: A Problem of Access. In M. Friedman, J. P. Das, and N. O'Connor, eds., *Intelligence and Learning* (New York: Plenum), pp. 515–529.

Cole, M. 1979. Reply. In D. Sharp, M. Cole, and C. Lave, Education and Cognitive Development: The Evidence from Experimental Research. *Monographs of the Society for Research in Child Development* 44.

Cole, M. and S. Scribner. 1974. *Culture and Thought*. New York: Wiley.

Coleman, J.S. et al. 1974. *Youth: Transition to Adulthood*. Report of the Panel on Youth of the President's Science Advisory Committee. Chicago: University of Chicago Press.

Davis, R.B. and C.C. McKnight 1979. Modelling the Processes of Mathematical Thinking. *Journal of Children's Mathematical Behavior* 2, 91–113.

Donaldson, M. 1978. *Children's Minds*. London: Croom Helm.

Flavell, J.H. 1978. *Cognitive Monitoring*. Paper presented at the Conference on Children's Oral Communication, University of Wisconsin.

Flower, L.S. and J.R. Hayes. 1980. The Cognition of Discovery: Defining a Rhetorical Problem. *College Composition and Communication* 31, 21–32.

Gallagher, F.M. and R.S. Mansfield 1980. Current Developments in Adolescent Psychology. Fourth edition. Boston: Allyn and Bacon.

Hadamard, J. 1945. *The Psychology of Invention in the Mathematical Field.* Princeton, NJ: Princeton University Press.

Huizinga, J. 1954. *The Waning of the Middle Ages.* Garden City, NY: Doubleday.

Inhelder, B. and J. Piaget 1958. *The Growth of Logical Thinking from Childhood to Adolescence.* New York: Basic Books.

Kahneman, D. 1973. *Attention and Effort.* Englewood Cliffs: Prentice-Hall.

Karmiloff-Smith, A. and B. Inhelder 1976. If You Want to Get Ahead, Get a Theory. *Cognition* 3, 195–212.

Kitto, H.D.F. 1951. *The Greeks.* Baltimore: Penguin.

Lakatos, I. 1970. The Methodology of Scientific Research Programmes. In I. Lakatos and A. Musgrave, eds., *Criticism and the Growth of Knowledge* (Cambridge: Cambridge University Press), pp. 91–195.

Luria, A.R. 1973. *The Working Brain: An Introduction to Neuropsychology.* London: Penguin.

Moffet, J. 1968. *Teaching the Universe of Discourse.* Boston: Houghton Mifflin.

Muller, H.J. 1967. *The Uses of English.* New York: Holt.

Neches, R. 1979. Promoting Self-Discovery of Improved Strategies. Paper presented at the annual meeting of the American Educational Research Association, San Francisco, April 1979.

Norman, D.A. 1976. *Memory and Attention.* Second edition. New York: Wiley.

Odom, R.D. 1978. A Perceptual-Salience Account of *Décalage* Relations and Developmental Change. In C.J. Brainerd and L.S. Siegel, eds., *Alternatives to Piaget: Critical Essays on the Theory* (New York: Academic Press).

Osherson, D.N. 1975. *Logical Abilities in Children.* Vol. 3. Hillsdale, NJ: Erlbaum.

Pascual-Leone, J., D. Goodman, P. Ammon, and I. Subelman. 1979. Piagetian Theory and Neo-Piagetian Analysis as Psychological Guides in Education. In J. M. Gallagher and J. Easley, eds., *Knowledge and Development,Volume 2: Piaget and Education* (New York: Plenum).

Piaget, J. 1928. *Judgement and Reasoning in the Child.* New York: Harcourt Brace.

———. 1970. *Science of Education and the Psychology of the Child.* New York: Orion.

———. 1977. *The Development of Thought: Equilibration of Cognitive Structures.* New York: Viking.

Pribram, K.H. 1976. Self-Consciousness and Intentionality. In G.E. Schwartz and D. Shapiro, eds., *Consciousness and Self-Regulation: Advances in Research* (New York: Plenum).

Price, L. 1968. *An Investigation of Transfer of an Elementary Science Process*. Unpublished doctoral dissertation, University of Southern California.

Robinson, F.G., J. Tickle, and D.W. Brison 1972. *Inquiry Training: Fusing Theory and Practice*. Toronto: OISE Press.

Rohwer, W.D. 1973. Elaboration and Learning in Childhood and Adolescence. In H.W. Reese, ed., *Advances in Child Development and Behavior, Vol. 8* (New York: Academic Press).

Scandura, J.M. 1973. *Structural Learning*. New York: Gordon and Breach.

Scardamalia, M. 1981. How Children Cope with the Cognitive Demands of Writing. In C. H. Frederiksen and J. F. Dominic, eds., *Writing: The Nature, Development, and Teaching of Written Communication* (Hillsdale, NJ: Erlbaum), Vol. 2, pp. 81–103.

Scardamalia, M., and C. Bereiter. 1983. The Development of Evaluative, Diagnostic, and Remedial Capabilities in Children's Composing. In M. Martlew, ed., *The Psychology of Written Language: Developmental and Educational Perspectives* (London: Wiley), pp. 67–95.

Scriber, S. 1979. Modes of Thinking and Ways of Speaking: Culture and Logic Reconsidered. In R.O. Freedle, ed., *New Directions in Discourse Processing, Vol. 2* (Norwood, NJ: Ablex).

Wallas, G. 1926. *The Art of Thought*. New York: Harcourt Brace.

Wilke, T. 1977. Brain Mechanisms of Attention Control. Paper presented at the North American Society for the Psychology of Sport and Physical Activity, Ithaca, NY, May 1977 (ERIC Document Reproduction Service No. FD 148 816).

About the Contributors

CARL BEREITER received his education at the University of Wisconsin at Madison, graduating with a Ph.D. in comparative literature. He soon switched to education and psychology, however, and became celebrated as the co-author (with Siegfried Engelmann) of the controversial *Teaching Disadvantaged Children in the Preschool* (1966), an account of a highly successful preschool they had designed and run at the University of Illinois at Champaign-Urbana. Bereiter then moved to the Ontario Institute for Studies in Education, where he has remained, and is now a professor in the Department of Human Development and Applied Psychology. He is also a co-director of the Education Commons at that institution, where he heads development of the Laboratory Network for Technology in Education, and is also a founding member of the Institute for Knowledge Innovation and Technology. In the late 1960s he was recruited as a curriculum author by Blouke Carus, and has ever since been deeply involved in creating a succession of curriculum programs in elementary reading and mathematics, as well as, with Marlene Scardamalia, the computer learning environment, *Knowledge Forum*. He is the author of many articles in education and cognitive science journals, as well as (with Marlene Scardamalia) *The Psychology of Written Composition* (1987) and *Surpassing Ourselves* (1993). Most recently, he has published *Education and Mind in the Knowledge Age* (2002), a more detailed elaboration and defense of his contributions to the present volume. He has been a Guggenheim Fellow, was twice a Fellow at the Center for Advanced Study in the Behavioral Sciences at Stanford University, and is a member of the National Academy of Education.

A.W. CARUS has degrees in philosophy, history, and economics from the universities of St. Andrews, Cambridge, and Chicago. He has published a number of papers on the philosophy of the Vienna Circle in scholarly journals and conference proceedings, and is at work on a book about Carnap's logicism. He is Blouke Carus's son, and has collaborated with Carl Bereiter on a number of projects, including the development of the Open Court elementary reading program, now published by SRA-McGraw Hill. He is Chairman and Publisher of Open Court Publishing Company.

JEREMY EDWARDS holds degrees in economics from both Cambridge and Oxford Universities. He is Reader in Economics at the University of Cambridge, teaching public economics and microeconomics. His research interests include public economics and corporate governance, with a sideline in economic history. He has co-edited *The Economic Analysis of Accounting Profitability* (Oxford: Clarendon, 1987) and *Banks, Finance, and Investment in Germany* (Cambridge: Cambridge University Press, 1994). He is working on the relationship between corporate governance and executive pay in present-day Germany.

HAROLD HENDERSON graduated from Carleton College and has been a staff writer for the *Chicago Reader* since 1985. He has published numerous articles on Illinois and Indiana topics, social, historical, environmental, and political, in many Midwestern publications, as well as his many contributions to the *Reader*. He is the author of the historical study, *Catalyst for Controversy: Paul Carus of Open Court* (1993).

JAMES MILLER, Director of Liberal Studies and Professor of Political Science at the Graduate Faculty of the New School, is also editor of *Daedalus*, the journal of the American Academy of Arts and Sciences. His books include *Democracy Is in the Streets: From Port Huron to the Siege of Chicago* (1987) and *The Passion of Michel Foucault* (1992), both finalists for a National Book Critics Circle award, and *Flowers in the Dustbin: The Rise of Rock and Roll 1947–1977* (1999), winner of the ASCAP-Deems Taylor award and a Ralph J. Gleason music book award.

SHEILAGH OGILVIE has degrees in English, history, and economics from the universities of St. Andrews (Scotland), Cambridge, and Chicago. She is Reader in Economic History at the University of Cambridge, teaching economic history and the economics of modern developing countries. Her research focusses on the sources of economic growth and stagnation before and during industrialization, particularly in Central and Eastern Europe. She is the author of *Proto-Industrialisation in Europe* (Cambridge: Cambridge University Press, 1993) and *State Corporatism and Proto-industry* (Cambridge: Cambridge University Press, 1997) as well as articles on a wide range of topics in economic history. She is now working on a book on *The Economic World of the Bohemian Serf, 1550–1750.*

ERICH H. RECK was educated at the University of Tübingen, Germany, the State University of New York at Stony Brook, the University of Bonn, and the University of Chicago. He is Assistant Professor of Philosophy at the University of California at Riverside, editor of *From Frege to Wittgenstein: Perspectives on Early Analytic Philosophy* (New York: Oxford University Press, 2002), and author of several articles on the history of analytic philosophy, the philosophy of mathematics, and logic.

MARLENE SCARDAMALIA holds the Presidents' Chair in Education and Knowledge Technologies at the Ontario Institute for Studies in Education of the University of Toronto. There she also directs the Institute for Knowledge Innovation and Technology, an international network dedicated to research-based innovation in education and knowledge-based organizations. With Carl Bereiter, she co-authored *The Psychology of Written Composition* (1987) and *Surpassing Ourselves* (1993).

BARRY SMITH has degrees from the universities of Oxford and Manchester, and has taught at the University of Sheffield, the University of Manchester, and the International Academy of Philosophy (Liechtenstein). He is Julian Park Professor of Philosophy at the University at Buffalo, where he is also affiliated with the National Center for Geographic Information Science and the Cognitive Science Center. He is author of *Austrian Philosophy: The Legacy of Franz Brentano* (1994) and co-editor of *The Cambridge Companion to Husserl* (1995). In 2001 Professor Smith was awarded a two-million-dollar Wolfgang Paul Award from the Alexander von Humboldt Foundation, Germany, the largest single prize ever given to a philosopher.

GORDON WELLS was, prior to 1984, Director of the longitudinal study of language development 'Language at Home at School', at the University of Bristol, England. From 1984 to 2000 he was a professor at the Ontario Institute for Studies in Education of the University of Toronto. He is now a professor of Education at the University of California at Santa Cruz. His books include *Language, Learning, and Education* (1985), *The Meaning Makers* (1986), and *Dialogic Inquiry: Towards a Sociocultural Practice and Theory of Education* (1999). In 2002 Professor Wells and his co-author Hossein Nassaji were co-recipients of the Kenneth W. Mildenberger Prize, awarded by the Modern Language Association of America, for their article 'What's the Use of Triadic Dialogue?' in *Applied Linguistics*.

Index